# Zeppelins Over the Midlands

# Zeppelins Over the Midlands

## The Air Raids of 31 January 1916

Mick Powis

Pen & Sword
**AVIATION**

First published in Great Britain in 2016 by
Pen & Sword Aviation
an imprint of
Pen & Sword Books Ltd
47 Church Street
Barnsley
South Yorkshire
S70 2AS

ISBN 978 1 47383 419 4

Typeset in Ehrhardt by
Mac Style Ltd, Bridlington, East Yorkshire
Printed and bound in the UK by CPI Group (UK) Ltd,
Croydon, CRO 4YY

Pen & Sword Books Ltd incorporates the imprints of Pen & Sword
Archaeology, Atlas, Aviation, Battleground, Discovery, Family
History, History, Maritime, Military, Naval, Politics, Railways, Select,
Transport, True Crime, and Fiction, Frontline Books, Leo Cooper,
Praetorian Press, Seaforth Publishing and Wharncliffe.

For a complete list of Pen & Sword titles please contact
PEN & SWORD BOOKS LIMITED
47 Church Street, Barnsley, South Yorkshire, S70 2AS, England
E-mail: enquiries@pen-and-sword.co.uk
Website: www.pen-and-sword.co.uk

# Contents

# Dedication

To my Nan who told me when I was a little boy, half remembered stories, about that frightening night when she visited Aunt Rose, and made me determined to find out more.

# List of Plates

1. The Killing Machine. Zeppelin L.21, in her shed at Nordholz (photo: *Wolverhampton Express and Star*)
2. *Kapitanleutnan*t Max Dietrich, commander of L.21 (photo: *Tonder Zeppelin Museum*)
3. The likely home of William and Mary Greenhill (photo: *Wolverhampton Express and Star*)
4. Union Street, Tipton, as it is today (photo: *Mick Powis*)
5. Bradley Pumping Engine House, on the Wolverhampton Union Canal (photo: *Mick Powis*)
6. Nelly, Thomas and Ina Smith, victims of L.21's bombing of Wednesbury (illustration: *the Daily Sketch*)
7. The Smith family home, 13 King Street, Wednesbury (illustration: *the Walsall Pioneer*)
8. Wednesbury Road Congregational Church (photo: *the Wolverhampton Express and Star*)
9. Mary Julia Slater, Mayoress of Walsall, the best known victim of L.21 (photo: *the Wolverhampton Express and Star*)
10. Bradford Place, Walsall, the morning after the raid. (photo: *the Wolverhampton Express and Star*)
11. A 50kg bomb of the type dropped by L.21 (photo: *Mick Powis*)
12. Walsall Cenotaph, built on the spot where the last of L.21's bombs fell (photo: *Mick Powis*)
13. *Kapitanleutenant* Odo Loewe (photo: *Wikimedia Commons*)
14. Zeppelin L.19 commanded by *Kapitanleutenant* Odo Loewe (photo: *the Wolverhampton Express and Star*)
15. British trawler *King Stephen* encounters the sinking L.19 (illustration: *Wikimedia Commons*)
16. 109 Shobnel Street, Burton-on-Trent, where three people died during the raid (Photo : *the Wolverhampton Express and Star*)

# List of Maps

# A Note On Time

During January and February 1916 Britain was on Greenwich Mean Time, Germany kept to Central European Time, one hour later. In this book I have converted all winter times to GMT. One of the problems with a book of this sort is confusion about time. Most of the events described took place in a twelve hour period between midday and midnight on 31 January 1916. I have included often contradictory information about when things happened. In 1916 with the exception of the military everyone used a 12-hour clock. Strangely this included Military Intelligence at GHQ. To avoid confusion I have converted all times to a 24-hour clock system. I still use terms like midday and midnight but have changed to a 24-hour clock even if I quote an original document which said 8.15 pm., I quote it as 20.15.

A further source of confusion is that from 21 May 1916 to 1 October 1916, the UK introduced British Summer Time, a daylight saving measure. The Germans had already done this, but starting on 30 April 1916. Both sides had daylight saving in 1917 and 1918, but it started and finished on different dates, so for a few days of the year, Germany was either on the same time as Britain or two hours ahead. During BST dates, I quote all times according to BST.

# Introduction

The canal towpath near the old pumping station, in Bradley, near Wolverhampton is now a peaceful place, but totally evocative of the Black Country. The canal pumping station was once part of the Wilkinson iron manufacturing plant. It housed a steam-powered beam engine that pumped water into the canal. Walking along the path it is easy to imagine the days when the canal was surrounded by glowing furnaces, a vital part of British industry.

On the wall of the pumping station there is another reminder of the past, a reminder of war. A plaque unveiled in 1994 commemorates the death of two innocent civilians, Maud and William Fellows. The couple were killed by a bomb dropped by a Zeppelin airship on 31 January 1916 during one of the heaviest air raids of the First World War.

On a personal note, the mother of the author was a babe in arms when her mother took her to see her sister in Wednesbury. When I was a boy my grandmother often told me that she could clearly see the Zeppelin while the pair waited in Wednesbury for a tram to take them home to Wolverhampton. They were covered in dust by the explosion of the bombs. The trams stopped running after the bombings, so she and my mother had to spend the night at her sister's house. As no one had a telephone, my grandfather spent an anxious night waiting for news of them.

While tens of thousands of Midlanders saw the Zeppelins and even more heard the bombs, it is surprising how little is known about the events of that frosty, foggy night.

Nine Zeppelin airships of the *Reichskreigsmarine*, the Imperial German Navy, set out from their bases on the North West Coast of Germany to bomb the English Midlands. Liverpool was their primary target, though they didn't hit it. In all seventy people were killed in the bombing. About 113 people were injured.

Two Zeppelins bombed the Black Country: the L.21, between 20.00 and 20.30 and the L.19 at about midnight.

Three Zeppelins bombed Burton-on-Trent, probably L.15 at about 20.30, L.20 at about 20.45 and L.19 at about 21.30. There is some debate about this, which I discuss in chapter three. We know fifteen people were killed

One Zeppelin, L.20, bombed Loughborough killing ten people at about 20.15. It then went to Ilkeston where another two men died, at about 20.30.

Zeppelin L.14 bombed Derby at about midnight, killing five people.

Zeppelin L.13 bombed in the Stoke-on-Trent area, then, at about 23.00, went to the Scunthorpe area killing three people.

The raids led to considerable political pressure for adequate blackout and air-raid precautions, and considerable anti-German atrocity propaganda. Several coroners' juries rendered verdicts of 'murder' by the German Kaiser and Crown Prince. In the end the fear, anger, economic and political pressure generated by the raids led to the development of a successful air raid defence policy.

In this book I intend to try to bring together two lines of research, the military and the civilian. It is perhaps surprising that far more is known about the military aspects of the raid, than what happened to civilians on the ground. After the First World War, surviving Zeppelin crews were heroes in Germany and many books were written by them. These books along with enemy documents and British defence records were used by H A Jones in his magnificent series of books *War in the Air*. Jones not only documents all the airship raids on Britain, but also produces maps showing the route taken by individual aircraft.

Much of this information is taken from secret documents produced by GHQ (Home Forces). From various sources, interrogation of captured Zeppelin crews, spotters on the ground and police reports they piece together the route of the airships and the destination of their bombs. There is another factor – top secret at the time – which helps us. The War Office had a copy of a top-secret German codebook, and from intercepted Zeppelin radio messages knew that a force of airships had left their bases for a raid on Britain. Though they didn't know the target areas this meant that ground forces were on the alert, and good quality records produced of the route of each Zeppelin over England.

These GHQ documents really give you a feel for the times. Written by military men they are wholly balanced. Describing some Zeppelin commanders as brave and skilled, others as overly cautious, they give the unvarnished facts, and professional analysis. Each copy was a secret document designed for a small group of senior officers. Each had to be signed for. It is fascinating to read them alongside the national and local press. The concept that truth is the first casualty of war certainly applies to the public, but not those in command.

Another book was vital to my research, *The Zeppelin in Combat* by Douglas Robinson, an American historian who not only was able to study all the German combat records, but personally interviewed a number of Zeppelin crewmen, members of the *Marine-Luftschiffer-Kameradschaft*, the organisation of surviving airship crews, which met until the 1960s. While it does not give a complete detailed account of all the raids on Britain in the way that the GHQ documents do, the combination of British and German records makes Robinson's book very useful. One thing has to be noted about times in Robinson's book: he uses Central European Time as the Zeppelin crews did, and this has often led to confusion in local histories when trying to square Robinson with Jones, or with newspaper accounts.

Finding out what happened on the ground is more difficult. While it is fairly easy to find out some of the facts from contemporary newspaper reports, these do not give the names of the victims or the areas where the bombing took place. Newspaper reports were strictly controlled by the Defence of the Realm Act, known as DORA by journalists. As a footnote to history it is interesting to note that when I consulted some coroners' reports in Walsall and Wolverhampton I found telegrams from the Under Secretary at the Home Office to the coroners. They explained that the raid could be reported provided no names, addresses or locations were indicated.

A further problem with newspaper reports is that they refer to the raids occurring 'in an area in the Midlands' or 'an area in Staffordshire', or Derbyshire, Leicestershire or Lincolnshire. This has often led to confusion as different areas in each were bombed by different Zeppelins, but newspaper reports describe events from different areas in the same article, leading to considerable confusion.

In general local newspapers are far more accurate and useful than national ones. Most tend to report coroners' inquests almost verbatim, just leaving out names of victims and witnesses and places. The national press, and local newspapers reporting on areas other than their own are unreliable, they shamelessly copy other newspapers' reports but sadly don't do it very well, leading to confusion and often inaccuracy. Reading a lot of newspapers from the time certainly disabused me of the idea that there was a golden age of fair and accurate reporting – bias and sensationalism are not new.

Coroners' inquest reports are perhaps the most valuable records. I was able to consult some of them in Walsall and Wolverhampton. Sadly those for most of the other towns where casualties occurred are lost. In some cases, not knowing the names of the victims, I was forced to rely on cemetery records.

In a few of the towns, local historians wrote articles about the raids shortly after the war and these provide valuable information, not only about what happened but the names of many of the people involved. They are however variable in quality and some include myths, probably caused by inaccurate newspaper reporting at the time, and gossip.

Another very useful source of information has been personal recollection, though there can be hardly any people alive who remember the bombing. The Zeppelin raid has entered the 'folk memory' of many regions. People told their children and grandchildren about the events of that night. On many occasions when I told friends about this article they volunteered half remembered childhood conversations. I am grateful to include some of them here.

Other useful sources of information have been local history magazines and newspapers. Over the years they have published a number of articles based on research, or until a few years ago, readers' memories of the events. There are several internet sites, in English and in German, that provide information on Zeppelin technology and operations. Many local history sites mention the raids and often record witness accounts.

Research on the Zeppelin raids has been made more difficult by the fact that the records are distributed in the local history and archives departments of the library services of the many different local councils, and I have travelled around the towns and walked the different sites. During my research staffs at all these local history sections were unfailingly polite and

All the bases were near the East Frisian Coast of Germany. On the 31st January 1916, four ships L.11, L.14, L.17 and L.21 set out from Nordholz. Three ships L.13, L.15 and L.16 set out from Hage. Two ships L.19 and L.20 set out from Tondern. Ahlhorn and Wittmund were used later in the War.

The Zeppelin Bases on the German Coast.

helpful. It is particularly important to ensure that all aspects of our history in these local history archives are preserved. Local history preserves and helps all of us understand the past. I hope that this work plays a part in the preservation of the history of the towns that were bombed, and helps us understand something about the time when ordinary people were involved in extra-ordinary events, as the horrors of total war reached the heart of British industry.

*Chapter One*

# A Noise like Thunder and Lightning

## 20.00: Zeppelin L.21 bombs the Black Country

Maud and William Fellows were sweethearts – though they had the same surname, they were unrelated. Both lived in the Coseley/Bradley area. Maud was a 24-year-old. She lived at 45 Daisy Street, Bradley and worked in a butcher's shop for Udall and Son in Bilston. William was twenty-three. He lived at 33 Castle St, Coseley and was employed as a stoker. Before this he had been a deliveryman for Wardells Mineral Waters.

Like thousands of sweethearts before and since, they walked along the towpath of the Wolverhampton Union canal. We will never know what they talked about as they walked hand in hand, at 20.00, on that frosty foggy Monday evening. Perhaps they talked about the war. The First World War was eighteen-months old. On the Western Front the battle of Verdun would begin in a few weeks. The battle of Loos had just ended. Almost a thousand local men of the South Staffordshire Regiment had perished, killed by a fatal combination of machine guns, shells, poison gas and high-level incompetence. On the home front, London had been bombed by Zeppelins in October 1915 and seventy-one civilians killed. The Wolverhampton *Express and Star* reported that on the previous night Zeppelins had attacked Paris. It hastened to reassure readers that 'in spite of this the morale of the citizens remained unshaken.' Perhaps closest to home was the fact that the government was planning to introduce conscription. Maud and William knew that soon their lives would be changed unpredictably by war.

We can only guess at what they talked about that evening; perhaps it was just the inconsequential chatter of lovers. We know from Maud's deathbed statement what happened next. She told her brother that at about 20.10 she heard a sound like 'thunder and lightning'. She and her young man ran to seek shelter as a bomb dropped. They may have heard the bombs dropped by the Zeppelin on Tipton a few minutes earlier, or more likely one of the five bombs reported to have fallen on Bradley. As they sheltered by the wall of the pumping station a high explosive bomb landed a few feet from them on the towpath. It killed William outright and fatally injured Maud.

The first people on the scene saw two bodies on the ground. Arnold Wolverson, who worked at the nearby Britannia Iron and Steel works, reported to the coroner's inquest that he heard an explosion and dashed for safety to the canal side. He heard someone crying for help. He found Maud – who was injured – lying across the breast of William who was quite dead, his head almost severed. There was a five-foot deep crater rapidly filling with water about eight-feet away. Maud was taken to the nearby Old Bush Inn, still existing today, in Bradley Lane where she was given first aid on a pub table. She kept asking how her "young man" was. She had wounds on her right side, her loin and all over her back. She was taken to the Wolverhampton General Hospital, where she died several days later on 12 February 1916, from septicaemia.

While researching this book I had the privilege of meeting the granddaughter of Maud Fellows. She told me that Maud was one of eleven children and well-remembered by her family as a brave determined woman. She had a difficult life as she was a single mother. She did two jobs to support her son, Wilfred, one in the butcher's shop and the other, a part-time job, as a barmaid in the Old Bush Inn. After she died, Wilfred was bought up by Maud's parents, then by one of her sisters. Wilfred trained as a printer and had a printing business in Bilston. He was one of the local historians responsible for the memorial plaque at the bomb site.

It is unlikely Maud and William saw the Zeppelin – flying almost two miles high – that killed them. We can be certain L.21's crew never saw their victims. From his combat report we know that her commander, *Kapitanleutnant* Max Dietrich of the Imperial German Navy, was hopelessly lost. He had been flying for more than nine hours and believed he was bombing the docks in Liverpool.

We know quite a lot about Max Dietrich. He was born on 27 November 1870, at Angermunde north of Berlin. Aged forty-five he was old for a combat officer. His background was different from most other Zeppelin commanders. He came from a solidly middle class family. One of sixteen

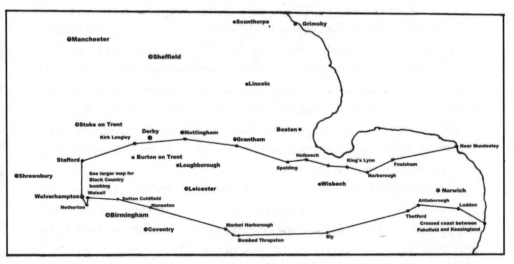

**16.50** crossed the coast near Mundesley, with L.13. **17.00**. She was seen over Foulsham. **17.20** Narborough. **17.25** King's Lynn, then south of Sutton Bridge and over Holbeach. **18.05** Spalding. **18.30** She was seen south of Grantham, then south of Nottingham and south of Derby. **19.00** She was seen near Kirk Langley, then Stafford. **19.45** flew over Wolverhampton, **19.55** over Netherton. **20.00** Bombed Tipton. **20.10** Bombed Bradley. **20.20** Bombed Wednesbury. **20.30** Bombed Walsall. **20.35** She was seen near Sutton Coldfield. **20.55** Nuneaton, then seen near Market Harborough and near Kettering. **21.15** Bombed the Islip furnace at Thrapston, she then flew north of Huntingdon. **22.00** She was seen near Ely. **22.35** Thetford. She was seen between East Harling and Attleborough then north of Bonwell and Long Stratton. **23.25** She was seen north of Lodden. **23.35** She crossed coast south of Lowestoft, between Pakefield and Kessingland.

*The route in this map is probably very accurate. I use a combination of information from the G.H.Q reports and the work of H A Jones, in 'War in the Air'. Most ground observers were soldiers waiting to be deployed to France. While they were able to accurately give their own position and the time they saw or heard a Zeppelin, they had no way of identifying which ship flew over them. When the information got to G.H.Q they drew the most likely route based on: where the bombs fell, radio intercepts and the later interrogation of captured crews. Radio signals could generally identify airships, but only give a very approximate location. Police reports on bomb damage are generally very accurate on where the bomb hit and damage, but less accurate on the exact time when they hit. Writing after the War Jones could use additional information, including German combat reports, so his routes are more accurate, but are not infallible.*

The route of Zeppelin L.21.


children he went to sea at the age of seventeen. He did well as a merchant seaman, becoming the youngest captain in the North German Lloyd shipping line. He commanded a number of ocean liners before the outbreak of war. He was regarded as a hero early in the war when he broke through the British blockade, sailing from America in the SS *Brandenburg*. He was awarded the Iron Cross 2nd Class for the exploit. As an officer in the merchant service, he was also a reserve officer in the Imperial German Navy. It is said his exceptional skill as a navigator led him to the Zeppelin Service. He had commanded two Zeppelins before L.21, winning the Iron Cross 1st Class in the process. His first airship was Zeppelin L.7 with which he was involved in a daylight naval action against a British minelayer on 9 August 1915. In November 1915 he had been given command of Zeppelin L.18, but she was destroyed in her shed at Tondern when being topped up with hydrogen. A member of her crew was killed in the accident. On a more trivial note, Max Dietrich was the uncle of Marlene Dietrich, though she was an unknown teenager when he set out on 31 January 1916.

L.21 left her base at Nordholz, near Cuxhaven, on the North German coast at about 11.00 GMT. Max Dietrich's orders were to bomb Liverpool. The Zeppelin crossed the English coast near Mundesley, Norfolk, at about 16.50. Dusk was falling. Observers on the ground noted L.21 over Narborough at 17.20 and King's Lynn at 17.25. She passed south of Grantham at 18.30, and then flew south of Nottingham and north of Derby just before 19.00. Dietrich was flying south-west thinking he was over the Irish Sea, when he saw the bright lights of two towns separated by a river, which he took to be Liverpool and Birkenhead. The lights were actually the lights of the Black Country, not at the time subject to any blackout regulations. The river must have been one of the many canals. Dietrich aimed his bombs at the glow from the foundries he glimpsed through the clouds. His target when Maud and William Fellows were killed may have been the Capponfield Foundry across the canal from the bombsite. Witnesses stated five bombs were dropped on Bradley.

In his report after the raid Max Dietrich said he bombed docks, harbour works and factories, with thirty-five 50kg (110lbs) high explosive and twenty incendiary bombs. He claimed to have seen the explosions of all the bombs and wrote that good results were clearly seen from on board.

The L.21 was the pride of German technology. She was a new aircraft, first flown only three weeks before on 10 January 1916. The Black Country raid was her first operation. A 'Q' type airship, she had been built at the Zeppelin *Werk* at Lowenthal. She was a massive machine: 585ft long and 61ft in diameter. She had a cotton fabric covered duralumin frame, and was kept in the air by some 1,264,400 cubic feet of hydrogen gas, contained in eighteen gas cells.

With a crew of seventeen, Zeppelin L.21 carried about 4,910lbs of bombs. It was powered by four 240-horsepower Maybach engines, which gave a top speed of 59mph. Though slower than opposing fighter aircraft, its service ceiling of 13,800ft made interception very difficult for the aircraft of early 1916. As we shall see this was to change during 1916, and the hydrogen in the Zeppelins' gasbags made them very vulnerable to incendiary bullets. However in January 1916 Zeppelins were able to roam freely over England, relatively safe from the Royal Flying Corps.

From Derby L.21 flew south-west, passing over Rugeley before reaching Stafford at 19.25. Observers reported that she then suddenly turned south, heading for Wolverhampton at high speed. She passed over Wolverhampton, then subject to a partial blackout, at 19.45. We have an eyewitness account of the airship passing over Wednesfield. Jack Burns told his grandson many years later that he was in his back garden when he saw the Zeppelin heading towards Fibbersley Bank: 'flying so low he could have almost stuck his pitchfork in the bugger.'

L.21 reached Netherton at 19.55 and hovered over the town for about three minutes. It is probable that Dietrich then spotted the lights and furnaces of the Black Country, which was not subject to any blackout restrictions. He turned north, passing over Dudley, reaching Tipton just after 20.00.

This is where the killing started. The bomb aimer was the second in command *Leutnant zur See* Christian von Nathusius. Using a bombsight made by the famous optical manufacturer Karl Zeiss of Jena, he dropped three high explosive bombs on Waterloo Street and Union Street, quickly followed by three incendiary bombs on Bloomfield Road and Barnfield Road. In Waterloo Street some outbuildings at the rear of houses were destroyed, and one person was killed. In Union Street two houses were completely demolished and others damaged. The gas main that ran under the road was set alight. Thirteen people were killed. The incendiary bombs fell in yards and gardens and failed to ignite. Walking around the Union Street area it is easy to see why Dietrich thought he was bombing docks. The area is between two levels of the Birmingham Canal, the street lights probably glittered on the water, making it a tempting, if misleading target.

Probably following the Great Western railway line, or the Wolverhampton level of the Birmingham Canal, L.21 then dropped three incendiary bombs on Bloomfield Brickworks. Two of the three bombs failed to ignite and no damage was done. The Zeppelin then reached Lower Bradley and dropped five high explosive bombs. They exploded between Potlatch Bridge and the Bradley Pumping Station. One landed on the canal bank killing two people: Maud and William Fellows. The bomb blast damaged the canal bank and pumping station, as well as breaking a considerable number of windows in the area.

Dietrich then turned L.21 east, bombing Wednesbury at about 20.15, killing fourteen people in the area of King Street near the Crown Tube works. Other bombs fell at the back of the Crown and Cushion Inn in High Bullen, and along Brunswick Park Road. Damage was done to the Hickman and Pullen brewery, railway wagons and buildings in Mesty Croft Goods yard, where one person was killed. Slight damage was also done to Old Park Colliery.

From Wednesbury Max Dietrich flew on to Walsall. Reaching the town at 20.25, he dropped seven high explosive and four incendiary bombs. A bomb hit the Wednesbury Road Congregational Church. A few hundred yards later incendiary bombs landed in the grounds of the General Hospital. Others landed in Montrath Street, damaging houses and the Elijah Jeffries Saddlery Works. The last bomb landed in Bradford Place, outside the Art and Science Institute. A number of people were killed in the Bradford Place area, and the public toilets were completely demolished. After the war the Walsall Cenotaph was built on the spot where the bomb landed.

The bombing run of L.21 probably lasted about twenty-five minutes, from Tipton to Walsall. The Zeppelin generally flew a curved seven-mile course at her cruising speed of 40mph, though observers on the ground reported that it seemed to circle looking for targets, and probably would have slowed to a hover while dropping bombs for a better aim.

Max Dietrich's combat report shows that he dropped thirty-five high explosive and twenty incendiary bombs. War Office GHQ records show that thirty-five people were killed in the Black Country and twenty-nine injured. We cannot be absolutely sure how many were killed by L.21, and how many were killed by Zeppelin L.19 that bombed the Black Country at about midnight. This Zeppelin, however, dropped many of its bombs in other areas. There is no doubt the majority of casualties were caused by the L.21.

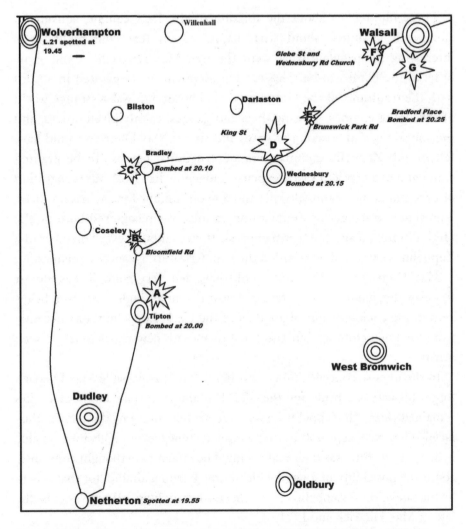

19.45 spotted over Wolverhampton, 19.55 spotted over Netherton. **'A' 20.00** Bombed Tipton 3 HE and 3 incendiary bombs, 14 people killed, mainly in the Union Street and Waterloo Street area. **'C' 20.10** Bombed Bradley, Dropped 5 HE bombs between Potlatch Bridge and the canal bank. 2 people killed, on the canal bank. **'D' 20.15** bombed Wednesbury, 15 people killed, mainly in the King Street area. **'E'** Bombed Brunswick Park Road **'F' 20.25** Wednesbury Road Congrgational Church and Wednesbury Road area. Dropped 7 HE bombs. One man killed on the corner of Glebe Street and Wednesbury Road. **G' 20.30** The Bradford Place area in Walsall town centre, 3 people killed. **20.35** spotted over Sutton Coldfield.

The route of L.21 over the Black Country.

These blunt facts about the mission of the L.21 cannot, considered alone, tell us much about what happened on that cold night. It is interesting to speculate what went through Max Dietrich's mind as he ordered the bombs to be released. His Zeppelin was operated in accord with the traditions of the German Navy. The airship was a strange world of throbbing engines, glowing dials and gauges, calmly given orders, and the squeaking and creaking of wires and struts. Max Dietrich would have felt proud: Zeppelin commanders were national heroes. To be granted command of a new and vastly expensive machine like L.21 was recognition of exceptional navigational skills and a great honour for any naval officer. The skill and danger of Zeppelin operations was recognised both by the High Command and the German press. It was said that every member of a Zeppelin crew would be awarded the Iron Cross after a successful mission.

Max Dietrich and his crew would have felt very cold. It was almost freezing at ground level, operating almost two miles high it was well below zero in the enclosed control gondola of the L.21. Zeppelin crews not only wore fur-lined clothing, but also lined them with newspaper to try to keep warm.

In the intense concentration of his bomb run it is possible Max Dietrich forgot his patriotic pride and the cold. It is almost certain another emotion remained: fear. All Zeppelin crews were acutely aware of the danger they faced. They were kept aloft by over a million cubic feet of highly inflammable hydrogen gas. Fire was their real enemy. They must have thought constantly about the possibility of a terrible death in a burning airship, for that was to be the fate of most Zeppelin crews. On another night in 1916 it was to be the fate of Max Dietrich and L.21.

Dietrich was probably even more aware of fire than other Zeppelin commanders. In November 1915 his previous airship, Zeppelin L.18, had blown up in its shed, while being filled with hydrogen. A crew member was killed and many others seriously burned.

If the crew of L.21 felt constant fear, what of the Black Country folk below? There is no doubt they experienced shock and terror. At first most people failed to realise what was happening. In an article in the *Blackcountryman* magazine, Bilston writer Tom Cope described the events, which happened when he was a schoolboy. He was in the Parish Room of St Martins Church,

Bradley taking part in a school choir practice. Suddenly there was a terrific bang and all the windows were shattered. Someone shouted, 'It's a boiler explosion.' The children dashed outside, the choir-mistress fainted. As Tom Cope walked home he saw a youth climbing a lamppost to extinguish the gaslight. He looked up and saw the Zeppelin: 'a huge silent cigar shape.' Like the author's grandmother, his parents were very late arriving home. They had been to the theatre in Wolverhampton and had to walk back, as all the trams had stopped running.

A number of people wrote of their experiences some seventy years after the raids in letters to the *Black Country Bugle*. Mrs V Owen was in Bradley; she said she saw what looked like a 'flash of lightning, followed by something like a thunderclap'. Several people on their way home from Bilston Market said there had been a boiler explosion. Later the police travelled around telling people there had been an air raid, and ordering them to blackout all lights and take shelter in cellars. Mrs D Griffith said she remembered the bright moonlit evening, the canal was like a silver thread, which the Zeppelin seemed to follow, scattering its bombs everywhere.

Many of our descriptions of events come from newspapers at the time. Mainly the Wolverhampton daily *Express and Star* and the weekly *Dudley Herald* and *Tipton Herald*. There is a problem using newspapers. Because of wartime censorship they were unable to name the victims or identify locations. However, they widely reported the bombing. The stories are full of human interest, and are taken from inquest or eyewitness accounts and are well worth quoting, even though they lack some personal detail.

The *Express and Star* described the events as happening in an 'area in Staffordshire'. This leads to another problem. The bombings are correctly reported as having occurred in a number of towns and villages in Staffordshire. However, there were two distinct Staffordshire areas bombed by different Zeppelins: the Black Country and Burton-on-Trent. In press reports incidents from the two areas are described together, and have in the past confused researchers, who have combined separate events.

We know for certain that Tipton was the first Black Country town bombed. The main casualty area was Waterloo Street/Union Street. In 4 February 1916 edition the *Express and Star* reported that the first air raid started between 8 o'clock (20.00) and 9 o'clock (21.00), and the second at about midnight. No damage of a military nature was done, 'though twenty-six innocent civilians, many of them women and children were sent to immediate and violent deaths, while a number lie on beds of pain, in the agony of wounds received from flying fragments of the bombs or the collapse of buildings'. The report goes on to tell us there was no panic, indeed the only moral result that the bombing engendered was an even stronger resolve on the part of the people to bring the War to a speedy and successful conclusion.

Be that as it may; the reports certainly give a flavour of the time. There is no doubt that the *Express and Star* is referring to Tipton when it tells us that at ten past eight bombs began to rain down on the poorest residential area of a Staffordshire town. The occupants were mainly coalminers or ironworkers, paying a rental of five to six shillings (25p to 30p) for their tightly packed houses. In one street all the houses were damaged more or less. One house was completely demolished; two or three partially destroyed, and about a hundred had windows broken by the force of the explosions. Thirteen people were killed and seven injured. A very poignant passage tells us that hanging on the wall of one wrecked house, open to the street, was a cage containing a canary which 'continued to whistle exuberantly directly the smoke and dust had cleared away'.

A police sergeant described the scene for the inquest. He had heard an explosion on Monday night and visited the area. He found several bodies lying in the roadway, and subsequently rescued others from the debris of the wrecked buildings. Another officer said he heard a succession of explosions and the whirring of aircraft engines. He did not see any machine. At the scene of the bombing, a huge crater had been formed in the road. A gas main had been fractured and was on fire. Several houses were wrecked. A search of the district found that five high explosive and three incendiary bombs had been dropped. One had landed on the railway line near the passenger station.

The *Tipton Herald* interviewed several people who had seen the Zeppelin, they all said it had flown very low, one said he could almost have hit it with a brick. This is almost certainly an optical illusion. Though we do not have precise detail it is likely that, like most Zeppelins, L.21 bombed near to its maximum altitude, perhaps at 9000ft. People on the ground could not appreciate its enormous size. By 1916 people were used to seeing aircraft flying overhead; they would have used these as a comparison to judge the height of the airship. Most aircraft were single or two seat biplanes about 20ft long with a wingspan of 25ft to 30ft. The Zeppelin was some thirty-times longer at 585ft, as people naturally underestimated the size; they perceived it as flying much lower than it actually was.

A coroner's inquest was held on Thursday 3 February 1916 on thirteen victims in Tipton: six men, four children and three women. Before the inquest the coroner warned the press he had no control over what they published but expected that they would deal with the matter with suitable discretion. (In fact this was certainly not the case, both the coroner and the editors knew that anyone who printed details contrary to the Defence of the Realm Act would find themselves in jail very quickly indeed.) I have not been able to find the records of the Tipton coroner's inquest on the victims of the raid, so most of my material comes from the local press. By combining newspaper stories with burial records for Tipton cemetery, I have been able to positively identify some victims, though the circumstances of the death of others remain uncertain.

The first witness at the Tipton inquest was Thomas Morris of 10 Union Street. He was described as a fine strong working man. He told the Court that his wife Sarah Jane Morris, aged 44-years, and two of his children Nellie Morris aged eight and Martin Morris aged eleven were killed by the Zeppelin. His mother in law Mary Greensill, aged 67-years and father in law William Greensill, aged 64-years, were also killed. He had gone to the pictures while his wife had taken their four children to her mother's house, Number 1 Court, 8 Union Street. He returned to find the house in ruins, the five victims among the debris. They had been sitting around the fireplace when the bomb landed. Their bodies were terribly mutilated. Death must have been instantaneous.

Another witness had identified her son killed in the shop where he worked. A bomb had hit the pavement in front of it, wrecking the whole place. She saw her son lying dead in a pool of blood. He was probably Arthur Edwards, a boot repairer aged 26-years of 69 Union Street. Also killed was Daniel Whitehouse, aged 34-years, of 31 Union Street.

Another witness, an old man, identified his daughter, the wife of a soldier. She had left the house about half an hour before the raid. He next saw her lying dead on the footpath, a few yards from a bomb crater in the roadway. She could have been Elizabeth Cartwright aged 35-years, of 1 Coppice Street.

Another person was killed standing in the doorway of her mother's house; she could have been Anne Wilkinson aged 44-years, of 18 Owen St. Another woman was seriously injured by a bomb, at 15 Waterloo Street, Tipton; she was Louisa Yorke, aged 30-years, and later died of her injuries in Dudley Guest Hospital.

Another victim was described as a well-known professional man. He was Thomas Henry Church, aged 57-years, an estate agent of 111 Dudley Road, Tipton. He was visiting the area and was hit by shrapnel when a bomb landed. He was probably on his way to Tipton Conservative Club, in Union Street, where he was a well-known member. The explosion blew out all the windows in the club. A witness said that Thomas Church was taken in to a house, where it was suggested a car be obtained to take him to hospital. He replied, 'It's all right don't bother,' then fainted and passed away.

Almost as if to keep a political balance another victim was, according to his obituary, a stalwart of Tipton Liberal Club. He was Benjamin Goldie, aged 43-years, a fender manufacturer of 58 Queens Road, Tipton.

Other tragic casualties were two children, aged twelve and nine, killed in the street while on the way to visit their grandmother. The twelve-year-old was George Henry Onions of 66 New Road, Great Bridge, the nine-year-old Frederick N Yates, of 5 Queens Road, Tipton.

At about 20.10 Zeppelin L.21 moved away from Tipton, probably following the canal to Bradley, where Max Dietrich dropped the bombs that were to kill Maud and William Fellows. The dead remained behind in Tipton, and work began to search for survivors. Little did the rescuers know that just after midnight they were to be visited by another Zeppelin, which was to bomb virtually the same area, fortunately with far fewer casualties. We shall consider that raid later.

From Bradley the killing continued in Wednesbury, where another fourteen people died. Twelve of them in King Street, another working class area, just off the Holyhead Road. We have a very full account of the events in Wednesbury. Local historian Frederick Hackwood wrote of the raids in an article for the *Borough News* in 1920. This was later re-published in his *History of Wednesbury.*

King Street was described as an area of artisans' houses. At one end stood the James Russell Tube Works. A number of its workers were on strike on 31 January 1916, otherwise casualties could have been far greater. The story of the raid was described in evidence to the Coroner's Court, presided over by Mr G C Lewis, the South Staffordshire coroner. The inquest, which lasted two days, considered twelve Wednesbury victims.

At Number 14 King Street lived the family of Joseph Horton Smith, an iron-turner. At about 20.15, Mrs Jemima Smith heard an 'alarming loud report', she ran out of the house to see what was happening, leaving in the house her husband, her daughter Nelly, aged 13-years, her son Thomas, aged eleven, and her daughter Ina, aged seven. It appeared they followed her out of the house, for when she returned they had all disappeared.

The bodies of Joseph, Nelly and Thomas were found later that night in the ruins of number 13 King Street, which suffered a direct hit by a bomb. The fate of little Ina was even more tragic, her body as not found until the next morning, it had been blown on to the roof of the James Russell Works by the explosion.

Everyone at number 13 was killed. The residents included Edward Shilton, a tube maker, and his wife Betsy, and Mary Ann Lee aged 57-years and Rachel Higgs, aged 36-years, who both worked as charwomen. At the time of their death Mrs Shilton and Mrs Lee were lying upstairs, ill in bed, when the bomb struck.

Miss Rebecca Sutton, who kept Huckster's shop, at 28 King Street was also killed. Her chest was pierced by a piece of shrapnel. Particularly sad was the death of another little girl. Ten-year-old Matilda May Birt, of 40 Dale Street, went out to play, with another child, who had been sent to the post box by her parents. The bombs fell as they walked along King Street. Matilda May's parents next saw her shattered body in the mortuary. The last victim identified by Hackwood was Susan Howells, aged 50-years, of 12 King Street.

From the burial records of Wednesbury Wood Green Cemetery I have found details of another Wednesbury victim. His body seems to have been found in the High Bullen area. He was Albert Gordon Madeley, a furnace-man, aged 21-years, of 48 Great Western Street. He was probably the man described in the *Wednesbury Herald* as 'walking to the house of his fiancée when he was lifted several yards into the air by the (bomb) blast'. He sustained severe abdominal injuries, and later died in hospital.

There were also stories of near misses. At 7 King Street, William Upton was sitting by the fire, when a piece of shrapnel came through the window and smashed an ornament on the fireplace. Though the house was badly damaged, a blackbird in a cage was completely uninjured. As in Tipton cage birds seemed to have had charmed lives in Wednesbury. Houses at number 6 and 8 King Street were badly damaged but a linnet and a canary were rescued without damage to a single feather.

Many of the humans weren't so lucky. Hackwood writes that fragments of human flesh were found several streets away from the place of explosion, when daylight came. Many of the witness reports from the inquest were harrowing. Harry Doige, a seaman, of 7 Foster Street, said he was walking Holyhead Road towards Moxley, at about 20.00. He heard three or four loud explosions, the first in the direction of Moxley, the next at the end of King Street. This explosion about 150-yards away blew him off his feet. The next two explosions followed immediately. He got up and walked up King Street, finding a human body on the footpath. He struck a match to see if he could help, but the body was so mutilated, he couldn't even tell what sex it was. A few yards further on he found another person, nothing but a trunk, the arms and legs blown off. He told the Court that three or four houses in King Street were completely destroyed. He helped to remove four bodies from the debris.

Police Sergeant Frank Robinson was on duty at the Market Place, when he first heard the explosions. He said he heard six explosions at some distance, then saw the flash and heard the bang of three more. He went to King Street and found that several houses were wrecked, there was a large deep hole in the road by the James Russell Works, and several bodies lying in the street. He later helped to move ten bodies, most of which were quite shattered, to the mortuary. The next morning he helped recover the body of little Ina Smith from a rafter on the roof of the James Russell Works.

Police Sergeant James Harris reported that he was by the Bulls Head Inn when he heard several loud explosions. There was an explosion with a flash that rose above the Russell Works. This shattered a number of shop windows in the area. Another bomb fell at the rear of the Crown and Cushion Inn, in High Bullen, making a hole four-feet deep. Other bombs fell in the area of Brunswick Park Road, at the back of Aston's Beerhouse, by the railway embankment and in Oldbury Street. These bombs caused property damage but no more casualties.

An incendiary bomb landed in the back garden of the Beerhouse. The landlord found it, half burned, spitting and spluttering. Getting his small son to hold a candle to illuminate his work, he promptly proceeded to extinguish it by steadily shovelling earth on it.

Three bombs were dropped in the area of the railway embankment in Brunswick Park Road. One hit the embankment, causing a large hole and damage to surrounding property, another one damaged brickwork on the railway bank, while the third damaged a telegraph pole. There were railway lines near all the areas bombed by L.21, and most of the bombs landed near to railway lines. It is a fair guess that Max Dietrich followed the railway lines, and bombed the more brightly-lit areas. This would certainly account for the fact that most of the bombs fell very close to Tipton, Wednesbury and Walsall town centres.

Another witness at the inquest was a Wednesbury man residing some distance from the town centre in Newton Road. He and his family had an Australian soldier as a guest. When they heard the first heavy report they went into the garden and saw, first in the direction of Tipton and Oldbury then Wednesbury, flashes of light, followed by loud reports. The bangs seemed to shake the buildings, even though at Newton they were two or three miles away. The Australian soldier experienced in such things was able to tell them they were undergoing an enemy air raid. Everyone was greatly perturbed by this, and all lights were quickly put out. The family heard twenty explosions before the Zeppelin passed over Walsall, as if it was going in the direction of Burton-on-Trent. The family also heard the bombs of a second Zeppelin, which passed over at about midnight.

After leaving Wednesbury, Max Dietrich headed north for Walsall, probably following the railway which still runs from Wednesbury, via

Bescot, to Walsall town centre. We have a very detailed description of the bombing of Walsall. In 1919 the Reverend W L T Merson wrote an article on the bombing for the Borough of Walsall Official Programme of Peace Celebrations. Much is contained in the excellent book published by Walsall Local History Centre: *Walsall at War*. This contains a section on the Zeppelin raid, some of it compiled from interviews with survivors, taken in the 1980s, some seventy years after the event.

Walsall's first bomb landed on Wednesbury Road Congregational Church, on the corner of Wednesbury Road and Glebe Street. In interviews conducted after the war the scene of chaos was pieced together. A preparation class from a local primary school was working in the church parlour. The class was taken by Miss Winifred Palmer; she said she saw a small piece of ceiling fall from the roof, then 'a blinding flash more vivid and fearsome than any lightning' she had ever seen. Then a terrific explosion and utter bewilderment. The bomb had struck the centre of the church roof, and severely damaged the interior. Pews were splintered, windows blown out, and the floor broken up.

The church was seriously damaged, the explosion so powerful that lead from one of the windows was later found twisted around the arch of the church gates. Miraculously no one inside was killed or seriously injured. Not so lucky was a man living nearby, Thomas Merrylees, aged 28-years, a template-maker of 55 Hillary Street, Pleck. He was killed on the corner of Glebe Street by flying debris from the church. At the coroner's inquest Police Constable Joseph Mason said he had been informed of a man lying dead at the corner of Wednesbury Road and Glebe Street. He attended the scene quickly after the explosion that wrecked the Congregational Chapel. Mr Merrylees was lying in the gutter on his face. He was quite dead, with the back part of his head and brain blown away.

After bombing the church Max Dietrich flew toward the centre of Walsall. An incendiary bomb landed in the grounds of the General Hospital. It was quickly extinguished by a policeman. Another bomb damaged houses in Mountrath Street, while another blew a hole in the wall of the Elijah Jeffries Saddlery Works. The last high explosive bomb landed right in Walsall Town Centre, outside the Art and Science Institute in Bradford Place. We have a number of accounts of this, from *Walsall at War*.

A K Stephens was a student attending an evening class in chemistry at the Art and Science Institute. In a tape he made seventy years later, for the Walsall Archives Service, he recalled the bombing. At almost 20.30 he heard a series of bangs. He looked through one of the big windows facing Bradford Place, after about thirty seconds there was a terrific bang and a huge flash. All the lights quivered and there was a fearful sound of breaking glass. All the chemistry apparatus disappeared, everything in the lab was blown to smithereens. It was pandemonium, but there was no panic. The students dashed down the stairs. Mr Stephens remembers a woman completely covered in blood. He later found he was injured, and was taken to the General Hospital, where there were two or three surgeons at work. He was given stitches ('a very painful process') and later taken home.

A number of people outside the institute were injured. A Pelsall woman, 14-years-old at the time, recalled how she was injured. With a friend she was window shopping, watching a clockwork train in the window of Halfords, outside the Arcade Chambers. She heard a buzzing in the sky, suddenly there was a big flash and all the lights went out. Something hit her on the head, which started bleeding. Someone came out of Halfords and told them to go into the cellar. When they came out, she saw that the bomb in Bradford Place had blown the public toilets away. The roof of the Arcade was caved in, and the floor covered with about three-inches of broken glass.

Many of the casualties were passengers on a number 16 tram. They included the most famous victim. Though most of the victims of L.21 were working class Black Country people like Maud and William Fellows, her bombs were no respecters of persons. Mary Julia Slater was the Lady Mayoress of Walsall. She was a passenger on the number 16 tram. From her hospital bed she told her husband she had travelled into town with her sister and sister-in-law. They caught the tram at the Black Lion public house on the Pleck Road. The tram stopped several times, as there were loud explosions. When it reached Bradford Place there was a violent explosion, all the glass windows in the tram shattered, the lights went out, and she felt something hit her. She got up and found it difficult to breathe; she thought there were fumes of gas in the tram. She was taken to a shop and given first aid. She was bleeding heavily and suffering from severe wounds to her chest and abdomen. She was taken to hospital and died several weeks later, on Sunday, 20 February 1916, from shock and septicaemia.

Mary Julia Slater was the last casualty of the bombing to die. It is one of the coincidences of war that she was from a German background, and had often travelled there. Her grandmother came from Bremen, not far from the Zeppelin bases on the north German coast. Her husband Samuel Mills Slater was a prominent solicitor. He was the Liberal Alderman for Pleck Ward, and in 1916 Mayor of Walsall. She was the daughter of C T Saunders a Birmingham solicitor. Aged 55-years, the mother of five children, including a son serving in France as an army officer, she was well known as a watercolour artist, and was an active fundraiser for the Red Cross. She lived at The Elms, Bescot Road, Walsall. She was buried in Goscote Cemetery, on 24 February 1916, the day that would have been her fifty-sixth birthday.

As well as Mrs Slater two men also died from injuries received in Bradford Place. They were two friends in town for a night out. Frank Thompson Linney, aged 36-years, of 12 Perry Street, and Charles Cope, aged 34-years, of 87 Crankhall Lane, Wednesbury. Both were master dairymen. Police Constable Frank Mason told the inquest he had found Frank Linney in Bradford Place with severe leg injuries. With the assistance of a number of civilians he was able to remove him to hospital. Sadly he died at 21.30 on 31 January 1916 from shock and loss of blood.

His friend Charles Cope was with him when he died. He had been less seriously injured. He told a friend he had been standing by the public toilets in Bradford Place when he was hit in the back. Though injured he was able to walk to hospital. A doctor told the inquest that Charles Cope had seemingly been recovering from his injuries, when he took a turn for the worse, and died at Walsall General Hospital on 3 February 1916.

A very sad case was that of John Thomas Powell, aged 59-years, of Pleck. Formally a gunlock-maker he was in failing health, and had declared himself destitute, and was an inmate of Walsall Workhouse. It was reported to the coroner's inquest that he was suffering from pneumonia on 31 January 1916, he was considerably alarmed by a number of loud explosions and died at 20.40 that night.

The bomb in Bradford Place was the last dropped by L.21 on the Black Country. It is fitting that Walsall Cenotaph now stands on the spot the bomb landed. With the killing over, Max Dietrich turned the L.21 for home, travelling at high speed. She was reported over Sutton Coldfield at 20.35 and over Nuneaton at 20.45. The last attack took place at about 21.15 at Thrapston, Northamptonshire where Max Dietrich ordered her six remaining incendiary bombs to be dropped on a blast furnace. They missed, landing in fields and causing no further damage.

L.21 was spotted over Ely at 22.00 and over Thetford at 22.35. She crossed the English coast, south of Lowestoft, between Pakefield and Kessingland, at 23.35. Her crew spent another exhausting eleven hours crossing the North Sea, arriving back at their base at Nordholz at about 10.45 on 1 February 1916. L.21 was one of the last Zeppelins to return. She had covered 1,056 miles in just over twenty-three hours.

After debriefing and breakfast most of the crew went to bed exhausted after a 24-hour mission. When they awoke on the evening of 1 February 1916, their relief in survival and pride in a successful mission was sullied by concerns about their comrades in Zeppelin L.19. This airship, the last to bomb the Black Country, had not returned. The last message sent by her commander *Kapitanleutnant* Odo Loewe, had been received at 16.05 that afternoon. It read: 'Radio out of order, three engines out of order, approximate position Borkum Island...' Then silence.

The death of the Smith children in Wednesbury illustrates how little information people in the Midlands had been given about air raid precautions. The children, and their father, heard a loud bang and ran outside to see what happened. Another bomb landed a few yards away and killed them. This happened in several different places that night. The Zeppelin commander, at about 9000ft, would have slowed his engines and dropped a bomb while virtually stationary. The bomb-aimer watched for the explosion and any effects and then dropped another. What probably happened in King Street is that Christian von Nathusius the bomb-aimer saw the explosion, and then a flash of light as doors opened, so he dropped another bomb. While Zeppelins often failed to find their target, when they could see a target they could bomb very accurately. Unlike an aeroplane which drops a stick of bombs as it flies over the target, a Zeppelin would aim very precisely.

After the air raids in London the Government issued posters and placed newspaper advertisements telling people what to do in the event of an air raid. Essentially: seek shelter and stay inside – most people were killed by shrapnel or flying debris. This information clearly hadn't reached many people in the Midlands.

By the end of the week the press was full of instructions as to what to do if the Zeppelins attacked again. Edgar Wallace wrote in the *Birmingham Post* that the most important thing was to go home and stay there. In a small house the cellar was the safest place. In a big house the floor or first floor were the safest, as long as you stayed away from the windows. If caught outside people should seek shelter, if none was available they should lie face down on the ground. This was sound advice. Shrapnel from a bomb flies upwards in a cone shape from the impact point and you are less likely to be hit flat on the floor. The last thing seems amusing, but recognised that people would go to look at the Zeppelins no matter what the government said. If you looked out from your front door, so long as you could see the Zeppelin, without cricking your neck, you were perfectly safe, but the moment you had to strain your neck, ever so slightly to get a view, you were in danger and needed to get inside and close the door and wait until more adventurous neighbours told you the Zeppelin had passed.

Before I started looking at the statements made by witnesses on the ground, I had assumed that Zeppelins dropped their bombs like fixed-wing aircraft, making bombing runs and dropping bombs as they moved. This may have been the case in London, or over the coast, where there was considerable opposition and the commander was trying to avoid searchlights or gun fire. But in the January Midlands raid where there was no opposition, there seems no doubt that the Zeppelins hovered and were virtually stationary when they bombed. Probably the engines were slowed to a tick over and the side propellers put into reverse, a manoeuvre similar to that used when landing. There is a distinct pattern to a number of the deaths. People inside a house heard a bomb drop nearby. They ran outside to see what was happening, and they were then killed by another bomb which fell a few seconds later. I do not think this was done deliberately in that the Zeppelin bomb-aimer could not see individuals on the ground, it was similar to naval gunnery practice where the first shot was a ranging shot, and subsequent shots based on observing where this fell. It is interesting to note the language used by Heinrich Mathy in his interview for the *New York World*, when he talks about bombing London when he ordered the bombs dropped he used terms like slow or rapid fire. Essentially Zeppelin crews were pioneers in a new form of warfare; they were adapting techniques they knew like naval gunnery to the new type of aerial warfare.

*Chapter Two*

# Like a Great White Mountain

**Midnight: Zeppelin L.19 bombs the Black Country, and meets a watery grave.**

The last Zeppelin to bomb the Black Country was L.19; she was also the only airship to fail to return from the mission. Zeppelin L.21 left behind a frightened and confused Black Country population. Though the press claimed there was no panic this is certainly an exaggeration. Tens of thousands of people had heard the bombs, and thousands had seen the Zeppelin. Before long people found out there had been an air raid, though very few knew exactly what had happened. The fires caused by the bombs could be seen for miles around, many of the streetlights had been extinguished, and the trams had stopped running. Though the police toured the area advising people to take shelter in cellars, there were many people out on the streets, walking home or trying to find out what had happened. Rumours spread rapidly, it was said that King Street, in Wednesbury had been completely destroyed, and that Owen Street in Tipton was running with blood.

A Walsall witness 'GH' quoted in *Walsall at War* described how when he walked with his father down Corporation Street and Wednesbury Road at 23.00 everywhere was in total darkness. When they reached the ruins of Wednesbury Road Congregational Church, they asked a policeman what had happened. He said he didn't know. All he knew was that the church was smashed to the ground. When they got near to the town centre they saw there were people still drinking, by candle light, in the Turf Tavern.

Another witness, a Wednesbury woman, quoted in Hackwood, said she was in West Bromwich at the time of the first bombing. She saw several flashes of light and heard loud reports. The trams were stopped so she started walking home at about 21.00 She met numbers of people who informed her in panic-stricken tones that Zeppelins had razed Wednesbury to the ground. As she got into Wednesbury the town was crowded. She described the scene: 'the time of slumber seemed as busy as the day.' The footpaths were crowded with people discussing the terrifying events of the day. She heard more explosions accompanied by flashes of light, apparently in the sky over Great Barr. This was almost certainly the bombing of Burton-on-Trent, which took place between 20.45 and 21.45. Zeppelin L.19 was the last of three Zeppelins to bomb Burton. Though Burton is perhaps only about twenty-five miles from Wednesbury, it was to take L.19 more than two hours to reach the Black Country, its next target.

It is very fortunate that Zeppelin L.19 didn't reach the Black Country until after midnight; otherwise casualties would have been much greater. By the time L.19 reached Wednesbury, most people were aware there had been an air raid. After the initial excitement and shock, very few people were still on the streets. Many were sheltering in cellars; most of the others were in bed. Though this would have made little difference if a bomb directly hit a building, as the majority of casualties were the result of shrapnel wounds or flying debris, bed was the safest place to be.

In his article in the *Blackcountryman* Tom Cope wrote that when his parents arrived home in Bradley, after walking from Wolverhampton, everyone went to bed. He was woken in the middle of the night by more explosions, but the sounds seemed further away. Because of this, instead of going to the cold dank cellar, all the family huddled together in one bed, fearfully awaiting further bombs. They heard no more.

The Zeppelin responsible for this fear was L.19 commanded by *Kapitanleutnant* Odo Loewe, with *Leutnant zur See* Erwin Brunhof as his executive officer. Loewe was an experienced commander, a veteran of three earlier attacks on England. He had previously commanded Zeppelin L.9, taking the ship over from Heinrich Mathy, in June 1915. The German Navy policy was that less experienced commanders got older ships, with the more experienced promoted to the newer models. Loewe raided the Humber area on 3 July 1915. He bombed Goole, thinking he was over Hull, destroying ten houses, damaging a number of warehouses and killing sixteen people. He set out in L.9 on 12 August 1915, but had to turn back because of mechanical

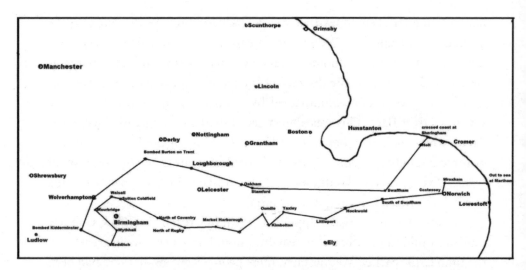

18.20 crossed coast near Sheringham. 18.25 seen at Holt. 19.05 Swaffham. 20.10 Stamford. Then seen to circle over Exton and Stamford, and then seen over Oakham. 21.30 seen near Loughborough. 21.45 Bombed Burton on Trent. She was then seen near Wolverhampton. 22.30 flew over Enville. Kinver. Wolverley. Bewdley. Bombed Kidderminster (bomb did not explode), then seen over Bromsgrove and Redditch. 23.00 seen over Wythhall, and then near Stourbridge. 00.15 (1 Feb 16) bombed Dudley, 00.20 bombed Tipton and Wednesbury. 00.25 bombed Walsall. 00.30 was seen over Sutton Coldfield. 00.40 Coleshill. 00.50 north of Coventry. 01.00 north of Rugby. Then seen over Market Harborough. Kettering and Oundle. 02.10 Kimbolton. 02.25 Stopped over Yaxley. Seen over Littleport. 03.10 Hockwold. Sutton Ferry. Spotted south of Downham Market. 03.40 south of Swaffham. 04.15 south of East Derham. 04.30 Wymondham 04.41 Costessey near Norwich. 05.15 Wroxham. 05.25 Crossed coast near Martham.

*This route is accurate in outline. GHQ and H A Jones agreed on the general course of Zeppelin L.19. What the map cannot represent is the fact that L.19 was reported as wandering and circling, in the 11 hours she spent over England. Though the times are accurate, and the order of the places she flew over seem likely, as she circled a great deal, probably as a result of trying to find targets, combined with engine trouble, this cannot be shown on a small scale map. In 'War in the Air Jones uses a 10 miles to the inch Ordinance Survey map to show her route, the draftsman attempted to show her circling but at that scale I think it was based more on artistic licence than evidence.*

The route of Zeppelin L.19.

failure. His last raid with L.9 was on 8 September 1915. His target was the Skinningrove Chemical Works near Loftus on the North Yorkshire coast, and he actually hit the plant but caused only minor damage and no casualities. (Due to changes to county boundaries Loftus is now part of Redcar and Cleveland.) As the works were built pre-war by a German firm it seems likely there were good quality maps. We know the works were bombed several times afterwards by Zeppelins.

Loewe took over the new Zeppelin L.19, in November 1915; she was a 'P' type – an earlier model Zeppelin than L.21, slightly smaller at 536ft long. He then spent a frustrating two months because of various sorts of engine trouble. Her engines – the newly developed, high compression, Maybach HSLu 240-horsepower engines – were proving very unreliable. This lack of action made Odo Loewe determined to have a successful mission, and go all the way to Liverpool. He could not know that engine problems were to prove fatal for him and his crew.

Zeppelin L.19, carrying a crew of sixteen, left her base at Tondern in Schleswig-Holstein at 11.15 for her rendezvous with the rest of the attack force over Borkum Island. She crossed the English coast over Sheringham, Norfolk at about 18.20. She seems to have been travelling more slowly than the other airships, though it is impossible to be precise as her combat log was lost. Her rather devious progress also caused problems for ground observers charting her progress. She was spotted over Swaffham at 19.05, over Stamford at 20.10 and over Loughborough at 21.30. From Loughborough Loewe seems to have seen the fires caused by other Zeppelins at Burton-on-Trent. He dropped a few incendiary bombs there, at about 21.45. It is not possible to say how many of the fifteen deaths in Burton were caused by L.19.

From Burton L.19 moved in a south-westerly direction passing near Wolverhampton. Between 22.30 and 23.30 she was reported 'wandering' about the districts south of Birmingham. She was seen or heard near Enville, Kinver, Wolverley, Bewdley, Bromsgrove, Reddich and Stourbridge.

There is an interesting story about a sighting of L.19 over Wolverley. In 1996 the author wrote an article for the Wolverhampton *Express and Star* to commemorate the 80th anniversary of the raid. I received a letter from an old lady from Wolverley. She told me she had been baptised on 31 January 1916, and had been told by her mother she had seen an airship over the village late that evening. Her mother saw the bomb doors of the Zeppelin open, but didn't see a bomb. However, in July 1939, an unexploded First World War German bomb was found on a river bank near Kidderminster by men of the Worcestershire Highways Department, erecting a coffer dam to repair the Old Iron Bridge. It was reported to weigh about 50lbs, and was about two-feet long, with fins. It was thirteen-feet down below the riverbank. It was live but hadn't exploded because it fell into soft ground.

Ground observers did not note the fall of a bomb in the Kidderminster area. They recorded L.19 as she passed over Wythall at 23.00 going towards Birmingham. Loewe failed to find Birmingham, which was in total darkness, and started his attack on Wednesbury at about midnight, possibly attracted by fires started by L.21. The official GHQ Home Forces report states he dropped a single high explosive bomb on the axle department of the Monway Works, doing slight damage to the building and machinery. An eyewitness interviewed by Hackwood after the war contradicted this report. The lady, previously quoted, who had walked from West Bromwich, had returned by midnight to her house in the Oakwood End area. She and her lady companions were all feeling very nervous having talked for an hour or so about their experiences on that dreadful night. There were rumours of the utter destruction of King Street, and the demolition of the James Russell Works. They all retired to bed just before midnight. Before anyone went to sleep there was a series of loud explosions that made the 'foundations of the house quiver and the windows rattle and shake so much it seemed they would fall out'. Shortly after the street outside was lit up, for a moment, by an intensely brilliant artificial light that seemed to travel in the direction of Hydes Road towards Hollies Drive. The women rushed down into the cellar and spent the rest of the night huddled together in the cold.

The fact the women saw a bright artificial light is interesting. There is some evidence from a Walsall witness that Loewe was using a searchlight and circling looking for targets. The very intense light was, however, unlikely to be a searchlight beam. It was probably a parachute flare, dropped by the Zeppelin and drifting in the direction the witness described.

From Wednesbury Loewe turned towards Dudley. He dropped five high explosive bombs on Ocker Hill Colliery, damaging the engine house and one dwelling house. He reached Dudley at 00.15 on 1 February dropping seventeen incendiary bombs, most of which fell in the Castle grounds or open fields. One fell on a grain shed at the Railway Station, causing £5 worth of damage. The site is now part of Dudley Zoo.

He caused much more damage when he flew north to Tipton, bombing almost the same area as L.21. He was probably able to see the still burning gas mains. The *Express and Star* reported that bombs fell 'scarcely before the dead and injured had been removed'. The GHQ Home Forces report states that Loewe dropped eleven high explosive bombs, at about 00.20 mainly in the western part of the town between the L&NW Railway Station and Bloomfield. He caused considerable damage to a number of houses, but caused no casualties. As well as damage to houses there was damage to the railway; rails and sleepers were blown some distance.

We can work out what happened in more detail by combining GHQ information with newspaper reports. One bomb fell in Union Street a few yards from the crater caused by L.21, another in the Waterloo Street area. Two more high explosive bombs fell near the Bush Inn at 127 Park Lane West, Tipton. The newspapers described in graphic detail the destruction caused by one of these bombs. It hit the roof of a house without exploding, and then bounced into the roadway where it detonated five-feet in front of the Bush Inn. The pub was completely wrecked by the explosion. Every door and window was smashed, the whole place rendered a ruin. We know exactly when the bomb was dropped as the clock in the bar was damaged, and stopped at 12.20 (00.20).

The *Tipton Herald* reported that the landlord, his wife and children all had a miraculous escape. Though they were cut and bruised by the flying debris, they were otherwise unhurt, even though every stick of furniture in the pub as destroyed. The landlord's wife described her experience to the press. She had been struck on the head, and believed she was unconscious for some time. She became aware of the shouting of people in the street, and told her husband 'I'm choking…I am on fire.' She and her husband were trapped in the wrecked bedroom by a broken door, until their son rescued them. According to Kelly's Directory of 1916, the landlord was Thomas Taylor.

The building that was the Bush Inn still stands in Park Lane West. It was a public house until the 1990s, but is now a grocery store. For many years the façade of the pub showed the scars of bomb damage. It was later covered in tiles. After the First World War a number of stained glass windows were installed illustrating the events of the night the Zeppelins came. Tipton

Green Junior School now occupies the site of the house opposite the Bush Inn, where the bomb bounced off the roof.

From Tipton Loewe seems to have followed the railway to Walsall. As with L.21 we have more details of what happened when L.19 reached that town. At about 00.25 on 1 February she dropped two high explosive bombs on Dora Street and Pleck Road, in Pleck. She then turned north and moved over Birchills, where she dropped another high explosive bomb, damaging Saint Andrew's Church and Vicarage in Hollyhedge Lane.

The son of a Pleck dairyman, known as 'GB' gave an intriguing interview, part of a series of oral history recordings collected by Walsall Local History Centre. They were published in *Walsall at War* some seventy years after the event. 'GB' was a boy of ten at the time of the raid. His family were aware of the earlier Zeppelin raid; they had seen burning buildings in Wednesbury. The children were sent to bed, but woken by their father in the middle of the night, and told to shelter downstairs under the table. As there were seven children it was quite a job. They waited some time and nothing happened. GB's father asked him to go outside and put a street lamp out. He climbed the lamppost, and extinguished the gaslight. Shortly after he heard a whirring noise, and looked up, seeing a Zeppelin in the sky. Suddenly it seemed a door opened on the machine and 'a light flashed down like someone with a big torch'. GB darted back into the house to tell his mum and dad. All of a sudden 'there was a crash, bang and then two more.' From the noise they assumed a nearby house had tumbled down, in fact it was their stable. The bomb had killed their horse, four pigs and about a hundred fowl. In a rather unusual display of dry humour the *Walsall Pioneer* commented in its report after the raid: 'With a fellow feeling for the rest of their kind, the Germans no doubt, would have spared the pigs if they had known.'

L.19 was partially responsible for one human casualty: William Henry Haycock aged 50-years, of 53 Bescot Street, Pelfrey. He was a retired police constable, very sick with rheumatism and bedridden. His wife told the coroner that bombs dropped by hostile aircraft at 8.15pm had greatly alarmed him, but afterwards he became calm and said, 'It would be all right, they won't come again.' When she heard another loud bang at about 00.30, she went to the bedroom and found him lying dead on the floor. The coroner

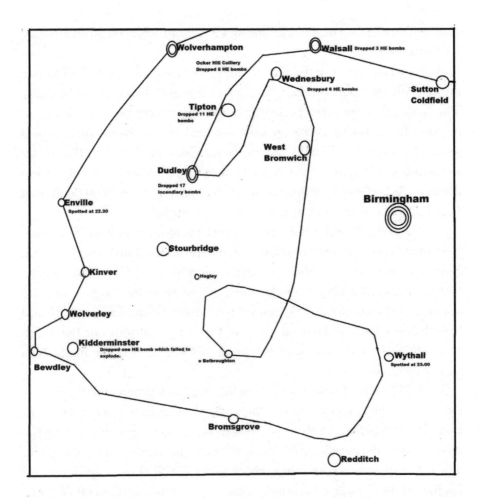

**21.45** bombed Burton on Trent then flew towards Wolverhampton. **22.30** spotted 'wandering' over Enville, Kinver, Wolverley and Bewdley. Bombed Kidderminster, the bomb did not explode. She then flew over Bromsgrove and Redditch. **23.00** spotted at Wythhall. Flew near to Stourbridge, and then bombed Wednesbury, one HE bomb fell on the Monway Works. She then bombed the Ocker Hill Colliery with 5 H.E bombs. **00.15** bombed Dudley, most of the 17 incendiary bombs fell in the Castle grounds. **00.20** bombed Tipton, 11 H.E bombs fell in the Union St and Park Lane area. **00.25** bombed Walsall, 2 HE bombs on Dora St in Pleck and one HE on St Andrew's Church and Vicarage in Birchills. **00.30** She was spotted over Sutton Coldfield.

*This diagram of the route of L.19 is based on a G.H.Q. map. Zeppelin L.19 spent about three hours in a relatively small area, and was described as wandering by the G.H.Q, though the times are accurate, and the order of the places she flew over seem likely, she circled a great deal, probably as a result of trying to find targets, combined with engine trouble.*

The Route of Zeppelin L.19 over the Midlands.

recorded that he died of shock following a hostile air aid, at 00.30 on Tuesday, 1 February 1916.

William Haycock was the last victim of the Zeppelin raid. Odo Loewe dropped his last bomb on Saint Andrew's Church and Vicarage in Birchills. The buildings were severely damaged, but there were no more deaths or injuries. In all Loewe seems to have dropped twenty high explosive and seventeen incendiary bombs on the Black Country. Jones in *War in the Air* wrote that Loewe 'inflicted no further casualties and did only minor damage'. As we have seen this is not strictly true, but there is no doubt that L.21 inflicted the majority of Black Country casualties.

After leaving Walsall Odo Loewe steered a course eastward for home. L.19 made very slow progress. She spent almost nine hours over England. Engine trouble seems to be the main reason for this, though she seems to have pursued a very devious route to and from her targets. On her journey to the coast she was spotted over Sutton Coldfield at 00.30 and Coleshill at 00.40. She passed north of Coventry and south of Bedworth at 00.50. She passed north of Rugby at 1.00. After this she made even slower progress.

At 02.23 (1 2 16) Loewe radioed his base for a navigation bearing. He was located between King's Lynn and Norwich. The Germans had radio stations from Tondern to Bruges. By a system of triangulation they could pick up the direction of radio signals, and crudely estimate the position of the Zeppelin. The information was then radioed back to the airship. Loewe again radioed his base at 04.37 to give his attack report: 'At 12 midnight (23.00 GMT) I was over the West Coast. Orientation and attack there were impossible due to thick fog; dropped incendiaries. 1,600kg [3,500lbs] of bombs dropped on several big factories in Sheffield.'

This shows very well the navigational problems he was having. He seems to have bombed Burton-on-Trent thinking it was Liverpool, and the Black Country thinking it was Sheffield. As for bombing factories most of his victims were killed in a stable.

L.19 crossed the English coast at Martham, Norfolk at 05.25, some hours after the other Zeppelins. She was spotted by a British observer who reported seeing a Zeppelin travelling very slowly and in difficulties. By this time it seems L.19 had three out of four engines operating on reduced power. British Naval vessels were sent to look for her, however, they found nothing.

Loewe requested another navigational bearing at 05.41, and the German Navy ordered three flotillas of destroyers to raise steam to search for her. It took L.19 another ten hours to cross the North Sea. At 15.05 on the afternoon of 1 February Loewe radioed to say he was on the German coast of the North Sea. His signal, again decoded by British Naval Intelligence read: 'Radio equipment at times out of order, three engines out of order. Approximate position Borkum Island. Wind is favourable.'

As a result of this the searching destroyers were called back to base, even though the bearings on Loewe's signal indicated he was further west than he thought. L.19 was in fact about twenty miles north of the Dutch Friesian Island of Ameland. This was radioed to Loewe; it is not known whether he received the message. It was to prove a costly navigational error.

Hardly able to steer or maintain forward speed because three engines were out of action, Loewe had probably given up hope of reaching Tondern. He almost certainly intended to land at Hage or crash-land when he reached German territory. Though only a few miles from the German coast luck was running out for Loewe and the crew of L.19. The crippled Zeppelin was pushed by the wind over Ameland Island, about thirty miles south of Borkum, at 16.00 on the afternoon of 1 February. Ameland was part of the territory of neutral Holland and heavily garrisoned. When L.19 appeared out of the fog, a number of Dutch soldiers fired repeatedly at her. The intense rifle fire caused no immediate casualties, but sealed her fate. The rifle fire punctured the hydrogen cells, causing gas leakage. It is probable that if her engines had been working properly L.19 could have reached German soil. However the combination of engine trouble and gas leakage meant she could not maintain speed or height. Virtually out of control L.19 sank towards the cold North Sea. Her crew had long before discharged all ballast, and then thrown overboard heavy objects, first the machine guns, then the useless petrol tanks. Finally anything not fixed to the structure of the Zeppelin. This was all in vain. At some time during the night of 1-2 February, perhaps 36-hours after leaving her base at Tondern, L.19 splashed into the North Sea.

On the morning of 2 February 1916, the German Navy sent out destroyers and seaplanes to try and find her, without success. Two seaplanes operating out of Borkum Island were lost, their crew, a pilot and observer in each aeroplane, adding four more casualties to the toll of the raid. A German destroyer found one of L.19's jettisoned fuel tanks, but there was no sign of the Zeppelin.

Nothing more was heard until 3 February when a British fishing boat reported seeing her, and became embroiled in a war crime controversy. The trawler *King Stephen*, out of Grimsby, had been fishing in a prohibited area. At 07.00 on Wednesday 2 February her crew spotted a large white object in the water. They sailed close to it and found the L.19 looking 'like a great White Mountain in the sea'. A group of men were in a roughly constructed shelter on top of the envelope and more seemed to be inside the hull. The crew of the *King Stephen* heard a knocking sound, probably the crew of L.19 trying to caulk leaks inside the hull. *Kapitanleutnant* Odo Loewe hailed the skipper Captain William Martin, and asked to be taken abroad. After consultation with his crew William Martin refused. The *King Stephen* had a crew of nine, he thought the Zeppelin had a crew of thirty (in fact it was sixteen). Captain Martin feared, probably correctly, that if he took the Germans aboard then they would take over his ship and sail her to Germany. William Martin later told the press that 'it went to a seaman's heart not to take them off', but he had to think of his crew and their families. Even though he reported that a German speaking perfect English had offered the crew £5 to rescue them, Captain Martin sailed away. He promised to report the position of the L.19 to the first warship he saw; unfortunately the *King Stephen* didn't come across any other vessels until she reached the Humber on 3 February. By then it was too late – the L.19 had gone down with all hands.

Once the fate of L.19 became known the propaganda changed. The German press promptly accused the skipper of the *King Stephen* of a war crime, the atrocity of leaving the crew of L.19 to perish in the North Sea. While this can be seen as typical propaganda, countering criticism of the sinking of the *Lusitania* by a German U-boat, as well as the bombing of civilians, the British position was not helped by the Bishop of London who, the press reported, supported leaving the Zeppelin 'baby-killers to drown in the cold North Sea'. To be fair to the Bishop, it seems what he actually said was that the whole of the British people ought to stand by the skipper of the trawler who came upon the ruined Zeppelin, and that you could not trust the word of the Germans. Had Captain Martin admitted the Germans, it was probable they would have turned on the crew and the whole German press would have applauded them for a clever piece of strategy. Any English sailor would have risked himself to save human life, but the sad thing was that the chivalry of war had been killed by the Germans and their word could not be trusted. The Bishop likely disagreed with the German who said he 'acted less as an apostle of Christian charity than as a jingoistic hatemonger,' though to the press on both sides 'jingoistic hatemonger' was probably seen as a compliment.

The end of the story of L.19 took another six months to discover. *Kapitanleutnant* Odo Loewe wrote a last report, which he put in a bottle. A Swedish yacht picked it up several months later. Loewe wrote:

'With fifteen men on the top platform and backbone girder of the L.19, floating without gondolas in approximately three degrees east longitude. I am attempting to send a last report. Engine trouble three times repeated, a light head wind on the return journey delayed our return and in the mist carried us over Holland where I received heavy rifle fire; the ship became heavy and simultaneously three engines failed.

February 2nd 1916, towards 1.00 PM, will apparently be our last hour.

Loewe.'

Two more messages from L.19 were later picked up on a Norwegian beach. One was from *Leutnant zur See* Erwin Brunhof, the executive officer. The other from a non-commissioned officer to his wife and mother. Brunhof wrote: 'Two days and two nights afloat. No help. Bless you. An English fishing steamer wouldn't rescue us. Erwin.'

The other crewmember Hans Constabel wrote: 'My Dear Ada and Mother. It is eleven in the morning, February second. This morning a fishing steamer, an English one passed by but refused to rescue us. It was the *King Stephen* out of Grimsby. Courage failing; storm coming up. Still thinking of you. Hans. At eleven-thirty we prayed and said farewell to each other. Your Hans.'

So German as well as Black Country mothers were left without sons and children without fathers. In the case of L.19, as in any war, it is difficult to decide who the victors are and who the victims are.

Two members of the crew of L.19 are buried in Denmark, it seems their bodies were washed ashore in July 1916. George Baumann is buried at Tranum, and Henrich Specht at Sonderho on Fano Island.

*Chapter Three*

# A Second Coming

## 20.30 to 21.30: Three Zeppelins raid Burton-on-Trent

The single town that suffered the most casualties on the night of 31 January 1916 was Burton-on-Trent. Three Zeppelins bombed it and fifteen people were killed and at least seventy-two injured. An understanding of what happened in Burton is very useful in understanding the Black Country bombings. At the time press reports described events in Burton and the Black Country as happening in areas in Staffordshire, without differentiating between the separate towns. We now know that the raids were mainly conducted by different Zeppelins. While one Zeppelin, L.19, bombed Burton and the Black Country, two more, L.15 and L.20, did not reach the Black Country.

It is generally thought that Burton-on-Trent was bombed by three Zeppelins L.15, L.19 and L.20, though because of sparse records this is not certain. Most researchers agree that L.19 and L.20 were certainly involved. There is more doubt about L.15; some argue L.13 was the airship involved. I will make the assumption L.15 was involved when I describe the raid, but will later discuss the movements of L.13.

The first Zeppelin was probably L.15. She arrived over Burton at about 20.30. L.15 was commanded by *Kapitanleutnant* Joachim Breithaupt; with *Leutnant zur See* Otto Kuhne as her executive officer, she had left her shed at Hage at 12.00 noon. She had engine trouble in her flight across the North Sea, with two of her four engines out of action. By the time she reached England they had been repaired in flight by her mechanics, and she then made good time. Though her flight was poorly recorded by British ground observers, she seems to have crossed our coast north of Mundesley at about 17.50. She then cruised directly westwards reaching Burton with a full bomb load. She seems to have reached Burton at about 20.30. The combat report of Joachim Breithaupt was very full and is worth quoting in some detail. He identified his target as Liverpool. He reported that he was over the West Coast at about 20.30, when he recognised a large city complex divided by a large sheet of water running north and south, joined by a lighted bridge. He identified this as Liverpool and Birkenhead. He dropped a parachute flare and most of the lights in the city went out. From a height of 8,200ft he dropped 3,100lbs of high explosive and 660lbs of incendiary bombs, mostly along the waterfront, in four bomb runs. All the high explosive bombs burst, but fires did not result. On the other hand the incendiaries worked well, and a huge glow of fire could be seen over the city from a great distance.

The next Zeppelin to reach Burton was L.20 commanded by *Kapitanleutnant* Franz Stabbert, with *Leutnant zur See* Ernst Wilhelm Schirlitz as her Executive officer. L.20 left her shed at Nordholz at about 11.00 on 31 January 1916, and headed across the North Sea. She reached the English coast at the Wash at about 19.00. Records show that Franz Stabbert dropped his first bombs at Uffington, near Stamford, breaking a few windows. He then continued in a westerly direction and was attracted by the lights of a large town, which he thought was Leicester. In fact, Leicester was subject to a blackout, which probably saved it. Stabbert had seen the lights of Loughborough. He dropped four high explosive bombs at about 20.05, killing ten and injuring twelve people. He continued west, probably following a railway line. Seven bombs dropped on Bennerly and Trowell. They damaged a cattle shed and a signal box. By 20.30 he reached Ilkeston in Derbyshire, where he dropped fifteen bombs on the Stanton Iron Works at Hallam Fields. He damaged the moulding and blacksmiths' shops, killing two men and injuring two more. From Ilkeston L.20 turned south and fifteen minutes later at 20.45 dropped about twelve incendiary bombs on Burton-on-Trent. As I discuss later it is interesting to note that Breithaupt reported seeing a huge glow of fire as L.15 left Burton, it may be he saw the incendiary bombs dropped by Stabbert, but did not see the Zeppelin.

The third Zeppelin to bomb Burton was almost certainly the ill-fated L.19 commanded by *Kapitanleutnant* Odo Loewe. She left her shed at Tondern at 11.15 and crossed our coast at Lower Sheringham at about 18.20. She moved west to bomb Burton at about 21.45, after this leaving for the Black Country, which she reached at midnight. She left our shores near Cromer at about 05.25 (1 February). She was the only Zeppelin to fail to return from the mission.

The other Zeppelin that some researchers consider bombed Burton was L.13, commanded by *Kapitanleutnant* Heinrich Mathy, with *Oberleutnant zur See* Kurt Friemel as her executive officer. She left her base at Hage at 11.45 on 31 January 1916, and crossed the English coast, along with Zeppelin L.21, north of Mundesley at about 16.50. She reached the English Midlands and bombed Fenton Colliery near Stoke-on-Trent at about 20.15, without causing any casualties. It is possible she then passed over Burton-on-Trent, possibly dropping bombs. We are fairly certain she then went on to bomb the Frodingham and Redbourn Iron and Steel Works near Scunthorpe, at 23.45, killing two men. In the town of Scunthorpe another person was killed when four workmen's houses were destroyed. L.13 left our shores at about midnight, arriving back at Hage at 08.50 the next morning.

While so many years after the event we will never know for sure exactly who bombed Burton, we have very good records of what happened on the ground, probably better than for any other town. Most of my information is taken from the very good local history *County Borough. A History of Burton-upon-Trent* by Dennis Stuart. He devotes a chapter appropriately entitled 'A shocking night' to the bombing. Also very useful was an unpublished work *Airs from Heaven* by John Hook.

We have a good record of the time warnings were received by various officials in Burton. Though the warnings didn't leave much time for things to be done, the lack of a plan and organisation led to a chaotic response, as in the other towns. At 19.44 the police contacted the gasworks manager: Zeppelins had been seen over Derby at about 18.55. He was requested to have the street lights put out. Though Burton had some electric street lights most were gas. He sent for the lamplighter. This was an honourable profession that has been overtaken by technology. Gas streetlights needed to be manually lit and put out in the evening and morning, by a man with a long pole. Most lamplighters supplemented their income with another job, 'knocking up' – they tapped the windows of factory workers with their poles to wake them up to get to work on time. (For the benefit of American readers I should point out, 'knocking up' has a different meaning in Britain than it does in the USA.) Sadly, as the Zeppelins approached the lamplighter couldn't be found. It took almost thirty minutes before another lamplighter was located. He then started to put out the street lights, but this obviously took time and the bombs were falling before he had finished. The situation was only slightly better with the electric lights. Streetlights were turned off centrally at about 20.30, but most lights needed to be switched off at the substation. These included the bright lights of the Picturedrome in Curzon Street and shop windows and a showroom. The electricity mains foreman, switched off a number of lights, but couldn't switch off the showroom lights, because he didn't have the substation key. The bombs continued to fall. By then the lights were probably irrelevant because there were fires started by the incendiary bombs for the Zeppelins to aim at.

When the bombing started members of the public tried to put the street lights out by climbing the lampposts, poking the flames with clothes line props, or throwing stones or bottles. If there is one real hero in the whole sorry tale of that frosty foggy night, it is a 13-year-old boy, Bertie Geary, who was blown off a lamppost he was climbing to put out the light, by a high explosive bomb, on the corner of Lichfield Street and Bond Street. While heroic, putting out the lights when the Zeppelins were overhead was probably counterproductive. We have accounts from Zeppelin commanders which tell of a bomb exploding and the lights all around going off. Seeing the effect the first bomb had they then dropped several more in the same area. As the Zeppelin was stationary almost two miles high, they couldn't see what was going on below but could see lights going off. This almost certainly happened in the case of Bertie Geary.

We have very little concrete information about when the different bombs were dropped. British Intelligence GHQ reports were normally very precise about the time bombs fell at different locations, and hence the path of the Zeppelin. The raid by three airships in a short period at Burton confused them. All the report says is that 'Burton was visited by three airships between 20.45 and 21.45, 15 HE and 24 incendiary bombs were thrown.' Though we can't identify exactly when the bombs were dropped, we can identify groups of casualties, killed or injured at the same place. Almost all the bombs fell in a fairly small area close to the town centre. It is possible there were two aiming points: the first around Shobnal Street between the Trent and Mersey Canal and the railway line; the second further south between the River Trent and the railway. What seems certain is that the bombs were aimed by men who could see their targets, aiming at lights or fires started by incendiary bombs. The small area also indicates the ships were hovering when they bombed, and if three Zeppelins were involved later raiders would have used fires started by earlier ships. The few bombs dropped outside the main target area were probably dropped as the Zeppelins left.

We have a fairly definite time line from one witness, an engine driver, Harry Hawkes. He heard a noise coming from above, over the noise of his shunting engine. Almost immediately a bomb landed about fifty-yards away. He looked up and saw a great black object in the sky. The lights were on at Leicester Junction so he put out as many as possible. Then an incendiary bomb dropped on the Ind Coope bottling store, it immediately went up in flames, at 20.45 to 20.50.

The greatest number of casualties in Burton occurred in a church mission, allowing the press a field day in atrocity propaganda. Six people were killed, almost certainly by a single high explosive bomb. The Wolverhampton *Express and Star* reported that in 'another Staffordshire town a woman missionary was killed. She was the wife of a well-known vicar, and bible in hand, was addressing an audience of about 200 people. A bomb dropped between the church and its mission room. There was a blinding flash and then all was darkness.' The woman missionary was struck by a huge fragment of shell and killed instantly, another lady and a young girl were also killed on the spot. In the darkness the screams of the injured could be heard and many were trampled in the confusion. After the initial panic, calm was restored, and all worked heroically at the task of rescue. The injured were dragged out of the debris and taken to hospital. 'The doctors and nurses worked splendidly in the very centre of the danger zone.'

With the benefit of subsequent research it is interesting to note that, despite wartime censorship, the press report was very accurate. The bomb fell in Moor Street, Burton, between Christ Church and its Mission room. Mrs Mary Rose Morris, a missionary from Brighton was lecturing a crowd of about 200 people, mainly women and girls. She had held a successful mission during the previous week and had decided to stay over on Monday night to hold a thanksgiving meeting. There were several eyewitness accounts of the bombing. Elsie Chapman was then a young girl, in the meeting room. The congregation had finished a hymn and a prayer, Mrs Morris had just started her address on 'the Second Coming of Christ', and was quoting from the bible when the bomb struck. There was a terrific bang and the room was thrown into darkness, Elsie thought it was almost as if the 'Second Coming' had arrived. Another witness Sybil Hayward reported that everything went black, many of the seats were thrown up, and people were struggling on the floor. In the darkness the screams of the injured could be heard, and people were trampled in the confusion. A voice called 'You will remain where you are, just for a few minutes'. People started singing a hymn, *Nearer my God to Thee*.

People then got up, clinging to each other. Eventually they got to the door, which had been damaged and seemed 'just like a hole in the wall'. The work of getting casualties out of the mission room was difficult, as they had to be carried over the bomb crater, which was twelve-feet in diameter and three-feet deep. Elsie Chapman would always remember the terrifying moments as she walked out of the wrecked meeting room, clinging to her companions. In the dark she was convinced she was stepping on dead bodies as she stepped on coats lying on the floor, among the wreckage. The Vicar of Christ Church the Reverend W R Guest and the Curate the Reverend T Streeter were both injured in the explosion but it is reported continued to assist in the rescue.

There were six people killed in the mission room. Four died instantly, they were Mary Rose Morris (fifty-five) the Missionary. Ada Britain (fifteen) was sitting near the front in the audience. Margaret Anderson (sixty) the sister of a high-ranking civil servant Sir James Anderson, the Permanent Under-Secretary to the Colonies. The last person was an old lady Rachel Wait (seventy-eight). Two women died later from their injuries. They were Flora Warden (sixteen) and Elizabeth Smith (forty-five). Her husband dug her out of the wreckage, before she died.

Fairly nearby two young people were killed in Lichfield Street. Bertie Geary, from nearby Blackpool Road, was found dying, after being blown from a lamppost. A small boy said he was walking down Lichfield Street when he tripped over a 14-year-old boy in the dark. The boy said he was going to die. Evidence later showed that Bertie Geary died in hospital the next day, his injuries were a wound to the back and a perforated abdomen.

Lucy Simnett aged 15-years was also killed by the same high explosive bomb which fell near the corner of Lichfield Street and Bond Street. A witness told the coroner that Lucy was with her mother when the bomb exploded, a piece of shrapnel went through the witness's hat but she was uninjured.

Another young victim was George Stephens, also from Blackpool Road, aged 16-years he was spending his evening in the brightly-lit Black Cat billiard saloon in the High Street. A report in the *Express and Star* tells of a man and youth playing in a billiard saloon in an area in Staffordshire. A bomb crashed into the room and wrecked it. The man was killed, but miraculously the youth survived even though the billiard cue was knocked out of his hand by the force of the explosion. The manager of the Black Cat told the coroner's inquest that there were fifty people in the hall at the time, the bomb 'knocked one wall in' and George Stephens was found unconscious near the tables. The manager said the Black Cat was well lit, and there was a skylight.

A lot of bombs fell between the Trent and Mersey canal and the railway, it may be that this was the area described by Breithaupt as 'a large city complex divided by a large sheet of water, running north and south, joined by a lighted bridge'. We can identify six people killed in this general area: John Finney (fifty-three) was working at the Midlands railway Goods Shed at Derby Street, when a bomb killed him and injured three workmates. Two people were killed in Wellington Street, at number 32, a child, Edith Meashan aged 10-years was killed at home. Her neighbour Charles Gilson, a brewery worker, of number 34, ran into his backyard when he heard the bomb explode, he was killed by another bomb. A gruesome aspect of his death is that the explosion blew his pocket watch into his body. It stopped at the time of the explosion 20.45. His son also called Charles Gilson aged 15-years had his left arm blown off by the same explosion. There were three people killed when a high explosive bomb hit a house in Shobnall Street. Florence Jane Wilson aged twenty-three had gone to visit a friend at 109 Shobnall Street. When the bombing started her brother went to look for her to see if she was alright. When he got to the area he found a number of houses had been damaged, number 109 was demolished. Four people were buried beneath the rubble of the house, Florence and three members of the Warrington family who lived at number 108. After frantic digging Mrs Minnie Warrington, aged 36-years, was found alive. Two of her children

Mary Warrington, aged eleven and George Warrington, aged six were dead, as was Florence Wilson.

As in the Black Country there were some narrow escapes. The grammar school was hit and the headmaster and his family had a 'wonderful escape' when a bomb landed in front of his house, in Bond Street, blowing down the front wall. Everyone inside escaped without injury. One of the best known stories of the raid took place in the Town Theatre. An actress described what happened. During the second act of the play *Potash and Permuter* there was a crash and plaster started to fall from the ceiling. An incendiary bomb was found burning just outside the box-office. To avoid panic the band was ordered to play on and the play started again. At the end of the second act about half the audience remained in the theatre. Before they were sent home they cheered the cast for carrying on with the show and everyone sang *God save the King*.

The GHQ (Home Forces) intelligence report estimated that fifteen high explosive bombs and twenty-four incendiary bombs were dropped on Burton. Fifteen people were killed, three men, six women and six children. There was also a great deal of material damage. Nine houses and a malt house were completely destroyed. The malt house belonged to Ind Coope, the brewer. A church, a mission room and two breweries were badly damaged. The breweries were Bass, Allsopp's and Worthington's. Many other buildings were slightly damaged.

I think the best memorial to Burton is a poem, written by a teenage girl in the Christ Church Mission Hall when the bomb dropped. Whatever it lacks in literary merit, it makes up for as an illustration of the spirit of the time.

On this night stood Mrs Morris
So the dreadful tale began,
Telling the old, old story
Of God's love to all the World.
Little thought she and her audience
As they sat beneath the light
Drinking in the gospel message
Danger stalked ahead that night.
Crash! the building flew in splinters,

Torn as by a giant's hands,
Lumps of stone and metal fragments
Dealing death on every hand
And the airship buzzing loudly
Spread its terror and despair.
With its car of leering demons
Ten ton devils riding there,
What more can be said The Midlands
Mourn the loss of its dear ones,
Slaughtered without word or warning
By the Kaiser and his Huns
As to that dear lady preacher,
She had gone at Christ's command;
Sister Morris died in harness
With the Bible in her hand.
Lilian Ethel Adkin

*Chapter Four*

# The Bright Lights of Loughborough

### 20.15: Zeppelin L.20 bombs Loughborough and Ilkeston

T he saddest thing about the bombing of Loughborough is that it was totally unplanned. While in hindsight the bombing of brightly lit Loughborough, north of blacked out Leicester and south of equally dark Nottingham, seemed almost preordained, in reality it was more complex: the Zeppelin commander certainly saw the lights, but in the mist didn't realise he was bombing a town, he thought it was a gun battery. This was not known at the time and after the raid there was considerable criticism of businesses that had left their lights on, and the Council who had kept the town lamps lighted as usual. The town was unusual in that at about 19.00 the police were warned that a raid was in progress and suggested precautions should be taken. As in most of the other towns bombed there was no air raid planning, and no one had a defined role or responsibility to turn the lights off.

We know quite a lot about the raid from British intelligence reports and the combat report of *Kapitanleutnant* Franz Stabbert the commander of Zeppelin L.20. It was Stabbert's first raid on England. A regular naval officer, born on 13 February 1881, Stabbert was an inexperienced airship commander; his first command was Zeppelin L.7 in November 1915, which he 'inherited' from Max Dietrich. We don't know why he was assigned to a more advanced 'Q' type ship ahead of more experienced commanders, it was probably because the much more efficient 'R' type was due in service in a few months, and they were destined for those. Stabbart took over Zeppelin L.20 on 22 December 1915. She was a new airship, the first of the longer 'Q' type Zeppelins. These had a higher bomb load than the smaller 'P' type, but still had the problems caused by the Maybach HSLu 240-horsepower engines.

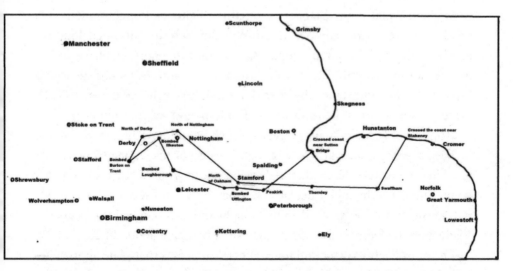

**19.10** crossed coast near Sutton Bridge in the company of L.11. **19.40** She was seen over Peakirk, She then bombed Uffington. She was seen north of Oakham, then north of Leicester. **20.00** Bombed Loughborough. She then bombed railway targets at Bannerley and Trowell. **20.30** bombed the Stanton Iron Works at Hallam Fields near Ilkeston. **20.45** bombed Burton on Trent. Was next seen north of Derby and north of Nottingham and then over Stamford. **22.30** She was seen at Thornley. **23.15** Swaffham. **23.45** crossed the coast near Blakeney. **23.52** Last seen from Cromer going out to sea.

*This map is probably very accurate. GHQ and Jones agree on the route of L.20. GHQ also had the additional advantage of being able to interrogate the second officer on L.20 Wilhelm Schirlitz. He was a very lucky man he had been repatriated to Germany when L.20 crash landed in the sea off the Norwegian coast. He became the second officer on L.33 and was captured when she was shot down.*

The route of Zeppelin L.20.

The route of L.20 was well monitored by the British. She left her base at Tondern at about 11.06. She was slowed down by engine trouble, the forward-engine was out of action for much of the flight over the North Sea, and the starboard ran irregularly. She also had to fly low at 6500ft because of heavy rain and snow, which caused icing on the hull. This further slowed L.20, but did not stop her reaching the English Midlands. The icing reduced as she flew overland and she was able to climb to about 9000ft. She was spotted crossing the coast at about 19.10 near Sutton Bridge in the company of Zeppelin L.11. She was spotted over Peakirk at 19.40, and then travelling west she bombed Uffington, at 19.45, dropping one HE bomb, which broke a few windows, but did no other damage. She passed north of Oakham and Leicester. Both Nottingham and Leicester had a full blackout, Loughborough did not.

At about 20.00 Franz Stabbert spotted the lights of Loughborough. The bomb-aimer *Leutnant zur See* Ernst Wilhelm Schirlitz dropped four HE bombs at 20.05, killing ten people. In his combat report Stabbart said he bombed an anti-aircraft battery which fired at him, and the bombs silenced it. It is difficult to understand why he said this unless he believed it were true. He made the report when he returned to Tondern, and was not under pressure to claim he only hit military targets – which would have been the case had he been a prisoner of war. He said that, because of his engine trouble, after bombing the battery, he made the decision not to go on to Liverpool, but to bomb Sheffield which he calculated was nearby. He turned north to do this, but was much further south than he thought and next bombed the Bennerley Viaduct on the Derbyshire–Nottinghamshire border at about 20.27.

The most likely explanation for Stabbert's report is that as he approached Loughborough he saw through the ground mist, flashing lights which he took to be gun fire. As we know the Empress Works were operating a night shift, other factories probably also did. An explanation for flashing lights could be welding flashes or intermittent light. Add to that anxiety, tiredness, restricted vision and the imagination takes over. On the same Monday night Stabbert's report was not unique. A number of British pilots flying over London reported seeing Zeppelins at a distance, or explosions on the ground. We know for certain that no Zeppelins operated over London that night. The reports even generated a name 'The Phantom Zeppelin Phenomenon'. We know the reports were written soon after the pilots landed, usually after an animated discussion with other pilots. There is no doubt they were absolutely honest recollections. The Zeppelins were probably clouds in searchlight beams, the explosions electrical flashes from underground trains, in the over ground sections seen through breaks in the fog – imagination did the rest. An admiral on reading a pilot's report said: 'Night flying must be most difficult and dangerous, and require considerable nerve and pluck, but this airman seems to have been gifted with a more than usually vivid imagination.'

One of the more bizarre results of these phantom Zeppelin reports which are available in *Pilots' Reports Relating to the Destruction of Zeppelin*, at the Imperial War Museum is that some have made their way to UFO internet sites.

It is interesting to note that a few months later the bomb-aimer Ernst Wilhelm Schirlitz was captured by the British. It seems he was a boastful young man, for he told them how skilled he was in using the complex bombsight.

Zeppelin L.20 did a considerable amount of damage in Loughborough killing ten people with four HE bombs. The British Intelligence report is quite explicit about the order in which the bombs were dropped, from this we can work out what happened. It seems she passed over Loughborough from east to west, and then cut her engines and slowed down looking for targets. We know the first bomb dropped in the Garden of the Crown and Cushion, a pub in Orchard Street. The second, a few seconds later, landed nearby in The Rushes, a main thoroughfare. It seems L.20 then circled and headed east – the last two bombs landed close together in the Empress Road area several hundred yards east of the first two, and according to witnesses about three minutes later. They were also dropped in quick succession. The third bomb dropped on an orchard in Thomas Street, causing no casualties but breaking a lot of windows in the area, and the fourth, seconds later, in front of the Empress Crane Works. It was noted in the British Intelligence report that the Crane Works did not put its lights out until the first bomb had dropped. Ten people, four men and six women were killed. About twelve people were injured. After dropping the bombs Stabbert opened the throttles on the engines and sped away to the north. Several witnesses noted the roar of the engines, but nobody saw the Zeppelin.

We know from some excellent research in the Loughborough Roll of Honour the names of all the victims and some of the circumstances of their death. The first victim seems to have been Martha Shipman aged 49-years of 5 Orchard Street, who was killed in the Crown and Cushion Inn when the first bomb exploded in the garden. According to the report in the local newspaper the *Loughborough Echo* she was taking refreshment when the bomb landed in the pub garden, it blew a wall down and Martha was killed by shrapnel. Sarah Oram wife of the licensee of the Crown and Cushion was in the same room but only injured. The next bomb landed in The Rushes – a street with a lot of shops. Annie Adcock aged 42-years, was killed at number 13 The Rushes, where her husband owned a brush-makers shop. Also killed in the area were a newly married couple Joseph and Alice Adkins, of Kingthorp

Road, Loughborough. Alice aged 29-years had gone to meet Joseph a fitter aged twenty-seven from work. It seems that Ethel Higgs aged twenty-five, a factory worker of 104 Station Street was also killed by the same bomb in The Rushes. A number of people were injured including James Stenson aged 45-years, a visitor to the town, who was staying at Gray's Lodging House, The Rushes and Rose Bartholomuch 38, an Italian ice-cream-maker.

The pattern of the bombing followed a pattern we have seen before: the bomb-aimer *Leutnant zur See* Scherlitz dropped his first bomb while the ship hovered. When he saw the explosion he dropped another close by. Witnesses said there were only seconds between the blasts.

The Zeppelin then moved slowly east, according to witnesses the third bomb was dropped about three minutes after the second, it fell in an orchard near Thomas Street, the fourth bomb followed seconds later. This landed in Empress Road, a mixture of factories and working class housing. Three members of the same family Mary Anne Page aged 44-years, her son Joseph Page aged eighteen and daughter Elsie Page aged sixteen were killed near their house at 87 Empress Road, the story was told to the coroner's inquest by Private Joseph Walton Page 'a stalwart looking soldier in khaki' who was a member of the RAMC and home on leave having been wounded in France. He said he was in the house when the windows were shattered by an explosion. On hearing this Mary Anne his wife and son and daughter ran to check on a neighbour who had been in a shop a few minutes before. Immediately they got outside another bomb hit the gutter a few yards from them. They were killed instantly, their bodies mutilated. Also killed by this bomb was Joseph Gilbert aged 49-years who kept a shop in Empress Road. His young son, with a bandaged head, manfully tried to control his emotions while telling the court he was in the shop with his father when the bomb exploded. His father was hit in the chest and fell to the floor. Joseph Gilbert's wife said she had taken him into the living room, but he died after a few minutes.

Most of the casualties occurred in the Empress Crane Works, just across the road from where the bomb fell. Only one man was fatally wounded. He was Joseph Turnill aged 50-years, a fitter of 83 Station Road, killed when heavy glass blown out of the roof hit him. There were a significant number of non-fatal casualties at the Crane Works. They included a soldier, Venus Hunt aged 48-years of Charles Street, William Humber aged 33-years employed as a turner; a machine-hand, Percy Measures aged 22-years; David Giles aged 28-years, electrician and a second soldier, John Thomas aged twenty-four. All these men were employed at the Herbert Morris Crane Works in Empress Street. The Empress Road bombs demonstrate a pattern we have seen in other towns. The Zeppelin bomb-aimer dropped one bomb, waited for the explosion and, if he saw any movement, dropped another in the same place. This certainly resulted in the death of the Page family, as it did the Smith family in Wednesbury. They heard the first explosion, ran outside to see what was going on, and were killed by the second bomb. It is notable that Private Page, a soldier, didn't run outside. He knew the danger: his wife and children didn't.

After the raid, two workers at the Empress Works were given bravery awards. Beatrice Smith was a crane driver, she was on duty when an air raid warning was given, and the works closed down. On leaving she forgot to pull the main electricity switch. She realised her error when she got home and, knowing it could cause a serious accident when work resumed, she went back to the factory in darkness and switched off. Her award was given for returning to her post at risk to her life in order to avert danger to the works.

Ernest Stubby was the works' electrician on the night of the raid; he remained at his post during the whole night. Both workers were awarded the OBE, which was presented by the Duke of Rutland.

The killing in Loughborough over, L.20 flew north at high speed, Schirlitz dropped one more bomb as he left the town; it landed in soft ground and didn't explode. Stabbert next saw lights at Ilkeston. He probably took Ilkeston for Sheffield, which he claimed to have bombed in his combat report. At Bennerly and Trowell he dropped seven HE bombs on the railway, where he damaged a signal box. He also bombed the Bennerley railway viaduct on the Derbyshire-Nottinghamshire border at Awsworth, but caused no casualties. The signal man in the Bennerly box was very lucky. He had been telephoned a few minutes before and told to stop all trains; he was walking along the track towards a waiting train to tell the driver to extinguish his lamps, when the bomb hit his signal box.

Stabbert continued west to Hallam Fields near Ilkeston where he dropped fifteen HE bombs on the Stanton Ironworks at 20.30. He did considerable damage to buildings and killed two men. We have reasonably good information about this, and can reconstruct much of what happened. There were two coroner's inquests on the victims: the one on James Hall on the Thursday, 3 February 1916, and the one on Walter Wilson the next day. Though the actual inquest reports are lost, the two Ilkeston local papers the *Advertiser* and the *Pioneer*, have virtually verbatim reports of the inquests, though obviously missing details like names and locations under the censorship of the Defence of the Realm Act. We can add to this the memories of people involved which were collected by the Local History Society many years later.

There seem to have been a number of common facts remembered by all the witnesses. It was a clear night – there was no mist in the area at the time of the raid. Almost everyone saw and also heard the Zeppelin. The explosions on the railway were heard and people saw the Zeppelin coming from the Bennerley area. There is also agreement that the Zeppelin spent a few minutes over the works, probably circling looking for targets. Several witnesses who were standing in the tram terminus with Walter Wilson one of the victims, said it dropped a few bombs and then went away. They heard more explosions in the distance, then the airship returned and dropped a few more bombs before flying away.

From this it seems likely that the first bombs were dropped near the works offices, and workers' housing a few hundred yards or so from Saint Bartholomew's Church. A number of the works offices, houses, a rifle range and a pub were damaged. It is certain Stabbert didn't know he was bombing offices and housing, but from 9000ft over a clear target Ernst Schirlitz, the bomb–aimer, probably saw lights and signs of activity. It seems he dropped five bombs in the first cluster. They damaged houses, offices and two pubs. We have a description of what happened at one of the pubs -it seems to have been the Stanton Hotel in Crompton Street. The local newspapers, one of which may have supported the temperance movement, reported what happened with some glee. The drinkers had a terrible fright when a bomb dropped in the pub garden, blowing out all the windows on that side. Bottles were thrown from the shelves, some of the beer barrels in the cellar lost their plugs, and there was a great deal of waste. The pub immediately cleared after the explosion, not many finishing their glasses. When people returned to tidy up in the gardens the next day they found a pigeon cote had been blown over. The birds trapped inside were considerably distressed. However, when the cote was re-erected the birds settled down as if nothing had happened.

Stabbert then turned away to the manufacturing area. A witness many years later said the bombs were dropped near the old works furnaces. The GHQ reports say the moulding shop was damaged. The first death occurred here. We have some fairly confused reports from the inquest of James Hall, aged 56-years, assistant furnace keeper, of Homer Cottage, 12 Frederick Street, Stapleford. This was held on Thursday, 3 February 1916, and presided over by Arthur N Whiston, the deputy coroner of Derby. The first witness had his hand bandaged and arm in a sling. He said he had been at work at about 20.30 with three other men when he heard 'a bit of a bump', two or three times. He didn't know what it was. He told the coroner he didn't hear any aircraft but next heard a very loud explosion about thirty yards away. He was hit on the arm and under the chin and got away as fast as he could. He did then hear the engines of an aircraft. He didn't see the body of James Hall for an hour as he was being treated for his injuries. When he did it was badly mutilated with the head blown off. Another witness said he was near James Hall. They were standing near the wall of a building when he heard people shouting about Zeppelins. It seems this was after they had heard the first explosions. They sought shelter, and were a few yards from each other when the next bomb fell, about thirty yards from them. The witness was unhurt, but in the dark, fell over the legs of James Hall. It seems the bomb hit a pile of pig iron and this added to the effect of the shrapnel from the bomb. James Hall was killed instantly, his body was badly mutilated, the top of his head blown off. The coroner said the death was the result of an abominable outrage.

Though the witness reports seem confusing we need to consider the circumstances behind them. It seems to me that what happened was that the men were working in a foundry shed, a noisy, dangerous environment where the glare of the furnaces would have prevented them from having much idea of what was happening outside. When they heard the first bombs and heard the warning about Zeppelins, the first thing they would have done was get away from the furnaces, and the molten metal. They were probably outside in the dark, trying to find shelter when the fatal bomb fell. It would have been a very frightening, very confusing situation.

We know more about what happened to the second victim Walter Wilson of 2 Albert Villas, Station Road Ilkeston. He was a 41-year-old furnace-loader, married with a large family. With three workmates he was waiting at the tram terminus opposite the church. He had finished work and was returning home. Saint Bartholomew's was built in 1895 as part of an estate for workers at the ironworks. The Zeppelin had bombed in the vicinity a few minutes before. It seems likely the men knew the trams had been cancelled and were getting ready to walk back to Ilkeston when Zeppelin L.20 returned and dropped two more bombs.

The first landed near the men, and they ran to find shelter, Walter Wilson sought shelter by the wall of Saint Bartholomew's Church. A few seconds later, in what seems like a frightening cat and mouse game, another bomb landed near them. The witness then described hearing a shrill whistle, an ear-splitting crash, and a blinding flash. The bomb hit the parish room, completely destroying it, and breaking a stained glass window in the church.

Walter Wilson was found lying against a wall near the demolished parish room. He complained about his back hurting. Several of the witnesses carried him to a hotel. The police were called; the officer reported to the coroner that he had been at home when he heard an explosion and the noise of an engine. He ensured his wife and family took shelter in his cellar, and then went to the hotel to examine the wounded man. He had a wound in his right buttock and had lost a lot of blood. He was conscious and able to talk. He said that when he heard the first bombs exploding he left work with the others to go home. He felt something hit him in the back and knock him off his feet. He was soon after taken to hospital, where he saw his wife and told her he was too badly injured to get better. He was operated on at Ilkeston Hospital. The doctor who attended to him said he was in a collapsed condition, and part of his intestine was protruding through a three-inch wound in his back. He never recovered from the operation and died on Tuesday afternoon, the day after the raid.

Like most of the towns bombed Ilkeston had its near miss story. The parish room at Saint Bartholomew's had been booked for a bible class for twenty teenage girls, but the wife of the curate, Mrs Cox was unwell, and so they were invited to the parsonage instead for a cup of tea.

Stabbert then flew to Burton-on-Trent, bombing the town at 20.45, the second of the three Zeppelins to do so. As by this time he had used all his high explosive bombs, he dropped only incendiaries. As three airships bombed Burton in a one hour period, with fifteen people killed, and a great deal of damage done, it is impossible to determine which airship was responsible for individual casualties. However, as Stabbard only had incendiary bombs it seems likely he caused fires and most of the casualties were caused by L.15 which arrived earlier. It is interesting to note that Breithaupt, the commander of L.15 stated in his combat report that he saw a huge glow of fire as L.15 left Burton. As far as we know there were no major fires in Burton. It may be that he saw the incendiary bombs dropped by Stabbert, but did not see the Zeppelin. Certainly neither commander reported seeing the other airship, though they must have been over Burton at much the same time.

After bombing Burton, L.20 suffered from more engine trouble, and made slow progress. She was spotted travelling in a north easterly direction passing north of Derby and Nottingham, and then she went south east to the vicinity of Stamford. She was spotted at Thornley at 22.30 and near Swaffham at 23.15pm. She crossed the coast near Blakeney at 23.45, and was last seen from Cromer going out to sea at 23.52. It seems she had more engine trouble because it took her 12-hours to cross the North Sea, arriving at Tondern at noon on Tuesday, 1 February 1916.

*Chapter Five*

# Rolls-Royce Town

## Midnight: Zeppelin L.14 bombs Derby

T he people of the Black Country towns, Burton and Loughborough were very critical of the police and local authorities in their towns. In fairness to them, it can be said they were either taken by surprise, or attempted to turn off the lights but didn't have the time or the resources to do it in time. In Derby there can be no excuse – they had four hours to plan, not only were some lights not turned off, but when a Zeppelin finally arrived after midnight, some had been turned on again. This was Zeppelin L.14, commanded by *Kapitanleutnant der Reserve* Alois Bocker. He was a very experienced naval officer, who had previously been a merchant seaman, serving as a captain with the Hamburg-Amerika shipping line. He was born on 12 May 1879 and survived the war. He had bombed Lowestoft on 15 April 1915, dropping high explosive and incendiary bombs on a timber yard, without causing any casualties.

Bocker took command of Zeppelin L.14 on 10 August 1915, and set out for England a week later. However, he had to turn back with mechanical trouble. He returned on 8 September 1915. He was again beset by engine troubles. He reached Norfolk but had to jettison his bombs near East Durham without causing any casualties. He then took part in the last raid of 1915, on 13 October. This time he got lost on the way to London, but bombed the Otterpool Army Camp near Hythe, killing fourteen soldiers, injuring twelve more and killing sixteen horses. He eventually reached Croydon, destroying houses and killing a number of civilians.

We have quite a lot of information about the route of Zeppelin L.14, on 31 January 1916. She crossed the English coast north of Holkham, Norfolk at about 18.15; she was sighted over Burnham Market at 18.20, Sandringham at 18.35. She bombed Knipton, south west of Grantham at

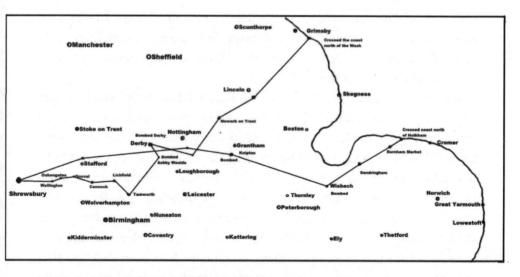

18.15 Crossed the coast north of Holkham, Norfolk. 18.20 seen near Burnham Market. 18.35 seen over Sandringham. 19.00 dropped one incendiary bomb at Wisbeach. 19.10 seen near Thornley. 20.00 Bombed Knipton, south west of Grantham. She was then seen south of Nottingham, south of Derby and north of Stafford. 22.05 L.14 seen over Shrewsbury, then over Wellington, Oakengates, Gnosal, Cannock, Lichfield and Tamworth. 23.35 Bombed Ashby Woulds, near Ashby de la Zouch. She then bombed Overseal. **Midnight** Bombed Swadlincote. 00.30 (1 Feb 16) Bombed Derby. She then flew south east of Nottingham. She was later seen near Newark and south of Lincoln. 02.10 Crossed the coast north of the Wash.

*This map is probably very accurate. GHQ and Jones agree on the route of L.14. Not only do ground observer's reports, radio interceptions and bomb locations confirm her position. Much of her route was based on the intelligence gained from the interrogation of her commander Bocker and most of the crew of Zeppelin L.33 shot down in September 1916, most of whom who had transferred from L.14.*

The route of Zeppelin L.14.

about 20.00, without any casualties. She then headed west for the Midlands, passing south of Nottingham and Derby and north of Stafford, where she was spotted over Shrewsbury at 22.05. She then wandered, passing over Wellington, Oakengates and Gnosal. It appears that Bocker thought the dark area of rural Shropshire to the West was the sea and he had reached the west coast. He turned east and flew over Cannock, Lichfield and Tamworth. At 23.35 he saw the light of furnaces at Ashby Woulds, near Ashby-de-la-Zouch. He dropped one high explosive and one incendiary bomb which fell on a cinder heap and did no damage. He reached Overseal in Derbyshire, at about midnight, where he dropped four high explosive bombs, three fell in open fields and one in a canal, and did no damage. A few minutes later at Swadlincote in Derbyshire, he dropped three high explosive bombs; they did a little damage, but caused no casualties. L.14 reached the town of Derby, which was showing many lights some four hours after the start of the raid.

We have very good reports about what happened in Derby which explain why the town was bombed when it was, and illustrate the chaotic planning and communication that was apparent in every bombed town that night. In fact, Derby acquitted itself better than the others that were hit. Derby police had been warned at about 19.00 of a possible raid and had arranged for precautions to be taken. Works' sirens were sounded, special constables reported for duty, trams stopped running and some works shut down. This almost certainly resulted in Derby not being bombed earlier that evening. Four Zeppelins flew close to the town, which must have been dark and they did not see it. L.21 passed north at about 18.55. L.13 passed over at about 19.45. L.20 passed close at about 21.00, while Bocker in L.14 flew just south at about 21.00 in his combat report he claimed to have seen Derby but decided not to bomb as his main target was Liverpool. He returned three hours later. Telephone calls to police in other towns seemed to confirm that the raids had ended and the danger was over. At some time between 22.00 and 23.00 a decision was made that the crisis was over. The special constables were sent home, the trams returned to their depots, and most works with a night shift turned their lights back on. Some of the street lights were put back on, too.

After a long night, L.14 still had an almost full bomb load. Though Bocker did not realise he was over Derby, it was a glittering prize for the German. We have very full reports from the ground of the bombing. According to the GHQ Report, Bocker reached Derby at about 00.10, ten minutes after he bombed Swadlincote. While the GHQ reports are detailed and state that Bocker dropped twenty-one high explosive and four incendiary bombs on Derby, they do not outline the route the Zeppelin took over the town. The GHQ report first discusses the events at the Midland Railway Locomotive Works, which might suggest it was the first target to be bombed – it was certainly the place where the most damage was done. It seems to me, however, using the map in the book *The Bombing of Derby in the Two World Wars* and after a very useful discussion with

Peter Kirk, one of the authors of that work, that the Locomotive Works was one of the last places to be bombed – it was the furthest north of all the target sites. Peter described the path of L.14 as like a reversed question mark about 1¼ miles by about ½ mile.

Bocker was travelling almost due north when he left Swadlincote, as he approached Derby from the south he would have crossed the Birmingham-Derby railway line and probably followed it into the city. If there were any lights showing he would have seen a mass of railway lines between the Osmaston and London Roads to the south of the city. In 1916 Derby was one of the principal railway towns in the country. The factories building railway engines and carriages were obviously connected by railway lines, but the whole area was like a huge goods yard. There were numerous branch lines and sidings to shunt and store the railway stock being built. It is unlikely Bocker would fail to see it from 9000ft. Witnesses on the ground said that the Zeppelin was over Derby for about ten minutes, dropping bombs in salvos of two or three every minute or two. No one reported that the Zeppelin was circling, so it seems likely she was flying slowly above the railway, and slowing down to a hover when dropping bombs. In Derby all the bombs were dropped in fairly small groups, the targets were railways, factories or workers' housing. It seems certain Bocker could see his targets, first from lights, and then possibly from fires he had started. It is likely the Zeppelin was stationary when the bombs were dropped.

Bocker flew north over Derby and the first bombs landed about a mile south of the city centre. The first targets of L.14 were factories around the Rolls-Royce Works on Nightingale Road, just west of the Osmaston Road. Bocker dropped a salvo of six high explosive bombs aimed at targets in the area. Two high explosive bombs obviously aimed at factory buildings hit waste land by the Rolls-Royce factory. Another high explosive bomb hit the motor car test track at the end of the Rolls-Royce factory; this did some damage to the workshops but caused no casualties. The next target was the nearby Metalite Works of the Derby Lamp Company in Gresham Road; the bomb-aimer *Oberleutnant zur See* Kurt Frankenberg dropped three high explosive bombs doing considerable damage to goods awaiting dispatch, and almost demolishing a building, but causing no casualties.

Bocker then continued a few hundred yards further north bombing the Midland Railway Carriage and Wagon Works (a separate enterprise to the Railway Locomotive Works some distance away) dropping five more high explosive bombs, doing some damage but causing no casualties. The next salvo was another few hundred yards north, it seems the Zeppelin first bombed the T W Fletcher Lace factory in Osmaston Road with two incendiary bombs; they landed in the factory yard and did little damage. Two more bombs hit the house of a Mr Sydney Fletcher, possibly the factory owner. Probably still hovering, Bocker then bombed some working class housing with four incendiary bombs. A house in Horton Street was set on fire by a bomb which went through the roof. It seems here that Bocker and Frankenberg could see enough to decide the type of bomb to use. Incendiaries were dropped on housing where they were more effective.

Still following the Osmaston Road, Bocker went a little further north. Frankenberg dropped one high explosive bomb on a large house, the Rolls-Royce Foremans' Club on the corner of Bateman Street and Osmaston Road. The bomb landed on the lawn, making a crater it was said 'big enough to put a horse and cart in'. The lawn later became the works bowling green, and signs of the crater can still be seen today. It is not recorded whether this gives a home advantage to Rolls-Royce teams.

Bocker then turned east across the London Road and over the railway yards. These were almost certainly well lit. He bombed the Midland Railway Locomotive Works off the London Road. This was the target where most damage was done. L.14 dropped nine high explosive bombs which killed three men outright and injured one so severely he died in hospital three days later. The British GHQ Intelligence report says that most of the bombs seemed to be aimed at trains in Chaddesden Sidings and a bomb hit the side of an engine tender. The men killed were all employed by the Railway Works. They were: William Barcroft, aged 32-years, a fitter of 34 Strutt Street Derby; Harry Hitherway aged 23-years, of 73 Devonshire Street, Derby, and James Gibbs Hardy, aged 56-years, an engine driver of 11 Strutt Street, Derby. The man who died three days later was Charles Henry Champion, an electrician, aged 41-years, of 33 Fleet Street, Derby. It seems the four men were killed by a single bomb. The coroner's report gives more detail. There were a number of witnesses who had been working with the victims, when the bomb fell. One said he and the victims had heard the engines of the Zeppelin clearly. It also seems Bocker was using a searchlight to look for targets. (He would have seen a train but not individuals at 9000ft.) The witness said he ran in one direction and the victims another. The men who died had sheltered under the engine tender, but the bomb landed a few yards from them. The witness was blown off his feet but not injured. Another witness was the departmental foreman who said he had turned up the lights in his department, as he saw another department do the same, and thought they had been given the authority to do so. When he heard the bombs he turned the lights off again, but obviously too late. As well as the four railway men, a woman died of shock. She was Sarah Constantine, aged 71-years, of Malvern House, Rose Hill Street. She was the widow of a Midland Railway official and a retired headmistress.

It is likely the last bombs to be dropped hit the works of the Derby Gas Company, south east of the Engine Works. Two high explosive bombs hit the gas works, and one incendiary bomb hit a coal heap, which failed to ignite, I think the bomb went off but the coal didn't burn. According to the GHQ report the bombs had no effect.

L.14 then left Derby and flew east. She was spotted south-east of Nottingham at 00.35, and near Newark and south of Lincoln, before leaving our shores north of the Wash at about 02.10 on 1 February, after almost eight hours in enemy territory. She had penetrated the furthest west of any Zeppelin on the raid. The raid on Derby showed the chaotic nature of decision making, but in another way the town was lucky. Had the lights been on earlier, there would have been more casualties, as people would have been out on the streets, as they were in other towns. The victims were shift workers – most people in the bombed area were tucked up safely in bed. Statistically they were much safer there than in the open.

There was a great deal of criticism of the actions of the local authorities and railway companies in putting the lights back on before midnight. While this was deserved, the real failure was at national level in the War Office. The route of L.14 from Shrewsbury to Derby was very well recorded, this meant that ground observers could see her and were sending accurate information by telephone to the War Office. The chaotic organisation and lack of an effective communication system meant there was no way to collate the intelligence and warn the authorities in the East Midlands that a Zeppelin was on its way back.

L.14 arrived back at Nordholz at about noon on 1 February 1916. The Germans said in a press release the next day, that Liverpool was the main target and had been hit by a number of Zeppelins. It is often thought that in his combat report Bocker claimed to have bombed Liverpool. According to Robinson this is not the case. Bocker said he identified Nottingham and Derby on his way west, but decided not to attack because his main target was Liverpool. He then flew into thick cloud. He thought he had reached the West Coast of England, when actually he had reached Shrewsbury. He then spent an hour looking for Liverpool, before deciding to turn back. This seems logical and explains the circling and rather devious route he took over East Shropshire and South Staffordshire. He then headed for home, dropping 415 lbs of bombs on big factories and blast furnaces he thought were in Nottingham, but were in fact in Derby.

The story does not end there. On Saturday, 23 September 1916, Bocker and many of the crew of L.14 were shot down in a new Zeppelin, L.33. The airship was hit by anti-aircraft fire over London. Luckily for them the ship did not catch fire and crash landed at Great Wigsborough in Essex. Twenty-two crewmen were captured. They were intensively interrogated. Bocker refused to say much, but many crew members talked openly. They all maintained that L.14 had bombed Liverpool, as had been claimed in the press communiqué. There seems no doubt that most of the crew genuinely believed this. The GHQ report says they all believed the claims made by their commanding officer and navigator on which they assumed the communiqué was based. However, it is unlikely many had much idea of the course of the ship – a man working in an engine gondola would have little idea of the position of the Zeppelin. Along with Bocker there was one man who did: the *Steuermann*, a warrant officer, responsible for navigation. After prolonged cross examination, he said he knew L.14 had not been to Liverpool, but said he had seen the lights of Manchester and Sheffield. It may be that while Bocker believed he was over the west coast, the *Steuermann* – who was an equally experienced seaman, responsible only for navigation – had a better idea of their location. However, he certainly didn't know the ship had bombed Derby. He said during his

**Map of the raid on Derby from 'The Bombing of Rolls-Royce at Derby in Two World Wars - with diversions'. By Peter Kirk, Peter Felix and Gunter Bartnick.**

*Map courtesy of Rolls-Royce Heritage Trust.*

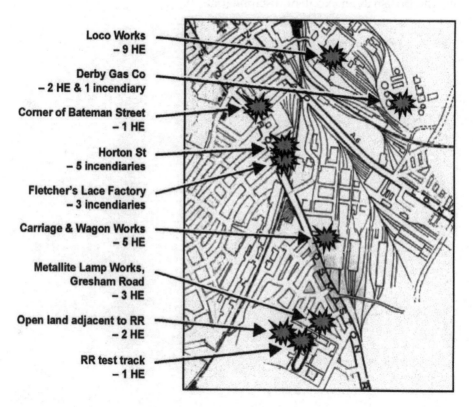

Loco Works – 9 HE

Derby Gas Co – 2 HE & 1 incendiary

Corner of Bateman Street – 1 HE

Horton St – 5 incendiaries

Fletcher's Lace Factory – 3 incendiaries

Carriage & Wagon Works – 5 HE

Metallite Lamp Works, Gresham Road – 3 HE

Open land adjacent to RR – 2 HE

RR test track – 1 HE

The bombs dropped on Derby by L.14.

interrogation that by compass readings and dead reckoning he was certain L.14 had bombed ironworks between Birmingham and Nottingham. The GHQ report says that this could only be the pipe furnaces at Ashby Woulds. This does indicate he had a better idea of the position of L.14 than Bocker, though neither correctly identified Derby as the target of their bombs.

Back at Nordholz after the raid, Bocker probably cared little about what the Propaganda Ministry said, and allowed the crew to believe they had bombed Liverpool. It seems very likely he discussed the route with the navigator, but we will probably never know if they agreed what it was. The *Steuermann* was unlikely to disagree with his commanding officer, described by the British as an excellent disciplinarian.

*Chapter Six*

# A Much Admired Man

**20.15 and 23.00: Zeppelin L.13 commanded by Heinrich Mathy bombs Stoke-on-Trent and Scunthorpe.**

K*apitanleutnant* Heinrich Mathy was regarded both by Peter Strasser, the Commander of the Airship Force, and the small group of British intelligence officers, with an encyclopaedic knowledge of the personnel and methodology of the German airship Service, in the GHQ as the best and bravest of all the Zeppelin commanders. Mathy was born on 4 April 1883 at Mannheim. He joined the navy when he was fifteen and was described as an exceptional cadet. He became a destroyer captain when still quite young, and was selected for a naval staff role. He went to the *Marine Akademie* in 1913 and 1914, and when he was there learned to fly in the DELAG Zeppelins. He was personally selected for the airship service by Peter Strasser, and joined in 1915. He had a reputation for boldness, determination and superb navigational skills. He was known in Germany and Britain as the man who had been responsible for the fires causing some £500,000 worth of damage in London. He was feted in the German press as a national hero. He had the status of a celebrity. The German press as a matter of policy tried to present the human side of heroic military figures, as a means of raising civilian morale. The Red Baron, Manfred von Richthofen was the best known, but other selected war heroes also became celebrities. As well as fliers these included U-boat commanders. Mathy was a handsome man with a very good looking young wife, Hertha. They had married in 1915 and had a baby daughter, Gisela.

As a Zeppelin commander Mathy was regarded as by far the best navigator, pressing on and finding targets long after his colleagues had given up. In his combat reports we get some idea of his methods. On a flight over England he tended to stop and hover every thirty to sixty minutes, often dropping a parachute flare to find his position. Once that was established he would plot a direct course and fly straight to his next waypoint, where he would drop another flare. By these means he went towards his objective. He had previously taken part in seven raids on England and was probably best known as the man who had dropped a 660lbs bomb on central London near the Bank of England, on 8 September 1915. Zeppelin L.13 killed twenty-two people that day; the German press claimed L.13 was a lucky ship, lucky for some anyway.

He first raided England on 14 April 1915 in Zeppelin L.9, bombing Wallsend, near Newcastle upon Tyne, injuring two people and causing minor damage. He entered the public eye on 6 June 1915 when he bombed Hull, in L.9. He did £44,795 worth of damage and nineteen people – five men, nine women and five children – were killed. Twenty-four more were seriously wounded. About twenty-four people died in all. The next day there were riots in Hull against businesses that had seemingly German names or connections.

Mathy took over a new Zeppelin L.13, which he would call his lucky ship on 25 July 1915. He set out three times to bomb England, on 9, 12 and 17 August that year, but each time he had to turn back due to engine trouble. On 8 September 1915 he bombed London, killing about twenty-two people. This was the raid we later describe in the von Wiegand interview. He was in action again on 13 September 1915, and had a lucky escape. He crossed the coast near Harwich but was hit by a six-pounder anti–aircraft gun based in Felixstowe. It damaged several gas cells. Mathy was able to reach his base at Hage but damaged the ship in a crash landing.

He had been summoned to Berlin on 18 September 1915 to meet Admiral von Muller, the Chief of the Kaiser's Naval Cabinet. The subject of the meeting shows what a strange society Germany was at the time. The Admiral said the Kaiser and Kaiserine had been alarmed by reports of bomb damage in central London, and wanted to be assured that no harm had been done to Buckingham Palace, churches or historic buildings. Mathy told von Muller all the bombs had been correctly aimed, and was told: 'Their Majesties would be greatly relieved.'

A mark of Mathy's celebrity status is that on 23 September 1915 he was interviewed by Karl von Wiegand the German correspondent of the *New York World*. The fact that he was allowed to give an interview to a newspaper from a neutral foreign country indicates the trust and status he had. While it is apparent in the interview that there were certain areas that could not be covered, Wiegand did gain some insights into Mathy's character, and a commander's eye view of Zeppelin operations. The fact that Mathy's Zeppelin was L.13 was described as 'something I cannot mention but which every superstitious believer in omens and signs would regard as a very magnet of disaster and ill luck'. This vagueness is difficult to understand. Almost everyone, certainly the British, knew Mathy was the commander of L.13, and if they didn't it wouldn't have taken a genius to work it out from the interview. Wiegand had previously interviewed a number of U-Boat commanders and had a fascination with these brave, intelligent professional killers.

He described Mathy as a man of about 34-years, with close cropped hair giving the appearance of an entirely bald, smooth-faced figure, as slender and supple as a young woman. Like the U-Boat captains Mathy seemed to live on his nerves. He was 'all nerves, nerves of steel'. We shall see later that was probably not the case. What can be said is that Mathy seemed to cope with the obvious stress he was under. It seems Mathy was superstitious; He said what he called 'luck' played a big part with him. That he regarded his ship Zeppelin L.13 as his lucky symbol, had been widely reported. In the past he said he had been assigned to Zeppelins which crashed, but chance had prevented him flying that day. At the time only two navy Zeppelins had crashed: L.1 had crashed into the sea on 9 September 1913 and L.2 crashed in flames at Johannisthal on 17 October 1913. It appears Mathy must have seen the aftermath of the Johannisthal crash because he remarked to Wiegand who had also seen it: 'Our eyes and mind must be concentrated on our work, for at any moment we may be plunged below a shapeless mass of wreckage and human bodies shattered beyond recognition.' With the benefit of hindsight it seems clear that this must have frightened and affected Mathy. We know for certain that at the time of his death he was suffering what we now recognise as post-traumatic stress disorder. It is possible this had set in as early as 1915 but Mathy was a man dedicated to duty, unable to accept weakness, especially in himself.

Mathy defended attacking cities as they were an integral part of the English war effort. He said London was a vast military centre, and a militarily defended city in every sense of the laws of war, written and unwritten. It had property usable for military purposes such as railway stations, banks, docks, shipyards and industrial establishments – all legitimate targets for aerial attack. He said he had strict orders to avoid hitting St Paul's Cathedral, and other churches, museums, palaces and of course residential districts.

He had some concerns about civilian casualities, and said he wanted it recorded that there wasn't an officer or man who didn't feel it deeply when he learned that women and children and other non-combatants were killed, however that was part of war. It was the same as when a gunner or commander of big guns hears that his shell didn't strike exactly where he wanted it to and resulted in the death or injury of non-combatants. He said that he would sooner be on the bridge of a torpedo-boat fighting ship against ship than attack a city from the air, though he emphasised this was not because of the danger – he recognised commanding a Zeppelin was more dangerous.

As the interview took place a few days after his raid on London on 8 and 9 September 1915, and his problem with anti-aircraft fire on 13 September 1915, most of the interview concentrated on it. He said the attack had been important because it was his 100th mission, including training trips, and he wondered whether he would safely round out his century. It is worth looking at the attack on London in some detail as it gives a commander's eye view and an insight into Mathy's thinking. We have to note, however, that London was a very different target from any other city. It was easy to find, Zeppelin commanders were very familiar with its geography, and it was also very heavily defended, with searchlights, anti-aircraft guns and fighter bases.

Mathy said it was getting dark as he approached the English coast. He could see other Zeppelins on either side of him as the light faded. Using a naval term he said his Zeppelin had a full magazine of bombs, not unlike the shells in a ship. He said that London was an easy target to find because of the river Thames which was an indestructible guide post. He had seen London from 60kms away as a reflected glow in the sky. He described in great detail the geography of London, and said he could hit any target he wanted. Mathy had spent a week in London in 1909, and obviously had a good sense of direction

He used the river to get his bearings, and could see many lights in the city. The residential areas were not much darkened, but there were dark spots that stood out. It was the dark spots he was after. At the height the Zeppelin flew there was no sign of life other than a few moving lights which were probably trains. Then there was a flash and it was as if the city suddenly came to life. If anyone doubted that London was well defended they should stand in the front gondola of his Zeppelin and look down. They would see the searchlights like glaring eyes, a narrow band of brilliant light reaching out from below. Before long there were more than a score of searchlight beams like criss-cross ribbons. Then the red flashes of guns, and the ominous crack of shrapnel shells which could be heard above the noise of the Zeppelin's motors and propellers. The searchlights were like tentacles seeking to drag the Zeppelin to its destruction.

When Mathy recognised he was in the area over St Paul's, and above the Bank of England, he ordered his executive officer at the bomb-sight to fire slowly. He saw the explosions and burst of flame of his bombs. He manoeuvred his ship over Liverpool Street Station, and ordered 'rapid fire'. There were numerous detonations and many fires. He said the attack on London took about ten minutes, the Zeppelin tactics of attack were to make a dash to points to be bombarded and quickly get away.

He talked more practically and probably honestly about what it was like to command a Zeppelin. There is an impression of speed, and it was very cold. There is little chance to move about much. Despite thick clothing 'the men get cold, very cold'. The crew carried hot coffee or tea in thermos flasks. 'Nothing stronger?' Wiegand asked. 'No, absolutely not,' said Mathy, 'We have to have clear heads and cool steady nerves up there.'

Asked whether he had ever been attacked by an English aeroplane Mathy said no, he had never been bothered by them. It took some time for an aeroplane to reach the height of a Zeppelin, 'and by then we are gone'. He said over England the crew manned the machine guns and watched for aircraft. Personally he was not much afraid of them, and thought if they attacked he could take care of them. We know of course how wrong he was, but it seems that at the time he was honestly reflecting what he thought. He was quite willing to say how much he feared anti-aircraft fire. It seems that crews in the airship service genuinely thought that aeroplanes were not a major threat – Zeppelins could out climb them and if necessary fight them off.

He talked about the future of aerial warfare. He saw part of his role as that of a pioneer. This was a new sort of warfare in which we had to more or less feel our way in aerial strategy and aerial tactics. Two years in the airship service had convinced him that 'we are only at the dawn of war in the air, and only at the beginning of a great era of development of aerial craft, which would have a great bearing on future wars.'

Wiegand asked Mathy if he thought a large force of about twenty-five Zeppelins could destroy London. Mathy said an attack without consideration of anything or anyone would be terrible: Zeppelins would fly higher if they could bomb anywhere. A large fleet would cause more than a thousand fires and would mean the destruction of a greater part of London. He didn't think there was any danger of that as the Germans had no wish to destroy indiscriminately, or to injure and kill woman, children and other non-combatants.

While it may seem Mathy was 'on message' repeating German propaganda when he talked about how destructive a fleet of Zeppelins could be, I tend to think that he absolutely believed what he said to be true. There is no doubt that Peter Strasser genuinely believed the Zeppelin was potentially a decisive weapon, and strategic bombing a road to victory. The Zeppelin crews must have discussed this often. It is only with the benefit of hindsight created by heavy bombing in the Second World War that we know how false it was.

As an example we can use area bombing by the RAF, though the London Blitz and Coventry also indicate what bombing could do. The best British bomber – the Avro Lancaster – carried about five tons of bombs, twice the load of a 'P' Class Zeppelin. It took several hundred bombers dropping a mixture of high explosive and incendiary bombs to set a city completely on fire and destroy large parts in a fire storm.

We don't know whether Mathy had an opinion on the new policy of 'frightfulness' in January 1916. By then he had completed one more attack on England, bombing London, in the heaviest Zeppelin raid of the war, on 13 October 1915. It seems he bombed the village of Shalford and then hit Woolwich Arsenal with a 300kg bomb. We don't know if there were any casualties caused specifically by Mathy. The raid was the heaviest of the war. Seventy-one people were killed. Most were killed by bombs dropped by Breithaupt, Bocker and Peterson.

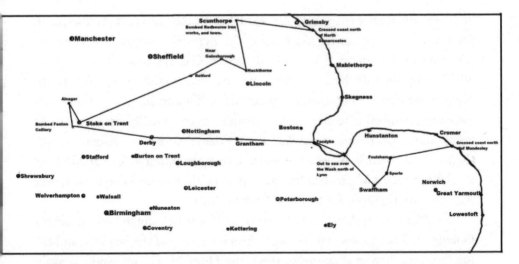

16.50 crossed the English coast, accompanied by Zeppelin L.21 north of Mundesley, The two Zeppelins then separated at Foulsham. L.13 was then seen over East Dereham. She was seen at **17. 15** over Sporle. **17.30** north of Swaffham. Then she flew out to sea over the Wash north of Lynn. **18.30** Back over land at Fosdyke, flew over Grantham. She was seen at **19.30** south of Nottingham. **19.45** Derby, then seen south of Cheadle. **20.15** bombed Fenton Colliery near Stoke-on-Trent then circled towards Newcastle on Lyme. **20.20** Dropped a flare at Madeley, and then flew over Alsager, Wolstanton and Basford. Seen going back in direction of Stoke. British observers then lose L.13. A Zeppelin almost certainly L.13 was seen at **21.50** near Retford. She was next seen near Gainsborough, then flying towards Lincoln. At **22.30** Mathy dropped a flare over Hackthorne. At **23.00** L.13 was over the Frodingham Iron and Steel works near Scunthorpe she bombed the closed Redbourn Iron and Steel Works, and the town of Scunthorpe. **23.35** seen at Humberston. She was fired on by the one pounder pom- pom gun at Waltham Wireless Station. **23.45** Crossed the coast north of North Somercoates.

*This map is based mainly on H A Jones, in War in the Air. GHQ reports confuse L.13, with L.11 and L.15. Ground observations track L.13 accurately until She reached Stoke, She is then lost in the fog. G.H.Q next reports her as bombing Burton, mistaking L.15 or L.20 for her. They then think she made for the coast, ascribing the bombing of Scunthorpe to L.11. In part the intelligence errors were probably a tribute to Mathy who was regarded by GHQ as such a good navigator he was unlikely to get lost.*

The route of Zeppelin L.13.

On 31 January 1916, Mathy left his base at Hage, in Zeppelin L.13 with a crew of sixteen, at about 11.45. We have good records of the early part of the flight. Zeppelin L.13 crossed the English coast, accompanied by Zeppelin L.21, at 16.50, north of Mundesley, Norfolk. The two Zeppelins then separated at Foulsham. Mathy took L.13 directly west, and she was spotted at East Dereham. She was seen at Sporle at 17.15, was north of Swaffham at 17.30. She then turned north-west and went out to sea over the Wash north of Lynn, then back over land at Fosdyke at 18.30. She flew directly west over Grantham, then was seen at 19.30, south of Nottingham. She was over Derby at 19.45 and then went south of Cheadle to Stoke-on-Trent. Witnesses in the town described seeing and hearing the Zeppelin approaching from the direction of Trentham. She bombed Fenton Colliery near Stoke at about 20.15, dropping six high explosive bombs, in a radius of seventy-yards, doing some damage but causing no casualties. This again demonstrates how Zeppelins bombed as to do this she must have been virtually stationary while bomb-aimer *Oberleutnant zur See* Kurt Friemel dropped his bombs. She then turned towards Newcastle-under-Lyme, dropping a flare at Madeley at 20.20. It seems Mathy had lost his way as he then circled northward, over Alsager, Woolstanton, Basford and back to Stoke.

British observers then lose L.13. It seems Mathy flew north-west, probably looking for Manchester, but failing to find it because of the blackout and the fog. He then flew east trying to reach the Humber. He was spotted again over Retford circling for some time at 21.50. He then went north near Gainsborough and then south-east towards Lincoln, dropping another flare over Hackthorne at 22.30pm. The airship then went at high speed north towards Hull.

In his combat report Mathy claimed to have bombed Goole, but in fact had found the brightly lit blast furnaces of the Frodingham Iron and Steel works near Scunthorpe. We have a detailed report produced by Harold Dudley, the local historian, who founded Scunthorpe Museum, written in 1931. The Zeppelin was heard at about 22.45. It seemed to be approaching at speed making a noise like a 'heavy goods train'. Newspaper reports suggest the Zeppelin was clearly seen right above the town. Dudley says that the authorities in the town had been warned that they were likely to be bombed and lighting had been reduced as much as possible in the various works and all the street lights turned off. It seems likely that because nearby Hull had been bombed, the authorities had plans in force for an air raid. The first bomb fell on workers' housing on Ravendale Street. It did considerable damage to the back of four houses, partly demolishing the washhouses and coal houses, and shattering all the windows within hundreds of yards. There were newspaper reports that a pig kept in the yard of one of the houses was decapitated by the bomb. Dudley mentions that a well-known local woman, a Mrs Sabina Markham, aged 86-years, widow of Enoch Markham the founder of the Scunthorpe Co-operative Society, of Trent Cottages, displayed courage and fortitude. It appears an incendiary bomb fell through the roof of Mrs Markham's house. Without panic she threw a bucket of water on the flaring object, which was then thrown through a window by a plucky neighbour. Her fortitude was not shared by many other townspeople, who fled to the surrounding countryside, 'some in their nightclothes'. The bombing didn't seem to have done any lasting harm to Sabina, she died in 1924 at the ripe old age of ninety-four.

It appears the airship was moving slowly after this as it bombed the nearby Glebe pit and the Trafford Street area, again breaking many windows. Mathy then circled over a number of different steelworks covering an area of several square miles. Dudley writes that two high explosive bombs fell in the vicinity of the North Lincolnshire Works, and then a single bomb hit the closed Redbourn Hill Steelworks killing two men. The men were Cyril J Wright, a laboratory attendant, aged 24-years, of 43 Ashby High Street, Ashby, and Thomas W Danson, an engine tender, aged 29-years, of 2 Park Street Scunthorpe. Danson was a noted footballer, the goalkeeper for Scunthorpe and Lindsey, the forerunners of Scunthorpe United FC. It seems Cyril Wright was killed outright, but Thomas Danson was severely injured and died later that night in Frodingham Hospital in Scunthorpe. Mathy then turned L.13 back towards the town, towards the Chemical Works. Dudley wrote: 'Many incendiary bombs and aerial torpedoes were released but little material damage was effected.'

Turning above the Chemical Works the Zeppelin passed above the (Frodingham) Steelworks, but the commander evidently failed to realise the unique opportunity for spoliation, these works entirely escaping. Mathy then dropped a single high explosive bomb which landed on a railway siding near the railway station, just a hundred yards from the Frodingham Works, injuring four railwaymen. L.13 then flew in a northerly direction over the old Lindsey Iron Works, dropping several more high explosive bombs near Dawes Lane where another man was killed and a number injured, by a bomb which fell in the road. The man who was killed was Ernest Wilkinson Benson, also a steel worker, aged 31-years, of 3 Ethel Terrace, Scunthorpe. He was a barrow filler, filling tubs with coke and ironstone before they were taken by hoist to the top of the blast furnaces. One of the men injured was a police officer, Superintendent Melbourne Holmes, hit in the leg by shrapnel. Dudley then says the Zeppelin turned and flew away in a southerly direction. It had been over Scunthorpe for between eight and nine minutes and dropped about twenty high explosive and fifty incendiary bombs. According to the GHQ Intelligence report, three men were killed, and seven people injured, five men and two women.

L.13 was again spotted at Humberston at 23.35 and fired on by the one-pounder 'pom-pom' gun at Waltham Wireless Station, without any damage. Mathy crossed the English coast at about 23.40, north of North Somercoates, returning to Hage by 08.30 the next morning.

Zeppelin L.13 remained in service until December 1917, taking part in a total of forty-five scouting flights and seventeen raids. Heinrich Mathy and most of the crew took over a new airship in July 1916 – the bigger and faster L.31. They were to die in it, over Potters Bar on 2 October 1916.

*Chapter Seven*

# England Shall be Destroyed by Fire

## The Operation of 31 January 1916

The raid of January 1916 was part of a strategic bombing campaign; it marked Germany's move to a policy of total war. In early 1916 Germany, like the Allied Powers, faced stalemate. Armies faced each other across the trenches of the Western Front. Both sides were planning attacks they thought would win the war, the Germans at Verdun, the British and French on the Somme. In Russia, the Germans were largely successful but they knew the war would not be won on the eastern front. Other fronts were equally peripheral to the outcome. In Macedonia the docks where British and French troops were landing at Salonika (now Thessalonica) were bombed by an Army Zeppelin on 31 January 1916. In East Africa and the Middle East the British fought Germans or their allies. But ultimately everyone accepted the war would be won or lost on the Western Front. The Western Front devoured hundreds of thousands of men, and millions of tons of materiel. Shells and gas, guns and grenades, bullets and bayonets.

The British had one huge advantage: her Navy. The British Grand Fleet at Scapa Flow and bases on the east coast of Scotland faced the German High Seas Fleet in her bases around Kiel, or on the Friesian Coast. Both Navies planned for the decisive battle, but neither would take the risk of an all-out attack, as neither side could risk losing. The Battle of Jutland, which employed all of the Zeppelins the Navy had, was not much more than a skirmish. The Royal Navy, however, had a trump card: the blockade. Gradually, day by day, ship by ship, Germany was starved of raw materials and food. The Royal Navy was strong enough to run an effective blockade, while the German Navy wasn't.

This was essentially the real threat the Germans faced, the root cause of her 'frightfulness'. She didn't have a Navy strong enough to raise the blockade, or to blockade Britain. What she did have was a large industrial workforce, and technical and scientific industry, closely tied to war production. She developed so called wonder weapons out of weakness not strength. New more efficient, more lethal weapons, like U–boats, poison gas and Zeppelins were ways to rebalance the numerical advantages her enemies had.

In 1914 the Kaiser's Germany was, more than any other power, the product of what President Eisenhower later called a military industrial complex. Eisenhower to his credit used the term in a negative sense; in the Germany of 1914 it was central to national pride, and a culmination of German history.

The Prussia of Frederick the Great was described as the 'Sparta of the North'. It was militarised fusion of the royal bureaucracy and *Junker* class – the landed aristocracy. From the side of the landed class came a conception of inherent superiority and sensitivity to matters of status. From the royal bureaucracy came the idea of the state as an institution over and above class and the individual. This was symbolised by the Prussian ideal of discipline, obedience and an admiration for the hard qualities of the soldier. With the unification of Germany under Otto von Bismarck, a crucial new factor was added. This was a rough working coalition between the landed aristocracy and the emerging commercial and industrial class. Large industrialists like Krupp and Zeppelin became an integral part of the authoritarian government. Anyone who doubts the truth of this analysis can do no better that look at the Krupp family. In 1810 Friedrich Krupp started a small forge in Prussia. By 1914 the vast Krupp Empire was run by Gustav Krupp von Bohlen und Halbach. Gustav had started life as a plain von Bohlen und Halbach. He had married Bertha Krupp, the principal shareholder and taken Krupp as his family name. It is said the Kaiser believed it unthinkable that Krupp should be headed by a woman.

Along with the changes in the upper classes, Germany was the first nation with a policy of *Sozialpolitik* – an embryonic welfare state. Bismarck introduced this both in response to working class organisation and agitation, and also to bind the peasantry and industrial working class into the ideals of nationalism and patriotism. Along with this came the introduction of an effective system of basic and technical education. The outcome of all these social changes was militarism, conscription, and the partnership of scientific invention and war production. This was the society that led to the rise of Count Ferdinand von Zeppelin.

Zeppelin came from an aristocratic family, he was a professional army officer born in Wurttemberg. He first flew in a balloon during the American Civil War. He served with distinction in the Franco-Prussian War. Douglas Robinson points out that the irony about his later life as an airship pioneer is that it started when he was forced to resign from the army as a general in 1890 after a memo he wrote protesting about the domination of the Wurttemberg Army by the Prussian War Ministry angered the Kaiser. Zeppelin had noted with alarm the success of a French dirigible, or steer-able, airship, *La France*. He felt Germany needed to develop a similar airship for military purposes and it was his patriotic duty to build it. He spent the next twenty years doing just that. By 1910 Zeppelin had built a number of reliable airships and set up the Zeppelin Foundation for the Promotion of Aerial Navigation, and the world's first commercial airline The German Airship Transportation Company, or *Deutsche Luftschiffahrts AG*, known by its German initials as DELAG. The machines built for DELAG were largely successful. Four ships the *Schwaben*, *Viktoria Luise*, *Hansa* and *Sachsen* had mainly been used for pleasure flights and by 31 July 1914, 10,197 passengers had been carried, on 1588 voyages covering some 107,231 miles. During this period army and navy crews were trained on these airships by DELAG. By this time Zeppelin, having been given the right to use aspects of design subject to patents by the rival Schutte-Lanz airship company, started to produce airships for the military.

The first Zeppelins purchased by the navy were the L.1 and L.2. Both crashed in late 1913. The first Leader of Airships drowned in L.1. This led to the rapid promotion of the man who was to have a crucial role in the development of the Zeppelin as a bomber, *Korvettenkapitan* Peter Strasser. Born on 1 April 1876 in Hanover, Strasser joined the navy at the age of 15. He attended the Naval Academy at Kiel. He quickly rose through the ranks and in the Imperial Naval Office, the German equivalent of the Admiralty, to a position in charge of shipboard and coastal artillery. Recognised as a rising star in the navy he took over the airship service in September 1913.

At the time of his appointment Strasser was himself learning to fly a Zeppelin, the commercial ship *Sachsen* while he completed theoretical studies on airships. He arranged that the navy chartered *Sachsen* to train other crews, and used his charm and considerable intellect to persuade the High Command to order another ship from the Zeppelin Company. One of the most impressive things about Strasser is that despite being of fairly junior naval rank, a *Korvettenkapitan* is equal to the army rank of Major; he was able to operate at an influential political level, possibly aided by Count Zeppelin in the early days, and divert resources to the Zeppelin programme. He was promoted on 28 November 1916 to *Fregattenkapitan*, equivalent to a lieutenant–colonel, but also given the title *Fuhrer der Luftschiffe* (Leader of Airships), with which came the privileges of an Admiral Second Class. This was done by the direct order of the Kaiser through the Naval Cabinet.

The navy commissioned another Zeppelin, the L.3 in 1914. She was put through a vigorous acceptance programme in 1914. She was a star performer at the Kiel Navy Week in June 1914, a celebration of balls, banquets and regattas, where the German Navy entertained as honoured guests a British Naval Battle Squadron. Some of the events were in the presence of the Kaiser on his racing yacht *Meteor*. The programme unfortunately came to an abrupt end, on 28 June 1914, when the friend and hunting partner of the Kaiser, Archduke Franz Ferdinand, heir to the Austrian throne, was shot dead in Sarajevo.

At the beginning of the war the German Navy had one Zeppelin, the L.3, which had a limited military function. However, the Zeppelin became a major weapon almost by default. The German Navy had always recognised it was outnumbered by the British, in war this soon meant that it lacked enough cruisers and destroyers to keep up constant reconnaissance patrols in the North Sea. The airship was seen as a solution. A Zeppelin could be built in three weeks, a cruiser took two years. 1915 saw a 'crash' programme of airship building. The Zeppelin Company built twelve machines for the navy and the Naval Airship Service grew to 3,740 men by mid-1915.

The Zeppelin, perhaps more than any other weapon of the First World War, symbolises both German scientific ingenuity and brutality. At the beginning of the conflict Germany was the only country that possessed a fleet of long range rigid airships. While the Zeppelin is best known as a bombing aircraft, its main function was aerial reconnaissance. The reason the Germany Navy was so enthusiastic about the Zeppelin is that it was highly efficient when used as the eyes of the fleet. Ernst Lehmann in his semi-autobiographical work *The Zeppelins* describes a mundane but vital task Zeppelins were involved in: mine clearance. A significant part of the British blockade was the laying of minefields. This was done at night or in stormy or foggy weather. In clear weather a Zeppelin could locate a minefield much more quickly than a surface ship. They could destroy single mines with machine gun fire, or drop buoys to mark a minefield, for mine sweeping flotillas. They were even able to put down on the sea to pick up an officer from a mine sweeper to help him get a complete idea of the extent of a large minefield. And then return him to his ship.

It is not so well known that the United States Navy used airships in a similar way during the Second World War. Goodyear Blimps, like Zeppelins, could stay aloft for days, and were widely used for anti-submarine reconnaissance. Using helium, Goodyear Blimps were certainly the most useful airships used as weapons of war, a lot more useful than Zeppelins. No allied convoy escorted by a Blimp ever lost a ship to a U-boat. They could sit aloft cruising at the speed of the convoy. If the crew spotted a periscope either visually or by radar, they could call a destroyer to kill the submarine with depth charges. The Americans operated the Blimp knowing it was completely vulnerable to aircraft attack. They were only used where enemy aircraft did not operate like the East or West Coast of the USA, or late in the war in the Straits of Gibraltar.

However, Zeppelins will be remembered as the first terror bombers, and its more normal and useful military role, as an observation aircraft will remain as a footnote to history. At the beginning of the War almost every German schoolboy could sing the Zeppelin song:

*Flieg, Zeppelin, Flieg.*
*Hilf uns im Krieg.*
*Flieg nach England.*
*England wird abgebrant.*
*Flieg Zeppelin*

\* \* \*

Fly Zeppelin Fly.
Help us in the War.
Fly to England.
England shall be destroyed by fire.
Zeppelin Fly.

During 1915 Zeppelins carried out a number of raids on England. At first the Kaiser insisted that bombing be restricted to military targets such as shipyards, arsenals, docks and military installations. But soon cities were seen as military targets, both as the concept of total war developed, and as military professionals realised that the ability of high flying airships to engage in precision bombing was limited, though it took a long time for them to understand *just* how limited. The first Zeppelin attack on England was on 15 January 1915 when two navy Zeppelins bombed Great Yarmouth, Snettisham and King's Lynn. Four people were killed and sixteen injured. By May 1915 the Kaiser agreed attacks on London could be made, but insisted the royal palaces be spared. The first raid on London took place on 31 May 1915. It was carried out by two army Zeppelins. During 1915 there were nineteen airship raids on England, killing about 182 people.

The largest raid was the last attack of 1915 launched on London on the night of 13/14 October. This killed seventy-one people and caused £80,000 worth of damage. Five Zeppelins all of which would attack the Midlands in January were involved: Zeppelin L.11 commanded by Horst von Buttlar, L.13 commanded by Heinrich Mathy, L.14 commanded by Alois Bocker, L.15 commanded by Joachim Breithaupt and L.16 commanded by Werner Peterson. During 1915 all raids had either been on London or the east coast, this led to a concentration of anti-aircraft defence on the coast or around London.

The raid of 31 January 1916 was the first Zeppelin raid on England since the bombing of London in October 1915. In January command of the German High Seas Fleet was taken over by *Vizadmiral* Reinhard Scheer, his operational brief was to pursue an aggressive strategy of total war against Britain's industrial capacity. Strasser saw an increased role for Zeppelin Force and its modern weapons, as a way to end the stalemate of the Western Front. It couldn't break the British blockade, but it could reduce the capacity of the English to make war, by hitting the civilian population, destroying both morale and industrial capacity.

The main thrust of the campaign was to be the introduction of unrestricted submarine warfare against merchant shipping, though because of concerns about America entering the war this didn't come into effect until 1917. Alongside this battle cruisers were to bombard British East Coast towns,

The killing machine, Zeppelin L.21, in her shed at Nordholz. She was a new machine commissioned on 10 January 1916. The front command gondola can be seen. A good estimate of her size is that the gondola is about the size of a bus. She has four 240hp engines; each of the engines drove a separate propeller. On the left we can see the propeller mounted on side brackets on the hull, and the drive shaft. *Picture from the Wolverhampton Express and Star.*

*Kapitanleutnant* Max Dietrich. Born on 27 November 1870 in Angermunde, Germany, shot down in flames on 27 November 1916, off the coast near Hartlepool. On 31 January 1916 he was the Commander of Zeppelin L.21. She killed thirty-five people in the Black Country towns of Tipton, Bradley, Wednesbury and Walsall. *Picture Tonder Zeppelin Museum. Website.*

This is thought to be the home of William and Mary Greensill, 1 Court, 8 Union St, Tipton. They were killed instantly when a bomb hit the house. Their daughter, Mary Jane Morris, and two grandchildren, Martin and Nellie Morris, also died in the house. *Picture from the Wolverhampton Express and Star.*

Union Street, Tipton, is almost completely changed from 1916; all the terraced houses have been demolished. The only building that remains is the Conservative Club, which is largely unchanged. All the windows were blown out by the bombs. Thomas Church, a committee member of the club, was killed just outside. *Picture Mick Powis.*

After bombing Tipton, L.21 flew to Bradley near Wolverhampton. This building is the Bradley Pumping Engine House, beside Wolverhampton Union Canal. In 1916, it housed a steam-powered beam engine. A courting couple, William and Maud Fellows, were killed by the white plaque on the left-hand wall. A 50kg high explosive bomb landed on the towpath as they were sheltering by the wall. There are still shrapnel marks on the brickwork from the bomb. *Picture Mick Powis.*

After bombing Bradley, L.21 flew on to Wednesbury. Her bombs killed fifteen people: four men, six women and five children. These were three of the victims: Nelly Smith, aged 13; her brother, Thomas, aged 11 and little sister, Ina, aged 7. They were killed along with their father, Joseph Horton Smith. *Picture from the Daily Sketch February 1916.*

This is where the Smith family died. 13 King Street, Wednesbury. *Picture Walsall Pioneer 12 February 1916.*

After bombing Wednesbury, L.21 flew to Walsall. A high explosive bomb hit Wednesbury Road Congregational Church. A bible study class was in progress when a bomb came through the roof. The teacher said there was a 'blinding flash more vivid and fearsome than any lightning'. Surprisingly, no one in the room was killed, though a man outside had half of his head blown off. *Picture from the Wolverhampton Express and Star.*

The best known victim of the raid was this woman, Mary Julia Slater, Mayoress of Walsall. She was a passenger on a tram when a bomb landed a few yards away, severely injuring her. She died a few weeks later. *Picture from the Wolverhampton Express and Star.*

This picture was taken in Bradford Place, Walsall, the next morning after the last bomb dropped by L.21 hit the public toilets, causing the crater we can see. *Picture from the Wolverhampton Express and Star.*

The damage was caused by a 50kg bomb. This specimen is in the Aeronauticum Museum at Nordholz. The bomb was hung from the ring on the tail in the bomb bay of the Zeppelin. *Picture Mick Powis.*

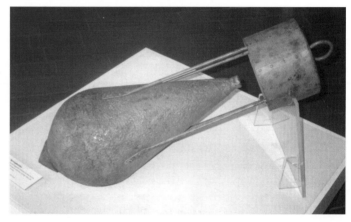

Walsall Cenotaph is built on the spot the last bomb from L.21 landed on Walsall. It killed three people. The tram stop was in the same place as the present day bus stops. The building behind is the Art and Science Institute, unchanged from 1916. All the windows were blown out by the bomb and several night school students were taken to hospital due to injuries caused by flying glass. *Picture Mick Powis.*

Lowe and his crew in Zeppelin L.19 were the only men not to return from the raid. L.19 bombed Burton on Trent, Tipton, Wednesbury and Walsall. Despite this it is not possible to determine how many casualties she caused. *Picture Wikimedia Commons.*

The problems of the Black Country were not over; a second Zeppelin, L.19, commanded by *Kapitanleutnant*, Odo Lowe, returned at about midnight. She had previously bombed Burton on Trent. It is unlikely she caused any human casualties, though a bomb killed a horse, four pigs and about 100 chickens in Walsall. L.19 was the only Zeppelin not to return; due to engine failure and loss of gas she ditched in the North Sea. All of her crew drowned. *Picture from the Wolverhampton Express and Star.*

On 2 February 1916 the British trawler *King Stephen* came across the L.19 with her crew on top of the sinking hull. Fearing that if he took the Germans on board they would take over his ship, the skipper, William Martin, refused to rescue them. This led to considerable atrocity propaganda by the Germans. A few hours later all the crew of L.19 drowned. *King Stephen* was later captured by the Germans. They threatened to put the crew on trial for a war crime but they ended up in a POW camp. *Picture Flight 10 February 1916. Wikimedia Commons.*

Burton on Trent was bombed by three Zeppelins. Fifteen people were killed: three men, six women and six children. This is 109 Shobnel Street. Three people were killed there: Florence Jane Wilson, aged 23, visiting a friend; Mary Warrington, aged 11; and George Warrington, aged 6. Several people were injured when buried in the rubble. The father of the children was part of the rescue party; he dug out his wife still alive but the children were dead. The house was a typical late Victorian terrace; the picture was taken from the backyard. The outhouse of the next house was badly damaged. The house was repaired and still exists. *Picture from the Wolverhampton Express and Star.*

This was the Christ Church Mission Hall, on the corner of Moor Street and Church Street, Burton. This is the most famous bomb site of the entire raid. Six people were killed here including the missionary Mary Rose Morris from Brighton. The same spot is now the home of the Burton Caribbean Association Community Centre. Church Street is now Uxbridge Street. The address today is 346 Uxbridge Street, Burton. *Picture Daily Sketch February 1916.*

A young hero died here. It is sad that Burton seems to commemorate the victims less than most other towns. This unprepossessing street corner near the ring road, where Bond Street joins Lichfield Road, is where Berty Geary, aged 13, of 89 Blackpool Rd, Burton, sustained the injuries which killed him. He was climbing a lamppost to put out the gas light when a bomb exploded a few feet away. His injuries were caused by shrapnel and the fall; he died in hospital the next day. A teenage girl, Lucy Simnett, aged 15, was killed here by the same bomb. *Picture Mick Powis.*

Loughborough and Ilkeston were bombed by Zeppelin L.20, commanded by *Kapitanleutnant* Franz Stabbert. The raid on 31 January 1916 was his first on England. *Picture Loughborough Roll of Honour.*

This gives a good impression of the size of a Zeppelin. L.20 is being taken out of her shed. The rails held a trolley that the airship was attached to as it was pulled out of its shed. *Loughborough Roll of Honour.*

Loughborough has the best records of any town attacked by Zeppelins. The first bomb dropped on Loughborough hit this building, The Crown and Cushion Inn. It killed one woman: Martha Shipman, aged 49, a customer in the bar. *Loughborough Roll of Honour.*

The next bomb landed in the main street, The Rushes. It killed four people, three women and a man. *Loughborough Roll of Honour.*

The shop on the left is the brush shop in The Rushes owned by the Adcock Family. Annie Adcock, aged 42, was killed just outside. It seems likely she ran out when she heard the bang of the bomb that hit the Crown and Cushion and was killed by shrapnel when the next bomb landed in the middle of the road. *Loughborough Roll of Honour.*

This newly married couple, Joseph and Alice Adkin, were killed by the bomb in The Rushes. *Loughborough Roll of Honour.*

After dropping its second bomb on The Rushes, L.20 took about 3 minutes to fly to the east of the town where she dropped two more high explosive bombs near the Herbert Morris Crane Works, killing five people: two men, one woman and a teenage boy and girl. This was the shop of Joseph Gilbert, aged 49, on the corner of Empress Road and Judge Street; he died a few minutes after the explosion. Three more people died a few yards away in Empress Road. They were: Mary Ann Page, aged 44; her son, Joseph Page, aged 18; and her daughter, Elsie Page, aged 16. They ran out of the house and were killed on the pavement. *Loughborough Roll of Honour.*

100 years later little has changed. Joseph Gilbert was killed in his corner shop, while Mary Ann Page and her son, Joseph, and daughter, Elsie, were killed on the pavement. The 'iron cross' memorial marking where the bomb landed is in the gutter. *Picture Mick Powis.*

The spot the bomb fell in Empress Road is commemorated by this stone 'Iron Cross'. The yellow line is an unwelcome modern addition. There is a similar stone in The Rushes. *Picture Mick Powis.*

After bombing Loughborough, Zeppelin L.20 bombed the Stanton Iron Works in Ilkeston. She killed two men, James Hall, aged 56, and Walter Wilson, aged 41. Walter Wilson worked as a furnace loader; he is the man on the left. *Picture Ilkeston Local History Society.*

This is the Old Furnace Section of Stanton Iron Works where James Hall worked. The picture dates from about 1880. *Picture Ilkeston Local History Society.*

Walter Wilson was killed sheltering against the wall of the Church school room, roughly where the car is standing. *Picture Mick Powis.*

Zeppelin L.14 killed five people just after midnight in Derby. The first bombs fell on a potentially valuable target, the Rolls-Royce Works in Nightingale Lane. This picture dates from about 1920 and shows factory buildings on the site of the test track, but otherwise shows the factory much as it looked from the Zeppelin. *Photograph Rolls-Royce Heritage Trust. Copyright Rolls-Royce plc.*

One HE bomb hit the test track and two fell on waste land near the factory. The only damage to the works were broken windows, which can be seen in this picture. *Photograph courtesy of the Rolls-Royce Heritage Trust. Copyright Rolls-Royce plc.*

The Metalite Works of the Derby Lamp Company in Gresham Street was badly damaged, though no one was killed. *Picture Mick Powis.*

This is the Birmingham to Derby railway line, taken from the Osmaston Road Bridge near Litchurch Lane. The picture shows roughly where the bombs fell. Anyone standing on the bridge would have had a grandstand view, if they survived. **A.** Five HE bombs landed on the Midland Carriage and Waggon Works, about 100 to 200 yards from the bridge. **B.** Three incendiary bombs fell on Fletchers Lace Factory about 100 yards from the bridge. **C.** Five incendiary bombs fell on Horton St, about 200 yards from the bridge. **D.** One HE bomb fell on the Rolls Royce Foreman's Club about 400 yards from the bridge. **E.** Nine HE bombs fell on the Locomotive Works, killing four men, about 850 yards from the bridge. **F.** Two HE and one incendiary bomb fell on Derby Gas Works, about 800 yards from the bridge. *Picture Mick Powis.*

This is the Fletcher Lace Works. Three incendiary bombs landed in the courtyard and five more in Horton Street just behind it. *Picture Mick Powis.*

The Roundhouse was part of the Locomotive Works where four men died. There were a number of roundhouses, indoor railway turntables. This was the world's first; though this one was not bombed, it stands as a memorial to the position of Derby as a major railway town. *Picture Mick Powis.*

Zeppelin L.13, commanded by *Kapitanleutnant* Heinrich Mathy, bombed Stoke-on-Trent and Scunthorpe. Three men were killed in Scunthorpe. *Picture Wolverhampton Express and Star.*

It is impossible to precisely determine where the bombs fell in Scunthorpe, as much has changed. However, the town can be proud that it still has a large steelworks which must look much as it did in 1916. Ernest Wilkinson Benson was killed near here in Dawes Lane, close to the old Lindsey Iron Works. The Parish Church of Scunthorpe, St John's, can be seen in the distance. *Photograph Mick Powis.*

Mathy and his crew were shot down in Zeppelin L.31 over Potters Bar on 2 October 1916. They are buried together at Cannock Chase German Military Cemetery. *Picture Mick Powis*

Cannock Chase Military Cemetery has a section where all the airship crews killed over Britain are buried; they were moved to Cannock from their original graves in the 1960s. I suppose 'Rest in Peace' would be the best epitaph. *Picture Mick Powis*

and the Airship Division was to intensify its campaign of bombing industrial cities.

Peter Strasser developed the details of the strategic bombing campaign. He had long been an enthusiast for the role of the Zeppelin as a bomber, able to significantly alter the course of the war. Clearly an intelligent man he faced up to, and justified, the moral dilemma of terror bombing in a letter written to his mother:

> 'We who strike at the enemy where his heart beats have been slandered as "baby-killers" and "murderers of women" … What we do is repugnant to us too, but necessary, very necessary. Nowadays there is no such animal as a non–combatant: modern warfare is total warfare. A soldier cannot function at the front without the factory worker, the farmer, and all the other providers behind him. You and I, Mother, have discussed this subject, and I know you understand what I say. My men are brave and honourable. Their cause is holy, so how can they sin while doing their duty? If what we do is frightful, then may frightfulness be Germany's salvation.'

A complex man with a strong sense of duty, Strasser thought it was necessary to go on combat operations with his crews, to maintain morale and maintain his tactical skills. He tried to fly on missions at least once a month. It is certainly the case he didn't have to go on operations, and it did not always endear him to the crew chosen to take him as a passenger. Nevertheless his willingness to put his life on the line made him a popular figurehead and charismatic commander.

Peter Strasser met with Admiral Scheer in January 1916, to agree the details of his 'frightful' strategy. There were three attack zones: England North: From the River Tyne to Edinburgh; England Middle: Liverpool across to the River Humber; England South: London and East Anglia. The raid of 31 January 1916 was the first conducted according to the new strategy. The plan was for nine navy Zeppelins to bomb industrial targets mainly in 'Middle England': Liverpool was to be their primary target.

Both the German Army and Navy operated Zeppelin and Schutte-Lanz airships. By 1916 the Army were becoming increasingly sceptical of their value as weapons of war. The *Reichskriegsmarine* remained enthusiastic. In many ways the operation of airships was second nature to sailors, they were so large and slow that they were not piloted, in the way that modern aircraft are, by one person. The commander gave orders, and crewmen followed his orders turning large wheels to operate the rudders and elevators as they would in ships, the officers and steering crew working in the enclosed front gondola of the ship. They communicated with the crew operating the engines, dropping ballast or manning the machine guns by speaking tubes or electric telegraph.

By January 1916 the Zeppelin Company had produced thirty-four of its 'P' and 'Q' type airships, nineteen for the army, and fifteen for the navy. By the standards of the time these were very effective bombing machines. There were two types of Zeppelin employed on the raid of 31 January. The 'P' Type was the smaller model, developed early in 1915. The 'P' Type airships belonging to the German Navy were numbered from L.10 to L.19. They were 536ft long, with a diameter of 61ft. They contained sixteen gas cells with a total capacity of 1,126,400 cubic feet of hydrogen. Each had four Maybach engines of 210 or 240-horsepower.

Zeppelins L.20 to L.24 were the later 'Q' Type. The diameter remained at 61ft, but the length increased to 585ft, allowing the fitting of eighteen gas cells with a total hydrogen capacity of 1,264,100 cubic feet. This increased the bomb load and service ceiling. The 'Q' Type ships had four 240-horsepower Maybach engines.

The Zeppelins were huge even in relation to present day aircraft. L.21 at 585ft was as long as two football pitches. A useful modern comparison is the Goodyear Blimp, used for advertising and television work at sporting events. This is just over 100ft long. L.21 was five times the size. Zeppelins are still the largest combat aircraft ever to have flown. A Zeppelin like L.21 would weigh about 53,000lbs empty. However, the 1,264,100 cubic feet of lighter than air hydrogen would provide lift of some 39,000lbs more than this, lifting the ship, crew, fuel, oil, ballast (used to control height) and the war load of about two tons of bombs.

Flying these huge lighter-than-air machines has been likened to an art rather than a science. They were strongly affected by weather conditions; the temperature affected the lift generated by the hydrogen gas cells. Lift was greater in cold weather. The night of 31 January 1916 providing perfect conditions for a full bomb load. The height of the Zeppelin was controlled by a combination of static lift, dropping ballast to balance the weight of the airship against the lift of the hydrogen gas, and dynamic lift generated by the forward speed of the airship. While Zeppelins were slower than opposing fighter aircraft, their most important defensive quality was their ability to climb much faster than the type of aircraft opposing them in 1916.

Probably the best way to understand how a Zeppelin flies is to recognise that technically it doesn't fly at all, rather it floats in the air. It operates like a very different weapon of war, the submarine. A submarine is fitted with flotation tanks which when it is on the surface are filled with air. When the captain wants to dive he orders the tanks opened to let in water. The boat will then sink because of reduced buoyancy. As it goes down the water pressure around it rises, until it gets to a depth of neutral buoyancy, it will then float at that depth. If the captain wants to go deeper he has more water put in the flotation tank, if he wants to go up compressed air forces water out, replacing water with air increases buoyancy, and the boat rises. By changing the buoyancy level the boat will float at any level the captain wants, from on the surface, to a depth where the water pressure could crush the submarine.

An airship operates in much the same way. The gas bags are filled with hydrogen making it lighter than air; it will float upwards until it reaches a point of neutral buoyancy. Obviously this operates in the opposite way to a submarine, as the airship rises, the air pressure decreases, as a submarine goes down the water pressure increases, but both float at the neutral buoyancy level. To go up the Zeppelin commander increases buoyancy, lightens the ship by dropping ballast. To go down he makes the ship heavy by releasing hydrogen. This is where the submarine-Zeppelin similarity ends. A submarine can pump in or pump out an unlimited amount of water. A Zeppelin is filled with hydrogen when it takes off, and if it releases any it can't be replaced until the airship returns to base. The same applies to ballast, which was usually water. This can usually only be replaced on the ground.

In practice a Zeppelin flight was a constant balancing act between height and weight. Before take-off the commander would calculate the weight of the ship and its movable cargo, fuel, ballast and bombs, and the lift expected to be generated by the hydrogen it carried. Crew were issued with a printed book of ballast sheets, to make this calculation before any flight. Problems occurred when the ship was subject to an unexpected weight change, such as ice or snow on the hull, or when the ship lost lift due to a hydrogen leak. In general a Zeppelin got lighter as a mission went on, fuel was used and bombs were dropped. The ship also lost hydrogen, as the gas cells expanded, as the ship flew higher and the air pressure went down. Each gas cell had an automatic pressure valve to cope with the change.

A Zeppelin commander would trim his ship to fly at neutral buoyancy at its cruising height, in the case of 'P' and 'Q' class ships about 9000ft. Minor changes in height would be made using the elevator. This brings us to our second technical term: dynamic buoyancy. The controls at the tail of a Zeppelin were very similar to those of an aeroplane. The ship had two rudders on its vertical fins, which controlled direction, and two elevators on its horizontal fins, which controlled height, or more technically the position of the nose. If the elevators were moved up, the nose rose and the ship climbed, if the elevators were moved down the ship dived. Like any other aircraft a Zeppelin could use its engine power to help it climb, trading speed for height.

In an emergency such as a fighter attack, a Zeppelin could climb very fast. The ship would drop ballast, and put the nose up on full power. In 1916 it could out climb any fighter, but by 1918 enemy fighters could fly higher and climb faster and that signalled the end of the Zeppelin as an effective bomber.

While we are considering these technical aspects it is worth considering an often asked question: could the Zeppelins have continued as bombers if the Germans had had access to helium, non-flammable gas? The short answer is probably no. Helium is the second lightest element after hydrogen. Hydrogen has a lifting capacity of 1.14kg per cubic meter (70lbs per 1000 cubic feet). Helium has a lifting capacity of almost six per cent less: 1.06kg per cubic meter (66lbs per 1000 cubic feet) which would have meant less fuel and fewer bombs. While hydrogen is highly inflammable, so was the rest of a Zeppelin. It contained petrol and oil, various sorts of incendiary and high explosive bombs, its envelope was covered in linen tightened with inflammable cellulose dope. In this way it was no different from the other aircraft of the period – aeroplanes were often shot down in flames, too. For the Zeppelin commanders in 1916, hydrogen was an acceptable risk. A Zeppelin could climb away, or fight off attackers with its machine guns. By 1917 the option of fighting off attackers had gone, but the new 'height-climbers' could still climb faster or fly higher. By 1918 both these advantages had gone and it was the end of the age of the Zeppelin as a bomber. For the Germans the wide wing-spanned, multi-engine Gotha and Giant bombers had taken over.

The structure of all Zeppelins was a streamlined rigid frame made of lightweight latticed duralumin girders, with steel wire bracing. The ship was kept aloft by hydrogen filled gas cells. Huge gasbags made from cotton lined with goldbeater's skins to make them airtight. Goldbeater's skins were thin membranes taken from the intestines of cattle. An indication of their nature is that as well as being used in airships, or by goldsmiths, Casanova is reputed to have had condoms made from them. For each gas cell goldbeater's skins from some 50,000 cattle would be needed. As a result gas cells were very expensive items. In 1916 each one cost around £2000. Zeppelin L.21 had eighteen gas cells, each containing about 70,000 cubic feet of hydrogen. They were held in the frame of the Zeppelin by wire and cord netting. It is important to note that a Zeppelin was not a single bag of gas like a Blimp. It had a rigid frame like an aeroplane, and the crew could move inside the envelope, climbing on ladders to machine gun positions on top of the airship. At the bottom of the hull was a keel which contained walkways. This was where the control and engine gondoliers were attached. To some extent a ship could be maintained and repaired in flight, and the crew had a sail maker to repair the envelope or gas cells, and mechanics to repair the engines.

The rigid frame of the Zeppelin was covered with lightweight cotton fabric, sewn and doped on the frame. The example of fabric I have seen in Nordholz Museum is natural linen, an off white colour printed with tiny blue dots or lines, to give a camouflage effect. Though later in the War the undersides of Zeppelins were painted black, this was not the case in 1916. The airship covered in this material was therefore a very pale blue colour. This indicated why almost all eyewitnesses described them as being silver or grey in colour. Seen in the reflected light of street lamps or fire from the ground, the Zeppelin would seem to be a silver grey. Other Zeppelins were covered in unprinted fabric and would be a cream or very light brown colour.

Attached to the hull of the Zeppelin were a command and front-engine gondola, and toward the rear about 200ft away was the rear-engine gondola. The front gondola was the officers' station – the commander and executive officer stood there. The gondola was enclosed, giving some protection from the elements, though as it was unheated it was bitterly cold. The front and sides had triplex glass or celluloid windows which gave a very good view forward and downwards. The commander stood near the front with his map table. He had an electric telegraph to order changes in engine speed from the mechanics in the engine gondolas. He had a number of speaking tubes to communicate with the crew in different parts of the ship. Behind the commander stood the rudder man operating a wheel to control direction. He had a compass to work to. Next to him stood the elevator man with a wheel operating the elevators. He had a number of instruments to measure the height, the rate of climb and the inclination of the ship (whether the nose was level or pointing up or down).

The second in command, the executive, or watch officer, operated the bombsight and actually dropped the bombs. He used a sight manufactured by Carl Zeiss of Jena. It was mounted by the front windows. It was a costly and complex instrument. It was calibrated for different weights of bomb; and could also be used to measure the drift or speed of the Zeppelin across the ground. There was a panel of electrical switches to operate the bomb release mechanism. The Carl Zeiss sight allowed very accurate bombing. The bomb-aimer could hit almost any target he could see, particularly when the Zeppelin was hovering. The operative words are 'see the target'. In cloud or misty conditions the Zeppelin was blind, which is why we get examples of very accurate bombing: two bombs dropped within yards of each other, if often on the wrong city. We have that when Mathy in L.13 bombed the Fenton Colliery near Stoke-on-Trent six bombs fell in a seventy-foot circle, probably from 9000ft.

Behind the command section was the radio room, used by the wireless operator and generally the executive officer. It was well insulated, to keep it quiet, and hence was warm, making it the best place to work on the ship. Zeppelins were fitted with powerful Telefunken radio sets able to receive and transmit signals by Morse code. They had long trailing wire radio aerials that could be wound in and out during a flight. It was normal practice to take the wire in if there was any danger of lightning. The radio room had a specialist wireless operator, though the executive officer often worked there coding and decoding messages. The radio also had another function, establishing the ship's position for navigation. The German Navy had a number of direction finding stations, most at the Zeppelin bases, but some further south at Borkum Island and in Bruges to improve accuracy. To establish the airship's position the radio operator would send a signal to these stations. They would then measure the strength and direction of the signal, and by comparing results from the different stations by a process of triangulation, estimate and send back her position to the Zeppelin. There were some problems with this. If the Zeppelin crew heard the position, so did the English who had radio stations on the East Coast directly linked by telephone cable to the Admiralty in London. The second more serious problem was that the radio positioning system was of limited accuracy, and it tended to lead to overconfidence about navigation among Zeppelin crews. At a range of 200 to 300 miles radio location was a crude measure. It could be as much as fifty miles out. This is why crews were so confident they had bombed Liverpool when they were fifty or sixty miles away.

It has to be recognised that radio like so much else in Zeppelin technology was in its infancy and many factors such as the effect of atmospheric conditions on the apparent direction of radio signals were unknown. The fact that the British could read their signals was soon understood and by the middle of 1916 radio discipline got better. Commanders remained overconfident about the reliability of the radio positioning system until the end of the war. The real problem occurred when the British started using large flying boats fitted with radio equipment to intercept Zeppelins. The Admiralty could pick up positional signals to and from Zeppelins and transmit their approximate positions to the interceptors. By 1918 the Germans were developing a radio positioning system in which the Zeppelin was silent, however, by then the Zeppelin was largely finished as a viable weapon, so it was not used in anger.

Behind the command gondola of the Zeppelin was the front-engine gondola which contained one engine, and the rear gondola which had three engines. Each engine was controlled by a mechanic who received his orders to set throttle position by an electric telegraph, operated by the commander. The front gondola engine and gearbox directly drove a propeller. In the rear gondola there were three engines one behind the other, the rear engine and gearbox directly drove a propeller. The other two drove a propeller on the port or starboard side of the hull. The propellers were mounted on outriggers – a tubular structure on each side of the ship. Though in pictures these structures looked flimsy, they were practical and strong. They added drag and were less efficient than direct drive, but had the crucial advantage of allowing the propellers to reverse direction to help with low speed manoeuvring.

Each engine had its own mechanic, able to maintain and often repair the engines in flight. The engine gondolas had one big advantage for the mechanics – they were usually warm, though a flight next to a very noisy engine, subject to exhaust and petrol fumes often left mechanics deaf or with headaches days after a flight.

During the 31 January raid engines were a problem for most of the Zeppelins. The early 'P' type ships, L.10 to L.14 were fitted with the Maybach C-X six-cylinder 22.6l sidevalve 210-horsepower engines. The C-X was a heavy engine with a poor power-to-weight ratio, and high fuel consumption. This limited the range or bomb load of the ships it was fitted in. It had one big advantage, however: it was well tested and reliable. As part of the programme to improve the performance of the Zeppelin fleet, the Maybach Company, which was a subsidiary of the Zeppelin Company at Friedrichshafen, developed a new engine, the HSLu. This was a more powerful high-compression 19l overhead-valve six-cylinder 240-horsepower engine. It was lighter, had a much better power-to-weight ratio and better fuel consumption. It was rushed from the design stage to production and installation in 'P' and 'Q' class Zeppelins, without a proper testing programme. This was disastrous. Everything that could go wrong with an engine went wrong. They overheated, seized up and burned out bearings. It was unusual for a Zeppelin to return from a mission without at least one engine out of order. On the 31 January 1916 raid engine trouble was the main cause of the loss of Zeppelin L.19, and to a greater or lesser extent, the cause of many of the problems the later model Zeppelins faced. By March 1916 Strasser had all the HSLu engines removed from the airships and returned to the factory. The problems were eventually sorted, and the HSLu became the principal Zeppelin engine with 490 being produced. The lessons about a proper testing programme were well learned by Strasser and the Zeppelin Company.

The fuel, ballast and bombs of the Zeppelin were attached to the keel, between the gondolas near the centre of gravity, so that when these were used the ship remained in balance. Petrol was kept in aluminium tanks distributed along the keel. In an emergency these tanks could be jettisoned, if no other ballast was available, the tanks just dropping through the covering to the ground. Most ballast was water carried in rubberised cloth sacks attached to the keel. The water was released by the elevator man in the control gondola, pulling toggles. We know that when L.21 set out from Nordholz on the 31 January raid, it was carrying 17,720lbs of ballast. This can be compared with the 4910lbs of bombs she carried.

A 'Q' class Zeppelin carried about two tons of bombs, in a bay with an opening bomb door. Reports from the ground often talk about seeing a light inside the airship, and this was probably seen through the open bomb door. The bombs hung from the keel in racks. They were dropped by an electrical release mechanism, controlled by the bomb-aimer in the front gondola. The bomb release mechanism was the only thing in the Zeppelin that was directly controlled by the operator. If the release mechanism went wrong bombs could be released manually by crew members stationed in the bomb bay. They had to be armed after the Zeppelin took off; this was done by the bomb bay crew just after the ship left the German coast and went over the North Sea.

There were two types of bomb carried by the Zeppelin. The first was high explosive, the second incendiary. High explosive bombs were pear-shaped and made from thick steel plate. They were often called Carbonit after the manufacturer. They had a round stabilising fin at the tail. The bombs came in standard sizes: 10kg (22lbs) 50kg (110lbs) 100kg (220lbs) and 300kg (660lbs). They were reliable and almost always exploded if they fell on hard ground. The explosion would throw a cone of shrapnel from the steel casing dozens of yards. Most injuries were caused by the flying shrapnel, or debris thrown by the explosion. The second type of bomb was the incendiary bomb. They were very different from the high explosive type.

They only weighed about 25lbs, were not explosive, and were, in effect, huge firelighters. In the centre was a tube of thermite, which was wrapped with a coil of rope covered in tar. When the bomb ignited the thermite would burn with a very hot flame, which would ignite the tar and rope which would burn for several minutes, setting fire to any building it was lodged in. Though there are a few reports of houses burning down after being hit by an incendiary bomb – there was one in Horton Street, Derby – it was very rare. There are more reports of people picking up burning incendiary bombs on shovels and taking them outside or covering them with earth. As far as we know all the deaths in the January raid were caused by high explosive bombs either directly, by shrapnel wounds or by being hit by flying debris or buried by falling masonry.

The idea of using high explosive and incendiary bombs together was that the high explosive bombs would open up buildings by blowing down walls or blowing off roof tiles, allowing the incendiary bombs to fall into buildings and set alight things such as roof timbers. This was what happened during the Second World War, different waves of bombers would carry carefully calculated mixes of high explosive and incendiary bombs, setting large areas alight. This only worked in large towns or cities with high densities of housing. The bombers only started the fires, which were then fuelled by inflammable material, usually wood, inside the houses. This incidentally was why Dresden was bombed in 1945. The targets were chosen by committees who not only looked at the strategic value and how well they were defended, but how well they would burn. As well as the obvious military personnel, targeting committees had people with expertise in historical architecture on them – who better to tell you how a city would burn?

The Zeppelins, however, were the first aerial terror weapon and they set out with the intention of destroying cities. Even though the amount of damage they could do was actually limited, neither the bombers themselves, nor those being bombed knew this for certain, and the huge silver looking cigar shape moving across the sky had a real effect on civilian morale.

The other weapons the Zeppelin carried were machine guns. Most navy airships carried six or seven 7.92mm Maxim guns. There was a gun on each side in both the front and rear gondolas. They fired through large windows, very like the waist gun positions in B.17 bombers in the Second World

War. Right at the back of the ship behind the rudders and elevators in the cruciform tail sat the look out and rear gunner. He had a very cold and lonely job, communicating with the command gondola some 400ft in front of him. He had the only clear view behind the airship, so had an important role when fighters were about. The coldest position on a Zeppelin was the upper gun platform, right on top of the hull above the control gondola. This was a flat platform with two or three machine gun positions, protected from the elements only by a canvas windbreak. The platform had speaking tubes and electric telegraphs to communicate with the commander. Wearing many layers of clothes to cope with the cold, for the gunners just getting to the gun position was difficult enough as they had to climb about 100ft up a ladder in an access shaft of canvas-covered duralumin rings.

Zeppelins had crews of up to twenty men. The commander, men operating the steering controls, the radio operators and some machine gunners worked in the control gondola. Other men were stationed in the vast envelope of the ship. There were usually two officers and two or three warrant officers in a crew, the other ranks tended to be non-commissioned officers. The officers and warrant officers remained on duty for the entire mission; the other ranks were divided into watches. Men off watch tended to man the machine guns, probably a colder and more arduous task then being on watch.

Whatever they did, the crew worked in bitterly cold conditions. They wore fur-lined clothing, and fur-lined rubber or straw boots to avoid causing sparks, or damaging the fragile aluminium frame of the Zeppelin. A number of photographs show officers wearing fur-lined leather flying suits. The crews had few creature comforts. A few hammocks were hung from girders in the hull, above the keel. The crews were usually well fed, much better than the blockaded civilian population. Sandwiches, sausage and chocolate were popular. Tea and coffee was available from thermos flasks as no heating of food was possible. Sometimes ships had cans of self-heating stew or soup. A special ballast bag supplied drinking water. Brandy was usually available although this was at the commander's discretion, and some took pride in running a dry ship. Last but not least there was a head or toilet near the back of the ship. Since this was quite difficult to get to for crew at the front of the ship, in bulky flying kit, it was augmented by relief tubes in most crew positions.

We have a number of crew lists from the interrogation of crews who survived after being shot down. The intelligence reports give a lot of personal details, and are noticeably free of the 'wicked baby killing Hun' view put over in the popular press. The crews generally come over as highly skilled intelligent men. Many were former merchant seamen, going to airships as naval reservists. They tended to be mature men, the crew of L.15 captured in April 1916 ranged in age between 23-years and 40-years. Breithaupt was thirty-three. The average age was about thirty. Much the same applied to the crew of L:33 shot down in September 1916. Their aged ranged between 23-years and 43-years. The commander Bocker was thirty-seven. The biographies in the reports are fascinating. While the officers were very correct, saying very little, afraid to pass on military information, many crew members were very chatty. They were proud of their skills and passed a lot of useful information, gained by oblique conversations about seemingly non-military matters.

The German Naval Zeppelin bases were on the windswept North-West Coast of Germany. There were three naval airship bases, used in the 31 January 1916 raid: Hague near Emden, a few miles from the Dutch border; Nordholz: near Cuxhaven, the headquarters of the Airship Service and Tondern: in Schleswig-Holstein near the Danish Border. (Tondern is now called Tonder. It was part of the territory ceded to Denmark in 1920 after the Schleswig plebiscite.)

For most of the war the Naval Airship Division headquarters was in Nordholz, but for about six months in late 1917 the headquarters moved to Althorn.

The Zeppelin bases were as much monuments to German scientific ingenuity as the airships themselves. The Zeppelins were kept in huge sheds each about an eighth of a mile long. Some sheds were capable of taking two Zeppelins moored side by side. So well-built were the sheds that some are still standing today. Each Zeppelin and ground crew had a specific home shed. These were given names to match the base. In 1916 Nordholz had sheds called Nobel, Norbert, and Normann. Nobel was a revolving double shed, turned according to wind direction by electric motors. Hage had Hanne, Hannibal, Harald and Hasso. Tondern had Toni, Tobias and Toska. This latter was another double shed, but it did not revolve – the mechanism of Nobel was too expensive to be generally used.

Though not built for the 31 January 1916 raid several commanders mentioned in our story were based at Ahlorn. This base was built as the Airship Service expanded and was not finished until September 1916. It was near Bremen and some sixty-miles from the sea. It became the headquarters of the Naval Airship Division between July 1917 and January 1918. By the end of 1916 it had four double sheds, Aladin, Albrecht, Alrun and Alix. Two more were built but were not completed until mid-1918. They were Alma and Alarich.

Another field mentioned in the text was Wittmund, near Wilhelmshaven which the navy took it over from the army in April 1917. This had two double sheds: Wille and Wunsch.

As well as the sheds, the bigger bases also contained large gasworks, which used the Messerschmitt process to produce hydrogen gas by passing steam over hot iron. Each base was easily identifiable from the air, because as well as having three or four huge airship hangers, they also had prominent gasholders, identical in appearance to civilian gasometers. These stored the hydrogen used to 'top up' the Zeppelins after their missions. The gas production plant at Nordholz was capable of producing 1.5 million cubic feet of hydrogen per day. Later in the war the bases were to become as vulnerable as the flying airships, subject to raids by carrier-borne British aeroplanes, but in early 1916 they provided a safe haven for the Zeppelins and their crews.

To service three or four Zeppelins each base required a large ground crew of about 500 men. Though the ships required a lot of repair and maintenance, it was during take-off and landing that the large ground crew was vital. The Zeppelins could not manoeuvre on the ground like modern aircraft. Especially in windy weather very large numbers of men were required to take each airship out of its shed and return it after its mission. For take-off specially trained crews of 300 to 400 men would walk the airship out of its hangar, pulling it along by ropes attached to its keel. For landing the Zeppelin would hover over the field, and drop landing ropes to the ground crew, who would haul it down and walk it into its shed, using the keel ropes to pull it.

Life in a Zeppelin base must have been strange. Nordholz was a huge shore base run in accord with strict naval tradition. It was busy and the ground crew of some 800 men had plenty to do maintaining the ships. But they lived in clean, dry barracks, eating far better than the civilian population. Flight crews had a gilded existence. They were popular heroes (many had the Iron Cross) and food was plentiful. Officers in particular lived a very privileged existence. Some lived off the base with their families. There was an active social life around the officers' mess or casino. Men dressed for dinner and drank good wine.

There was of course a price. Of the nine Zeppelins commanders who walked to their shed and climbed into their ships on Monday 31 January 1916, five would die in action, two would become prisoners of war, only two would see out the war in service.

Just after noon on 31 January 1916, the nine Zeppelins made their rendezvous near Borkum Island, on the German Friesian coast. All Zeppelin raids on Britain took place at night, almost always when there was little moonlight. A typical raid took twenty to twenty-four hours. About seven to eight hours crossing the North Sea, an average of about eight hours over Britain, and another seven or eight hours to get back to base. The raids were timed so the airships would cross the coast in darkness, and leave before dawn. This was not difficult in January with the long nights, so ships took off about noon. It was more difficult in the summer months – Zeppelins took off later in the afternoon and were vulnerable crossing the coast, and on the way back in the dawn light.

British Naval Intelligence knew at about noon there was to be an attack in strength. Though they knew there was to be a raid, they did not know where it was to take place. The police across the country were told an air-raid was possible. However, no public air-raid warnings were given. By 19.00, seven Zeppelins had crossed the coast and the authorities made the assumption that London was the target, a decision that was to have fatal consequences. Because of the foggy weather in the London area, British night fighter aircraft were ordered to take off from airfields on the outskirts of London. In all twenty-two sorties were flown, no pilot saw a Zeppelin, never mind shot at one. In the fog pilots were unable to find their landing flares and crashed. Six aircraft were wrecked and two pilots killed. Because of the early warning British defences were on the alert, and this led to an advantage for historians – the path of the Zeppelins over England were well tracked.

This is very useful, as the logs of the Zeppelin commanders were wildly out. Different commanders claimed to have bombed Sheffield three times, Manchester and Liverpool twice. In fact these cities were untouched by the raids. The majority of casualties were in Staffordshire, the Black Country and Burton-on-Trent. The excellent records kept on the route of the nine airships enable me to give a brief account of the individual actions of each of them, including those that didn't reach the Midlands.

The nine Zeppelins were approaching an almost undefended target. While a major thesis of this book is that the UK almost completely lacked an effective defence system, and that the 31 January raid acted as a significant catalyst in the development of one, it has to be accepted that the raid of 31 January was very different from any previous attack. Until then Britain had been subject to two types of air raid. The first were little more than a nuisance – daylight raids by aeroplane. They were mainly by float planes operating from near Zeebrugge and the targets tended to be around Dover. The first bomb to fall on Britain was dropped by a Friedrichshafen FF29 biplane on Christmas Eve, 1914. It landed in a garden near Dover Castle, causing no injuries, only breaking a lot of windows and causing about £40 worth of damage. The owner of the property was Mr Thomas Terson, an auctioneer and valuer. History does not record his views on the effect of air raids on house prices in Dover. The second type of air attack by Zeppelins was a very different matter indeed. By January 1916 airships had killed more than 200 people and caused about a £1,000,000 worth of damage. Most of the attacks were on the North-East Coast or on London. This is where British defences were concentrated.

The defences around London and on the East Coast were rationally designed and quite effective. The first line on the East Coast were radio direction finding stations (we consider these later in more detail). They intercepted radio signals from Zeppelins, and transmitted them by telephone cable to the Admiralty in London for decoding. They had some limited capacity to indicate the direction a signal came from.

The second line, also on the East Coast, was an interesting type of pre-radar early warning device, the sound mirror. These varied in design, but a typical example was a concrete block with a fifteen-foot diameter saucer-shaped dish cast into it. It looked like a huge version of a modern satellite

TV aerial. In the centre there was a microphone or sound locator; sound waves were reflected by the concave shape on to the microphone. It is said that in ideal conditions a sound mirror could pick up a Zeppelin twenty-five miles away. In normal conditions an effective range of eight to ten miles was usual, but it was a considerable improvement on the unaided ear. At night a Zeppelin could be heard several minutes before it was seen. The operator or listener had to have very acute hearing. It is interesting to note that experiments were done using blind men as operators, because their hearing was often better.

When the Zeppelins crossed the coast they were met with searchlights and anti-aircraft gun batteries. Amongst them were small calibre quick-firing pom-pom guns, but these were generally ineffective against Zeppelins. The larger guns were either 75mm or 3- inch. The most commonly used was the 3-inch, 20cwt, so called because 20cwt was the weight of the breech and barrel. These fired a 16lbs shell to an effective height of 16,000ft. By June 1916 there were 371 anti-aircraft guns deployed in Britain. Shells had adjustable fuses timed so they burst at a set height. This increased the chances of doing damage to the Zeppelins, but more importantly ensured the shell didn't return to earth intact. The main problem was hitting or getting close enough to do damage. In early 1916 the searchlight and anti-aircraft gun combination was the most effective weapon Britain had, but it was probably more important psychologically than physically. The combination of searchlights and gunfire was very frightening and there are many incidents where Zeppelin commanders would turn back to escape. Mathy who was undoubtedly the bravest commander talked in his interview with Karl von Wiegand of 'searchlights like tentacles seeking to drag the Zeppelin to destruction' and the red flashes of the guns and the ominous crack of shrapnel shell, louder than the engine of the airship.

In practice anti-aircraft artillery wasn't as dangerous as it seemed to be. There are a number of examples of Zeppelins being hit by shells and getting home, or at least landing safely. Mathy in his 'lucky ship' L.13 was hit by a six-pounder shell in September 1915, it damaged a number of gas cells, but Mathy was able to limp home. In 1916 Breithaupt in L.15 and Bocker in L.33 were hit by shells which damaged gas cells and forced the Zeppelins down, but most of the crews survived and were captured. What happened in these cases is that the shell went right through the Zeppelin without hitting anything solid enough to make it explode. It damaged the ship, causing a loss of gas, but did not cause a fire. If the crew were unlucky and the shell hit something heavy like an engine, it would explode and the resulting hydrogen fire would leave very little.

Over London searchlights either worked directly with anti-aircraft guns, or in areas where fighters were in operation were used to illuminate the airships and to direct fighter planes to them. The last lines of defence were the fighter bases. These were located around London and along the East Coast, later in the war they were the most effective weapon against the Zeppelin, but in January 1916 they were of limited value. We have to accept that fighters, guns and searchlights were limited resources, and were moved around to where attacks were expected. They were subject to constant dispute, not only where they should be deployed, but whether they should be used for home defence or moved to the Western Front. Decisions had to be made where to deploy these limited resources and generally places that had already been bombed were chosen. The Midlands had not, so it was largely undefended on 31 January 1916.

## Chapter Eight

# Target Middle England

## A Summary of the operation of each Zeppelin

Before we look at the action of each of the nine Zeppelins we need to look at the weather on Monday, 31 January 1916, as it had a major effect on the operation. It was described in the secret intelligence document produced by GHQ Home Forces: 'On the evening of 31 January the wind conditions over the Low Countries, the North Sea and England were exceedingly quiet, and calculations of the wind at 1,500ft show an almost complete calm throughout this area. There was a clear sky in the Midland Counties, but on the East Coast there were large patches of mist and fog, so thick in some places as to be reported as drizzling rain. In London the weather was inclined to be misty and the sky was not clear. There was no moon.'

I don't think this report fully describes the weather in the Midlands. We tend to get seemingly contradictory statements from witnesses. For some the Zeppelin appeared out of the mist, while others looked up to see the Zeppelin in the starry sky. Most people talked about a frosty, foggy night when the Zeppelins came. I think it was one of those rare winter nights when there is drifting ground fog. At times like these there is limited visibility on the ground, but looking up a bright, clear and starry sky.

| Zeppelin L.11 | 'P' Type |
|---|---|
| Length | 536ft |
| Diameter | 61ft |
| Engines | 4x Maybach C-X 210-horsepower. |
| Commander | *Oberleutnant zur See* Horst Freiherr Treusch von Buttlar-Brandenfels |
| Executive Officer | *Leutnant zur See* Hans Schiller |
| Crew | 18. This included *Korvettenkapitain* Peter Strasser, Commander of the Navy Airship Division. |
| Base | Nordholz |

Take off time        11.48 31 January 1916.
Landing time         9.50 1 February 1916.
Bomb load            4,730lbs

The young aristocrat, Baron Horst von Buttlar-Brandenfels, born on 14 June 1888, was one of the first Zeppelin commanders. He had been in combat as early as Christmas Day 1914, when truces were taking place all over the Western Front. On that day British seaplanes attacked the Nordholz base, dropping a few bombs but causing little damage. Buttlar in Zeppelin L.6 spotted the HMS *Empress* a British seaplane carrier and attacked it. He dropped a bomb which missed, but then engaged in a gun fight with the ship. He was fired on by rifles and replied with machine gun fire. When he returned to Nordholz there were a number of bullet holes in his gas bags.

In Zeppelin L.6 he then took part in the first bombing raid on England on 19 January 1915, when Great Yarmouth was bombed, but suffered from engine trouble and returned early. His next raid was on 15 April 1915, again in L.6. He was caught in a searchlight and fired on by cannon and machine guns, dropping his bombs near Maldon in Essex. When he returned to Nordholz he noted one of his gas bags was completely empty and he counted eight tears and seventeen bullet holes in the others.

He was assigned a new ship, Zeppelin L.11, in June 1915. He seems to have been developing the sense of caution that meant he was the only airship commander to serve right through the war. He set out to raid England on 15 June 1915, but had to return to Nordholz because of engine trouble. August was a busy month. On 9 August 1915 he crossed the coast near Lowestoft, was fired on by anti-aircraft guns, and quickly dropped his bombs: some fell in the sea, some on land without causing any casualties as far as we know. He was in action again on 12 August 1915, but had engine problems and did not cross the coast. On 17 August 1915 he crossed the English coast and bombed Ashford and Faversham in Kent. Though he dropped sixty-two bombs no casualties were reported. It appears that after the raid Buttlar claimed to have bombed London. Douglas Robinson, following discussion with Zeppelin crews many years after the events, says that Buttlar made false claims on occasions and it was just one of the reasons he was unpopular in the Airship Service.

He set out again on 7 September 1915, but had to return due to engine trouble. His last raid of the year was on 13 October, when he crossed the coast at Bacton, came under machine gun fire and jettisoned his bombs on the villages of Horstead, Coltishall and Great Hautbois in Norfolk. No casualties were recorded. It seems he again said he had bombed London, claiming to have bombed West Ham, the docks and Woolwich.

Zeppelin L.11 left Nordholz in good weather before noon on 31 January 1916. While Buttlar was nominally in command, he was accompanied by the Commander of the Navy Airship Division *Korvettenkapitain* Peter Strasser. It must have been difficult for Buttlar to command with his boss looking over his shoulder. Strasser was a popular charismatic figure much admired by the men of the airship service. He made a point of flying on as many raids as possible to share the dangers faced by his crews. It seems Strasser was an unpopular passenger, however much he was otherwise admired by Zeppelin crews. He had a reputation as a Jonah, many of the missions carrying him going wrong. He didn't bring L.11 much luck that day.

We know less about the route of L.11 than most other Zeppelins as she operated further north, and the fog which hampered her operation also hampered ground observations. There is no doubt that the GHQ report confuses part of the route of L.11 with that of L.13, however it seems accurate for the first part of the flight of L.11. She crossed the coast in the company of Zeppelin L.20 near Sutton Bridge at about 19.10, she had been slowed down and had been unable to climb because of a build-up of ice on her hull having flown through fog, snow and rain. In his combat report Buttlar said she had about two tons of rain and ice on her hull when she reached England. This cleared as she moved inland, but Buttlar could see very little because of the remaining fog. At 20.15 she passed a big city which Buttlar thought was Lincoln, and then headed directly west until about 23.00. His report indicated he thought he had reached the west coast, but it seems more likely he flew over the sparsely populated Peak District between Sheffield and Manchester.

The GHQ report indicates that L.11 took a separate route from L.20 at the coast. They report she dropped one incendiary bomb at Holbeach at

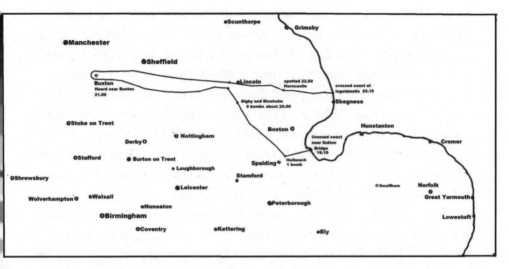

**19.10** crossed the coast near Sutton Bridge in the company of L.20. **19.40** Though Buttlar claimed to have taken all his bombs home as he couldn't find suitable military targets it is possible L.11 dropped one incendiary bomb at Holbeach, and at about **20.00** 3 HE and 1 incendiary bomb at Digby and 4 H E bombs at Bloxholme Park. **21.50** a Zeppelin believed to be L.11 heard but not seen due to the fog near Buxton in the Peak District. **22.50** Spotted near Horncastle then seen north of Lincoln. **23.15** Seen going out to sea at Ingoldmells.

*This route is very speculative. For much of the raid L.11 was lost in the fog, this made navigation and ground observations difficult. I use a combination of information from the G.H.Q report and the work of H A Jones. Most ground observers were soldiers waiting to be deployed to France. While they were able to accurately give their own position and the time they saw or heard a Zeppelin, they had no way of identifying which ship flew over them. G.H.Q thought that L.11 bombed Scunthorpe, in fact it was L.13.The most confusing thing about the route of L.11 is the claim Buttlar made after the raid that as he didn't find any military targets he didn't drop any bombs. The fact that Strasser was aboard makes this claim more likely, however, bombs were dropped in the area L.11 flew over just after crossing the coast and it is difficult to attribute them to other Zeppelins.*

The route of Zeppelin L.11.


19.40, and then turned North West, in the direction of the districts of South Yorkshire. The report says L.11 dropped one incendiary and three high explosive bombs on Digby in Lincolnshire and then four high explosive bombs on nearby Bloxholme Park, at about 20.00, without causing any casualties. The main problem with this account is that it is widely believed that the most remarkable feature of the cruise of L.11 is that she did not drop any bombs. Buttlar wrote in his combat report that because he failed to find any military targets he and *Korvettenkapitain* Strasser decided to bring their bombs home. This caused British historian H A Jones, writing after the War, to comment on his 'high conception of his duty'. This leaves us with the problem of which Zeppelin dropped the bombs on Digby and Bloxholme at that time. We can rule out L.13 – she was bombing Stoke-on-Trent at 20.15. The only candidates seem to be L.14 or L.19. Bocker in L.14 bombed Kipton near Grantham at 20.00. Digby is about twenty miles away from there. The other possibility seems to be L.19. She was reported south of Stamford at 20.10, but as her path was poorly observed and she was reported as circling she may have reached Digby and Bloxholme.

The other possibility is that GHQ got it right, L.11 did drop the bombs. The source of evidence Jones uses is the German naval historian Otto Groos, in his history of the High Seas Fleet, *Der Krieg in der Nordsee*. Much of this was based on official reports and commanders records. We know that Buttlar was not always accurate in his combat reports and it may be the bombs did come from L.11. We will probably never know.

Ground observers certainly lost L.11 after that. GHQ report that a Zeppelin they believed to be L.13 was creditably reported in the Peak District – heard at about 21.50 but not seen. The GHQ map shows her just west of Buxton, in Derbyshire. After that the GHQ reports seem to get more accurate, albeit still believing they were tracking L.13. Zeppelin L.11 was spotted over Horncastle north of Lincoln at 22.50, and crossed the coast near Ingoldmells at 23.15. Zeppelin L.11 returned to Nordholz at 09.50 the next morning.

| Zeppelin L.13 | 'P' Type |
|---|---|
| Length | 536ft |
| Diameter | 61ft |
| Engines | 4x Maybach C-X 210-horsepower |
| Commander | *Kapitanleutnant* Heinrich Mathy |
| Executive Officer | *Oberleutnant zur See* Kurt Friemel |
| Crew | 16 |
| Base | Hage |
| Take off time | 11.45 31 January 1916. |
| Landing time | 8.30 1 February 1916. |
| Bomb load | 4,850lbs |

Zeppelin L.13 had a much more exciting flight and we have better records, though GHQ confused her with L.11. She was commanded by *Kapitanleutnan*t Heinrich Mathy, generally regarded by the British as the bravest and the best airship commander. Mathy was 32-years-old, born on 4 April 1883.

L.13 crossed the English coast, accompanied by Zeppelin L.21, at 16.50, north of Mundesley, Norfolk. The two Zeppelins then separated at Foulsham, Mathy took L.13 directly west, and she was spotted over East Dereham. She was seen at Sporle at 17.15 was north of Swaffham at 17.30. She then turned north-west and went out to sea over the Wash north of Lynn, then back over land at Fosdyke at 18.30. She flew directly west over Grantham, then was seen at 19.30 south of Nottingham. She was over Derby at 19.45 and then went south of Cheadle to Stoke-on-Trent. She bombed Fenton Colliery near Stoke at about 20.15, dropping six high explosive bombs, in a radius seventy-yards, doing some damage but without causing any casualties. She then turned towards Newcastle-under-Lyme, dropping a flare at Madeley at 20.20. It seems Mathy had his way as he then circled northward, over Alsager, Woolstanton, Basford and back to Stoke. British observers then lose L.13, it seems Mathy flew north-west probably looking for Manchester, but failing to find it because of the blackout and the fog. He then flew east trying to reach the Humber. He was spotted again over Retford circling for some time at 21.50. He then went north near Gainsborough and then south-east towards Lincoln, dropping another flare over Hackthorne at 22.30. The airship then went at high speed north towards Hull. In his combat report Mathy claimed to have bombed Goole, but in fact had found the brightly lit blast furnaces of the Frodingham Iron and Steel works near Scunthorpe. He missed the Frodingham works, but hit the closed Redbourn Iron and Steel Works, at about 23.00, killing two men. L.13 then bombed the town of Scunthorpe, where four houses were destroyed and another person was killed. She was again spotted at Humberston at 23.35 and fired on by the one-pounder pom-pom gun at Waltham Wireless Station, without any damage. Mathy crossed the English coast at about 23.45, north of North Somercoates.

Zeppelin L.13 remained in service, until December 1917 taking part in a total of forty-five scouting flights and seventeen raids. Heinrich Mathy and most of the crew took over a new airship in July 1916 the bigger and faster L.31. They were to die in it, over Potters Bar on the 2 October 1916.

| **Zeppelin L.14** | 'P' Type |
|---|---|
| Length | 536ft |
| Diameter | 61ft |
| Engines | 4x Maybach C-X 210-horsepower |
| Commander | *Kapitanleutnant* Alois Bocker |
| Executive Officer | *Oberleutnant zur See* Kurt Frankenberg |
| Crew | 17 |
| Base | Nordholz |
| Take off time | 11.40 31 January 1916. |
| Landing time | 12.06 1 February 1916. |
| Bomb load | 4,130lbs |

Zeppelin L.14 was commanded by *Kapitanleutnant der Reserve* Alois Bocker. He was a very experienced naval officer, who had previously been a merchant seaman; he was born on 12 May 1879 and survived the war. We have quite a lot of information about the route of Zeppelin L.14. She crossed the English coast north of Holkham, Norfolk at about 18.15. She was sighted over Burnham Market at 18.20 pm, and Sandringham at 18.35. She bombed Knipton, south west of Grantham at about 20.00, without any casualties. She then headed west for the Midlands, passing south of Nottingham and Derby and north of Stafford. She was spotted over to Shrewsbury at 22.00. In reaching Shrewsbury she went further to the west than any other Zeppelin, according to the GHQ report over 180miles inland. She then wandered, passing over Wellington, Oakengates and Gnosal. It appears that Bocker thought the dark area of rural Shropshire to the west was the sea and he had reached the West Coast. He turned east and flew over Cannock, Lichfield and Tamworth. At 23.35 he saw the light of furnaces at Ashby Woulds, near Ashby-de-la-Zouch. He dropped one high explosive and one incendiary bomb which fell on a cinder heap and did no damage. He reached Overseal and Swadlincote in Derbyshire at about midnight, and dropped more bombs. They did a little damage, but caused no casualties. She reached the town of Derby, which, amazingly, was showing many lights some four hours after the start of the raid. She bombed many targets including the Rolls-Royce Works, the Metalite' Lamp Works, the Railway Carriage Works, the Gas Company, and the Midland Railway Locomotive Works, dropping nine high explosive bombs which killed four men and a woman who died of shock. The airship then flew east and went south-east of Nottingham near Newark and south of Lincoln, before leaving our shores north of the Wash at about 02.10 on 1 February, after almost eight hours in enemy territory. She had penetrated the furthest west of any Zeppelin on the raid.

Many of her crew were captured at Great Wigborough on 24 September 1916 when L.33 was shot down. They had transferred to the new ship with Bocker. On interrogation most of the crew believed they had bombed Liverpool on 31 January. L.14 arrived back at Nordholz at about 12.00 noon on 1 February 1916.

| | |
|---|---|
| **Zeppelin L.15** | 'P' Type |
| Length | 536ft |
| Diameter | 61ft |
| Engines | 4x Maybach HSLu 240-horsepower |
| Commander | *Kapitanleutnant* Joachim Breithaupt |
| Executive officer | *Leutnant zur See* Otto Kuhne |
| Crew | 17 |
| Base | Hage |
| Take off time | 12.00 Noon 31 January 1916. |
| Landing time | 10.05 1 February 1916. |
| Bomb load | 4,750lbs |

Zeppelin L.15 was commanded by 33-years-old Joachim Breithaupt. Born on 28 January 1883, he was an experienced professional naval officer. Like most airship commanders he had previously served in an older ship, the L.6 which he took over from Buttlar.

He was promoted to Zeppelin L.15 in September 1915. She was the first ship to be fitted with the new Maybach HSLu high compression 240hp engines. These engines had been introduced with little testing and were very unreliable. This didn't prevent her taking part in the last raid of 1915. Breithaupt attacked London on 13 October 1915. This was very successful. He attacked Central London in the so called 'Theatreland' raid, bombing around the Strand and Charing Cross, and killing about twenty-three people.

Though the mechanics did a lot of work on L.15 in the next two months, the engine problems remained. Two of her engines had been out of order as she crossed the North Sea on 31 January 1916, but had been repaired by a mechanic. The ability to repair an engine in flight was one of the few

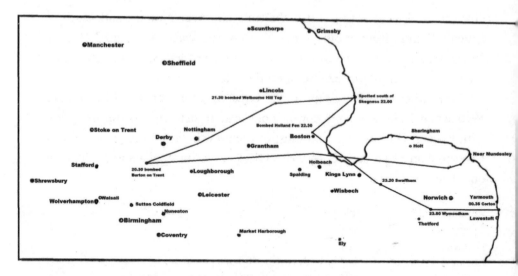

**17.50** crossed the coast at Maundesley. Seen north of North Walsham and Aylsham. G.H.Q observers then loose L.15. **20.30** Bombed Burton on Trent. **21.30** Probably bombed Welbourne Hill Top. **22.00** spotted south of Skegness. **22.30** Bombed Holland Fen near Boston. **23.20** spotted at Swaffham. **22.50** spotted at Wymondham. **00.35 (1 Feb 16)** crossed the coast at Corton.

*This map is based on the route suggested by Jones. There is more confusion about the route of L.15 than any other Zeppelin. GHQ were convinced that L.13 not L.15 bombed Burton. Jones thought it was most probable L.15 was involved, though he was not sure and thought she bombed at 21.15 not 20. 30 as I think likely. My theory is based on the evidence that Zeppelin L.15 had enough HE bombs left to kill 15 people. L.20 which bombed shortly afterwards had only incendiaries left. The other Zeppelin to bomb Burton was L.19, but she bombed later in the evening, and most witness statements report people being killed at about 20.30. Burton was definitely bombed by three Zeppelins, and though we know where all the bombs landed, there are differing statements about when the bombs fell and the order they hit. We do know that L.15 was shot down in March 1916, and her commander Joachim Breithaupt and crew were captured. During interrogation Breithaupt appears to have been convinced he bombed Liverpool, which we known he didn't. However, he very clearly described bombing a city, which could only have been Burton on Trent.*

The route of Zeppelin L.15.

advantages the Zeppelin had over a heavier than air machines. We have less detailed information on the cruise of L.15 than most of the other Zeppelins. She seems to have crossed the coast at about 17.50 north of Mundesley. Though there is some confusion in the reports it seems she flew over Walsham and Aylsham and then spent some three hours travelling to Burton-on-Trent where she dropped most of her bombs. There is some confusion about the time she arrived at Burton. Witnesses on the ground estimate heavy bombing started at about 20.30, though the GHQ report estimates it was between 20.45 and 21.45. In his combat report Joachim Breithaupt claimed to have bombed Liverpool. As he was known as one of the more reliable commanders it is worth quoting his combat report in some detail. He said: 'at about 9.30 pm (20.30 GMT) the ship was over the west coast; a large city complex, divided in two parts by a broad sheet of water running north and south joined by a lighted bridge was recognised as Liverpool and Birkenhead. After dropping a parachute flare the lights of the city mostly went out. From 2500m (8200ft) 1400kg (3100lbs) of explosive and 300kg (660lbs) of incendiaries were dropped in four crossings of the city, mostly along the waterfront. All explosive bombs burst but fires were not seen to result. On the other hand the incendiaries worked very well in my opinion, a great proportion seem to have burst. A huge glow of fire was seen over the city from a great distance.'

As we know Liverpool was untouched, and since three Zeppelins bombed Burton-on-Trent we can be fairly sure one was L.15. After this Breithaupt flew east to return to base. We have poor records of his course as his magnetic compass was faulty, and the ship was steered by the stars. This gives a good indication of the weather on the night over the Midlands, while patchy ground fog, often obscured the low lying areas, at height the sky was clear and bright. British records were very unreliable. They reported L.15 dumped forty bombs in the fenland north-east of Cambridge. These were almost certainly the bombs dropped by L.16. It seems they got it right, however when she was spotted south of Skegness at 22.00.

It is possible L.15 dropped nine incendiary bombs at Welbourne Hill Top, north of Sleaford at 21.30 and then went on towards Skegness. It seems that she then turned south and dropped a single incendiary bomb on Holland Fen, near Boston at 22.30. She went out to sea over the Wash and crossed the coast again near King's Lynn. She was spotted at Swaffham at 23.20 and over Wymondham at 23.50. She left our shores at Corton, at about 00.35 (1 February).

L.15 arrived back at Hage at about 10.05 on Tuesday 1 February. Like many of the Zeppelins fitted with the 240hp engines, she was out of action for some time as they were returned for modification to the Maybach factory at Friedrichshafen. She had modified engines fitted and was readied for action in March 1916.

| Zeppelin L.16 | 'P' Type |
|---|---|
| Length | 536ft |
| Diameter | 61ft |
| Engines | 4x Maybach HSLu 240-horsepower |
| Commander | *Oberleutnant zur See* Werner Peterson |
| Executive Officer | *Leutnant zur See* Karl Brodruck |
| Crew | 17 |
| Base | Hage |
| Take off time | 12.15 31 January 1916 |
| Landing time | 8.00 1 February 1916. |
| Bomb load | 4,010lbs |

*Oberleutnant zur See* Werner Peterson, born 24 July 1887, was a young professional naval officer. He was described by Robinson as popular with his fellow officers and renowned as the best ship handler. He had taken part in three previous raids on England. The first was on the 15 April 1915 in Zeppelin L.7. Hampered by strong headwinds, it seems he reached the English coast near Great Yarmouth but he was unaware of that because of the blackout. British observers reported he crossed the coast, but he didn't realise this and went back to base.

Peterson was assigned a new airship the L.12. He returned to England on 9 August 1915. He got lost crossing the North Sea and bombed Dover, thinking he was bombing Harwich. He injured three men and damaged some buildings. He was fired on by a 3-inch anti-aircraft gun. It fired ten rounds, and one was seen to hit L.12. Luckily for Paterson it didn't cause a fire, but severely damaged two gas bags. Paterson managed to return to German occupied territory and crash landed in the sea at Ostend. The Zeppelin was destroyed.

Peterson was given command of Zeppelin L.16 at the end of September 1915. He took part in the raid on London on 13 October 1915. He again got lost and claimed to have bombed London, but in fact bombed Hertford killing nine people.

Peterson's next raid was on 31 January 1916. Like most of the Zeppelins fitted with newer more powerful, high compression, 240-hp engines L.16 still suffered from engine trouble. She made slow progress as an engine failed before she reached the British Coast. She was also

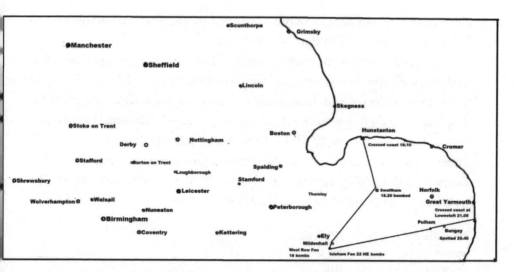

**18.10** Crossed the coast near Hunstanton. **18.20** bombed north of Swaffham. **19.10** spotted near Mildenhall. **19.15** Bombed West Row Fen. 3 H.E and 15 incendiary bombs.**19.35** Bombed Isleham Fen. 22 H.E bombs. Spotted over Pulham. **20.40** spotted near Bungay. **21.05** crossed the coast north of Lowestoft.

*Because of the fog there is confusion over the routes of L.15 and L.16. Using the routes suggested by Jones where they differ from the G.H.Q reports I think this is the most likely route.*

The route of Zeppelin L.16.

covered with snow and ice, and unable to climb above 7000ft. She was spotted when she crossed the coast at Hunstanton at 18.10. Because of the engine problems Peterson decided to abandon the mission target to bomb Liverpool, and bomb Great Yarmouth instead. There is some confusion in the British reports about her movements. She was reported as wandering about Norfolk, dropping two bombs near Swaffham, one of which did not explode, until she left our shores at 21.05 at Lowestoft. Peterson's combat report contradicts this. He claimed to have dropped all his bombs on various factories and industrial works at Yarmouth. While we know Yarmouth was not bombed that night, and he was lost in the fog, he would certainly know if he had dropped all his bombs. It seems likely that British ground observers watching Zeppelins sliding in and out of view in the mist, confused his bombing, and attributed it to another airship. It is probable the bombs dropped in the fenlands attributed to L.15 actually came from Peterson in L.16.

If this is the case we can confirm much of her route from where the bombs landed. A Zeppelin was spotted over Mildenhall at 19.10. She dropped three high explosive and 15 incendiary bombs at West Row Fen at 19.15. The Zeppelin then flew west to Isleham Fen where she dropped twenty-two high explosive bombs at 19.35. Probably because of the marshy ground only fifteen exploded, a hen house was destroyed and sixteen chickens killed. The Zeppelin was again spotted over Pulham at 20.30 and Bungay at 20.40. She went out to sea north of Lowestoft at 21.05.

| Zeppelin L.17 | 'P' Type |
| --- | --- |
| Length | 536ft |
| Diameter | 61ft |
| Engines | 4x Maybach HSLu 240-horsepower |
| Commander | *Kapitanleutnant* Herbert Ehrlich |
| Executive Officer | *Oberleutnant zur See* Dietsch |
| Crew | 18 |
| Base | Nordholz. |
| Take off time | 11.17 31 January 1916 |
| Landing time | 08.00 1 February 1916. |
| Bomb load | 4,430lbs |

This was the first raid on England by *Kapitanleutnant* Herbert Ehrlich. He seems to have been the commander with the least public attention. He was born on 20 March 1884, in Dresden. The son of Admiral Alfred Ehrlich, he was a senior teacher at the Navy Officers Training School in Cuxhaven. He won the Iron Cross 2nd class in 1914. He was a cautious and competent commander, who survived the war. He seems to have been well respected by Peter Strasser, who recommended him for technically difficult missions or experimental work. His first command was Zeppelin L.5 which he took over from Bocker in July 1915. He was assigned to L.17 on 27 October 1915.

Like the other Zeppelins fitted with the newer more powerful, high compression Maybach HSLu engines L.17 suffered from engine trouble. Two of her engines had seized before she reached the English coast. Her mechanics had spent much of the afternoon repairing the forward engine. His starboard engine also failed repeatedly. This led to *Kaptainleutnant*

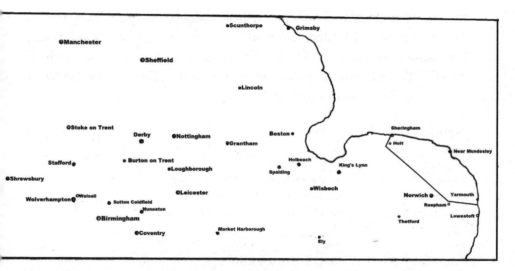

**18.40** Crossed the coast at Sheringham. A few minutes later L.17 was caught by the Royal Naval Air Station searchlight at Bayfield. As a result she dropped most of her bombs in an attempt to hit the searchlight, they fell in fields around Bayfield, a few hundred yards from the Air Station. She dropped the rest around Letheringset, damaging a barn and some houses but causing no casualties. It seems she then spent some time in the vicinity of Holt. She was spotted near Reepham at about **20.10** and crossed the coast south of Yarmouth at **20.30**.

*This is probably an accurate route for L.17 she spent little time over England, as she dropped most of her bombs on a searchlight soon after crossing the coast. GHQ and Jones agree on her route. I suppose the interesting thing is why she spent almost 2 hours over England, after dropping all her bombs.*

The route of Zeppelin L.17.


Ehrlich making very slow progress. Ground observers spotted L.17 as she crossed the coast at Sheringham at 18.40. In his combat report Ehrlich said he could not determine his position due to thick cloud, but saw the glow of blast furnaces to the starboard and steered towards them. He was then caught by a searchlight beam, and said he was fired on by small calibre guns. He said he made two runs over the industrial area, and that the battery was silenced and all lights were out by the end of his attack. He later calculated his position by dead reckoning, and thought he had bombed Immingham. She did not bomb there, the British in their GHQ report said L.17 was the only Zeppelin to be troubled by British defence forces, being caught in a searchlight beam, operated by the Royal Naval Air Service at Holt. This caused her to drop her bombs at Bayfield and Letheringsett. They missed the searchlight and landed mainly in fields, damaging a barn and a house, but causing no casualties. She left British airspace, south of Yarmouth, at 20.30. L.17 made slow progress back to Nordholz, taking over twelve hours to cross the North Sea to land safely.

| Zeppelin L.19 | 'P' Type |
|---|---|
| Length | 536ft |
| Diameter | 61ft |
| Engines | 4x Maybach HSLu 240-horsepower |
| Commander | *Kapitanleutnant* Odo Loewe |
| Executive officer | *Oberleutnant zur See* Erwin Braunhof |
| Crew | 16 |
| Base | Tondern |
| Take off time | 11. 15 31 January 1916 |
| Landing time | Failed to return. L.19 probably sank in the North Sea, off the Friesian coast, on the afternoon of 2 February 1916. |
| Bomb load | Not known. |

We covered the flight of L.19 in some detail in Chapter Two. She crossed the English coast at Lower Sheringham at about 18.20. She then made very slow progress, almost certainly due to engine trouble. Because of her failure to return, we do not have Loewe's combat report. We do have very good Intelligence records, probably because she was flying so slowly. We know her route better than any other ship. What is puzzling is how meandering it was, Loewe stopped and circled a number of times. Was he deciding whether to go on, or turn back?

It seems L.19 crossed the coast at Sheringham and was first spotted at Holt at 18.25. She made slow progress and was next seen at Swaffham at 19.05. She passed south of Stamford at 20.10, and then did a large circle, being spotted over Exton and then over Stamford again. She then pursued an uncertain course and was spotted over Oakham and seemed to circle several time until she reached Loughborough at 21.30. It seems that by then all the lights were out because she ignored the town and reached Burton-on-Trent at about 21.45, dropping incendiary bombs on fires started by other Zeppelins. She then turned south-west and flew near Wolverhampton. She was spotted several times between 22.30 and 23.30 in the area between Kidderminster and Birmingham. She was seen or heard near Enville,

Kinver, Wolverley, Bewdley, Bromsgrove, Redditch and Stourbridge. We can be fairly certain she dropped a bomb at Kidderminster, which didn't explode. It wasn't noted in the intelligence report but dug up almost twenty-five years later. She was over Wythall near Birmingham at 23.00. She then turned north to bomb Wednesbury, then circled again and bombed Dudley at 00.15 (1 February), then Tipton at 00.20, moving to Walsall at 00.25. It seems she used all her bombs in the Black Country.

L.19 then travelled very slowly using an equally devious route to the coast. She was over Sutton Coldfield at 00.30, Coleshill at 00.40, then north of Coventry at 00.50, north of Rugby at 01.00. She then took another indirect course, being spotted over Market Harborough, then Kettering, then Oundle. She was heard at Kimbolton at 02.10. She then turned north to the west of Huntingdon, then seemed to stop over Yaxley. At 02.25, she turned east over Littleport and Hockwold, where she was seen to circle again at 03.10. She then went over Sutton Ferry, south of Downham Market, south of Swaffham a 03.40.South of East Derham at 04.15, then to Wymondham at 04.30. She then seems to have avoided Norwich, turning north-east passing Costessey at 04.41. She then turned for the coast and was spotted over Wroxham at 05.15, crossing our shore at about 05.25, near Martham in Norfolk. She spent more than eleven hours over England. She was the only Zeppelin not to return. We can only guess at the reason for her route, it seems she was not simply lost, perhaps she was trying to stay over land as long as possible, only crossing the sea when she was as close as possible to Germany; whatever the reason was, the plan didn't work, and a day later all the crew drowned in the cold North Sea.

| Zeppelin L.20 | 'Q' Type |
|---|---|
| Length | 585ft |
| Diameter | 61ft |
| Engines | 4x Maybach HSLu 240-horsepower |
| Commander | *Kapitanleutnant* Franz Stabbert |
| Executive Officer | *Leutnant zur See* Ernst Wilhelm Schirlitz |
| Crew | 18 |
| Base | Tondern |
| Take off time | 11.06 31 January 1916 |
| Landing time | 11.00 1 February 1916. |
| Bomb load | 5,600lbs |

L.20 was the first of the longer 'Q' type Zeppelins. It had a better bomb load than earlier models, but still had the problems caused by the Maybach HSLu 240hp engines. The route of L.20 was well monitored by the British. Like most ships with the 240hp engine she had engine trouble. The forward engine was out of action for much of the flight over the North Sea, and the starboard ran irregularly. Her commander Franz Stabbard also had to fly low at 6500ft because of heavy rain and snow, which caused icing on the hull. This slowed L.20 down but did not stop her reaching the English Midlands. She crossed the coast at about 19.10, near Sutton Bridge in the company of L.11. She was spotted at Peakirk at 19.40, and then travelling west she bombed Uffington, dropping one HE bomb, and breaking a few windows. She passed north of Oakham and Leicester. Both Nottingham and Leicester had a full blackout, Loughborough did not. At about 20.00 Franz Stabbert spotted the lights of Loughborough. The bomb-aimer *Leutnant* Schirlitz dropped four HE bombs at 20.05, killing ten people. In his combat report Stabbart said he bombed an anti-aircraft battery which fired at him, and which the bombs silenced. He said that at that time he made the decision not to go on to Liverpool because of his engine trouble, but bomb Sheffield which he calculated was near. He was much further south than he thought, and next bombed Bannerley and Trowell in Nottinghamshire, where he dropped seven HE bombs on the railways, damaging a signal box, but causing no casualties. He continued west to Hallam Fields near Ilkeston where he dropped fifteen HE bombs on the Stanton Ironworks at 20.30. He did considerable damage to buildings and killed two men.

He then flew to Burton-on-Trent, bombing the town at 20.45, probably the second of three Zeppelins to do so. By this time he had used all his high explosive bombs and dropped only incendiaries. As three airships bombed Burton in a one hour period, it is impossible to determine which airship was responsible for individual casualties. However, as Stabbard only had incendiary bombs left it seems likely he caused fires and most of the casualties were caused by L.15 which had arrived just before him. In all a great deal of damage was done and fifteen people killed. After bombing Burton, L.20 suffered from engine trouble, and made slow progress. She was spotted travelling in a north-easterly direction passing north of Derby and Nottingham. Then she went south-east to the vicinity of Stamford. She was spotted at Thornley at 22.30 and near Swaffham at 23.15. She crossed the coast near Blakeney at 23.45, and was last seen from Cromer going out to sea at 23.52. It seems she had more engine trouble because it took her twelve hours to cross the North Sea, arriving at Tondern at 11.00 on Tuesday, 1 February 1916.

| | |
|---|---|
| **Zeppelin L.21** | 'Q' Type |
| Length | 585ft |
| Diameter | 61ft |
| Engines | 4x Maybach HSLu 240-horsepower |
| Commander | *Kapitanleutnant* Max Dietrich |
| Executive Officer | *Leutnant der Reserve* Christian von Nathusius |
| Crew | 17 |
| Base | Nordholz |
| Take off time | 11.00 31 January 1916. |
| Landing time | 10.45 1 February 1916. |
| Bomb load | 4,910lbs |

We have already covered the raid of Zeppelin L.21 in some detail. She crossed the English coast near Mundesley, with L.13 at about 16.50. Both were seen near Foulsham at 17.00, but L.21 was faster and they separated. At 17.20, she was over Narborough and at 17.25 over King's Lynn she travelled south of Sutton Bridge and Holbeach to Spalding at 18.05. She travelled at high speed south of Grantham (18.30) then south of Nottingham and Derby. She was spotted at Kirk Langley at 19.00 and then Stafford. She flew over Wolverhampton at 19.45, was heard over Netherton (19.55) then started he attack on the Black Country towns. She started her attack on Tipton at about 20.00, and finished her attack on Walsall at about 20.30. She probably caused more casualties than any other Zeppelin, killing thirty-five people in the Black Country. From Walsall she was seen over Sutton Coldfield (20.35) and Nuneaton (20.55). Passing near Market Harborough and Kettering, she bombed the Islip furnace at Thrapston, Northamptonshire at 21.15. As the GHQ report states she then went with a 'very definite and unswerving direction' north of Huntingdon, over Ely (22.00) and Thetford (22.35). She then was seen between East Harling and Attleborough. She flew north of Bonwell then turned towards Long Stratton and was spotted north of Lodden at 23.25. She crossed the English coast south of Lowestoft, between Pakefield and Kessingland at 23.35. She returned to Nordholz at about 10.45 the next morning.

## The Outcome

The raid of 31 January 1916 was the second heaviest of the war. Seventy civilians were killed and 113 injured. The raid is estimated to have caused £53,832 worth of damage. A total of 205 high explosive and 113 incendiary bombs were dropped. The raid of 13/14 October 1915 on London is generally regarded as the heaviest airship raid. There seventy-one people were killed, 128 injured and about £80,000 worth of damage caused. However, if we add the two British pilots killed in defence operations to the total, then seventy-two British people were killed, making the raid of 31 January the most costly. Looking back over the whole of the twentieth century the raid can be seen in the context of the carnage of the Western Front, and the massive loss of lives caused by air-raids in the Second World War. The total 'butchers bill' for the raid was small. Ninety-two people had died: seventy British civilians, two British airmen, sixteen crewmen from the L.19 and four German airmen sent to find them. But it was a portent for the future – terror bombing had reached the centre of British industry. War was no longer a matter for soldiers, something graphically illustrated by the fact that fifteen of the dead were children.

In press reports the *Reichskreigmarine* claimed the raid as a major success. Zeppelin commanders reported they had bombed Liverpool, and other cities of major military importance. The raid had given the English a bloody nose. The British Navy might be able to starve German citizens by their blockade, but the Zeppelins could kill English civilians and destroy their industry.

The German press communiqué of 1 February 1916 said:

'A German Naval airship squadron had dropped a large number of high explosive and incendiary bombs on and near Liverpool and Birkenhead docks, harbours and factories. Manchester was also bombed. Bombs were also dropped on blast furnaces at Nottingham and Sheffield, and on a number of industrial establishments at Great Yarmouth. At all places the effect was heavy and caused mighty explosions and violent fires. They went on to say "the airships were heavily fired on in many places, but they were not hit, one battery was silenced".'

In fact, in terms of military damage, the raid was a failure. The Zeppelins had wandered above England, hopelessly lost. England had not been destroyed by fire. The effect on civilian morale was more difficult to assess. There was some initial panic, and for a few months afterwards false air-raid alarms that affected industrial production across the country. Perhaps the most important effect of the raid was that it made the Government take the air defence of the nation seriously, leading to the destruction of numbers of Zeppelins from the autumn of 1916 onwards.

The raid cost the German Navy dearly. Zeppelin L.19 commanded by *Kapitanleutnant* Odo Loewe, one of its most experienced airship officers failed to return. Her crew drowned in the cold North Sea. Also killed were four German airmen, the pilots and observers of two seaplanes lost in the futile search for Zeppelin L.19 off the Friesian coast. The German Navy recognised they had made mistakes. The loss of L.19 was acceptable – the price of war is that some men die for the Fatherland. They recognised the error of fitting new and untried engines. One of the first things Strasser did after the raid was have strong words with the Maybach Company. He arranged for all the HSLu 240hp engines to be removed from the airships and sent back to the factory. They were to be accompanied by warrant officers and mechanics. Officially the men were on a course, in practice they were to work with the engineers to get the engines right.

They were much slower to recognise the failings of their radio positioning system. In a sense the technology worked, Zeppelins were able to get a rough estimate of their position by radio location. In practice, however, it was useless; given locations could be 50miles out. It gave navigators false confidence in technology, and had an overall negative effect. Most of all they believed that the Zeppelin, defended by bristling machine guns, could survive for long periods at night in hostile territory. The rest of 1916 showed just how wrong they were.

At the time the British saw the raid as a defeat. Zeppelins had roamed at will over the Midlands. There was far more public and political concern following the January raid, than the October 1915 raid on London. The capital was protected, surrounded by a ring of searchlight sites and anti-aircraft gun batteries, as well as fighter airfields. Though this had not prevented the bombing, the public could see something was happening. In the Midlands in January, Zeppelins had roamed unmolested over England for up to twelve hours. British defence forces were almost totally ineffective, only Zeppelin L.17 was troubled, dropping her bombs after being caught in a searchlight. The only searchlights and anti-aircraft guns were on the East Coast or around London.

To say the defence system did badly is being generous. In reality there was no defence system, just a series of *ad hoc* measures, resulting from inter-service rivalry and poor communication. It is very much to their credit that the British were willing and able to accept this and build an effective air defence system, which led to the complete defeat of the Zeppelin.

*Chapter Nine*

# Anger

## The aftermath of the raid

The raid of 31 January 1916 was the second heaviest airship raid on England in the Great War. Seventy civilians were killed and some 113 injured. Indeed if we add military to civilian casualties more people died that night, than in any other Zeppelin raid on England. Unlike earlier raids on London where the defence forces could be seen to be doing something with searchlights and anti-aircraft guns, not only had the Zeppelins caused considerable damage, but had also flown unmolested over Britain for up to eleven hours. There was a great deal of fear and anger, fuelled by rumour, amongst the local people. The extent of the fear can be seen in the advertisement columns of the local press. Local firms moved quickly to take advantage of demand created by the new situation. On 2 February Beattie's of Wolverhampton advertised blackout blinds in the *Express and Star*. The advertisement pointed that 'prudence and patriotism' demanded that people darken their windows. Beattie's could supply various types of dark blinds; all made to order in their own workrooms. Other companies offered different sorts of insurance. Jay and Company of 37 Digbeth, Walsall offered free insurance against Zeppelin or hostile aircraft raids on all furniture purchased on their deferred payment scheme.

People's anger was directed two ways, at the Germans and at the Government. It was not easy to take revenge on the Germans. Sadly in some cases any foreigner would do. A very distasteful incident took place at Cradley Heath, in the Black Country. Harry Harris, formally Hirsh Demboski was a naturalised Russian Jew, a refugee from Tsarist pogroms. With his wife Miriam, he owned a shop at 134 High Street, Cradley Heath. He was a draper and corset maker. On Tuesday, 1 February 1916 a hostile crowd gathered in front of his shop, people shouted 'they are Germans', and prepared to attack the shop. The police were called, Mr Harris was advised to close the shop, but was followed home by an angry crowd. The next day a crowd of several hundred people congregated in the area of the shop. They claimed Mr Harris had made pro-German comments. Stones were thrown, and about £20 worth of damage was done to glass and clothing. The police made several arrests.

At Old Hill Police Court the following week, Monday, 7 February 1916, a woman and a number of teenagers were summoned. Mrs Anne Jeavons was charged with standing in front of the shop shouting, "Bring out the Germans." She was bound over to keep the peace. William Bridgwater (18), Horace Corfield (17), Charles Homer (18), Gertrude Little (14), Marie Stringer (18) and Albert Wellings (17) were all charged with breaking windows. They were each fined ten shillings and ordered to pay damages of ten shillings each. The chairman of the magistrates said he thought Mr Harris should have taken steps to let the people know he was a Russian, not a German. We will probably never know if he tried to do this. There is one further twist to this sad little tale. Harry Harris appears in the Kelly's Directory for 1916. His trade is interesting, as well as a draper and corset maker he was also a pawnbroker. Probably many people in the crowd thought he was a German, but for some of his clients maybe the Zeppelin raid was an excuse for revenge of a more personal kind.

Another similar incident is reputed to have taken place in Bradley, where Maud and William Fellows had been killed. The *Black Country Bugle* reported in 1994 that rumours spread that an old lady, a factory owner, possibly of German origin, had guided the Zeppelin to its target by shining a light into the air. It was thought that the Zeppelin had several local works on its target list. An angry crowd gathered and stones were thrown at her house. She and her son were rescued by the local police who took them to Bilston Police Station for questioning. It seems the woman was later sent to Stafford Jail, but the details are lost to history.

Rumours spread in any war and sadly innocent people are often scapegoated. However, rumours can also be very funny. One circulating in Wednesbury certainly was. Hackwood related the affair of the captured gun. On Saturday, 22 January 1916, a German field gun captured in the battle of Loos was paraded through the town from Kings Hill to Wood Green, a route which also happened to be similar to that followed by the Zeppelin. A colonel, from Lichfield, led the procession, which included the City Fathers in their robes of office, the Fire Brigade, the Boy Scouts and Girl Guides, in fact virtually everyone in Wednesbury with a uniform. There were two military brass bands and many patriotic speeches. Less than two weeks later the Zeppelins came. It was the solemn conviction of many townspeople that the two events had to be connected. Berlin had found out about the procession in Wednesbury and sent their Zeppelins to avenge the insult. When less gullible souls questioned, 'How did the Germans know?' they were told that there were spies everywhere.

There was another similar spy story in Derbyshire, which appeared after the war in the *Derby Mercury* and is quoted by John Hook. At Melbourne, a small town between Loughborough and Derby, a Zeppelin was seen by four men returning from work. It was coming from the direction of Loughborough and the Charnwood Forest at about 21.00. At the same time the men saw a large grey car with men in white or light coloured overalls heading towards Derby. After some time they again saw a Zeppelin, this time flying in the opposite direction, and the grey car again, coming from the direction of Derby. They then said the car halted and a 'bunch of cluster lights, pointing upward were uncovered'. The car then drove off in the direction of Burton and the Zeppelin followed it. It was a fair supposition, the newspaper reporter said, that the car was directing the airship. If we accept that the four men honestly related what they saw it seems that the whole thing was a series of coincidences. There were at least three Zeppelins operating in the area at that time and almost certainly they saw one going towards Derby, and another flying away. The quoted times do not match with what we know about the movement of each Zeppelin, but there was considerable confusion in the records. We can be sure the car was not directing a Zeppelin, from the height they operated at a commander would not have seen a single car, or the lights at night.

Probably the best of these stories came from Loughborough. The commercial title of the Empress Crane Works was the William Morris Works. William Morris was a largely self-made millionaire. He had started a company making pulley blocks in 1889, with a German-born partner Frank Bastert. As manufacturing industry expanded the company rapidly diversified into making electric cranes. The company was called William

Morris and Bastert. Morris was a popular man, basically an inventor and salesman. Bastert was the man with day-to-day control of the works. He was known as a hard employer. Though Bastert sold up in 1911 and the company became William Morris Limited, the ill-reputation of Frank Bastert lived on. It didn't improve when war broke out. Several witnesses to the Zeppelin raid said they had seen Frank Bastert looking down from the Zeppelin and laughing as the bombs dropped.

Ilkeston had its own rumour on the night of the raid. A repertory company was performing a spy drama called *The Enemy in our Midst* at a local theatre. Part of the performance involved a model Zeppelin being lowered over the stage. The performance had to be halted when a real one appeared and the theatre emptied at about 20.30. For some people this seemed to be too much of a coincidence. Was it possible the cast were German spies? The touring company performed the play in Derby a few weeks later. The model Zeppelin remained the 'star' performer though the timing of its appearance was advised to protect patrons of a nervous disposition.

A few days after the bombing different coroner's inquests began their melancholy work. Newspapers were permitted to describe the events, but telegrams from the Home Office gave strict instruction that no names or addresses of victims be published, or anything that could identify the location of the bombing. The inquest on thirteen victims of the Tipton bombing took place on Thursday, 3 February 1916. The jury determined that the thirteen victims were killed by explosive bombs dropped by enemy aircraft and a verdict of 'wilful murder against the Kaiser and Crown Prince of Germany as being accessories before and after the fact'. The coroner argued that there was no evidence that the Kaiser or his son personally knew anything about the raid. He understood the jury's feelings, but they had to return a verdict on the evidence before them. A juror said 'He is the controller of Germany and as such orders these things.' After much argument the jury refused to change the verdict and the coroner reluctantly accepted it. Normally when a coroner's jury returns a verdict of murder against particular persons it is the duty of the coroner to issue the police with warrants for their arrest. It is not recorded whether the Tipton coroner did so. In this case it was a process hardly in keeping with the dignity of the office.

The jury in the case of Maud Fellows returned a similar verdict. The inquest was held at Wolverhampton Town Hall on 15 February 1916. The jury was made up of men mainly from the Graisley area of the town and recorded that Maud Fellows died of septicaemia following injuries caused by the explosion of a bomb dropped by an enemy aircraft. They were of the opinion that 'the Kaiser and Crown Prince were guilty of the murder of Maud Fellows as accessories before the fact.' The coroner, George Maynard Martin pointed out that there was no possibility of taking proceedings against the Kaiser, and asked if the jury would change its verdict. They refused, saying the verdict might have some weight after the war. The coroner accepted the verdict, but said he didn't intend to commit the Kaiser or Crown Prince.

The jury was somewhat better behaved at the inquest of William Fellows, adjourned until 28 February 1916. They returned a verdict of 'wilful murder against some person unknown' who in their opinion was acting on the instructions of Germans in authority. The coroner said he thought it 'a very sound and proper verdict'.

There was a further move towards the morality of total war at another inquest, probably that of Albert Madeley, in Wednesbury. The jury returned a verdict that the victim had died following the explosion of a bomb thrown from an enemy aircraft, by persons unknown. They added a rider that the government should adopt a policy of reprisals against German towns. It is recorded that two members of the jury dissented from this. The jury also made critical comments about the fact that no warning of the approach of the Zeppelins was given and asked if the Government had known the Zeppelins were coming.

Coroner's juries sat in Walsall on 2, 4 and 22 of February 1916. They were generally better behaved, following Coroner Addison's advice and recording verdicts that the six victims died as a result of bombs dropped from enemy aircraft.

There were a number of inquests in Burton. As always they were emotional affairs. The coroner told the Burton jury he hoped they would not return a verdict of 'wilful murder against the Kaiser and Crown Prince' as he would then have to issue a warrant to commit the Kaiser and Crown Prince to Stafford Assizes for trial, and 'issue a warrant to Superintendent Heath to arrest them'. He urged the jury not to be guilty of such foolishness, like the jury of another Midlands town. The jury behaved themselves, returning verdicts that 'death was due to explosive bombs dropped from enemy aircraft'. They recognised nothing could be done about the Kaiser, but pointed to some culprits closer to home. One inquest added the rider 'There was delay in carrying out necessary precautions in the lighting departments.' Another was stronger: it said 'The attack was entirely due to the railway companies keeping their premises lit until the first bomb fell.'

Much the same happened in Derby where a trade union representative asked if there should be central control for lighting, especially when it should be turned up again. He said he had been told by the police that when consulted they had advised against it. The railway had not consulted them. At other firms the lights were extinguished at about 19.30 and not turned on again until the next day. Trams had returned to their depots without lighting. The jury returned a verdict that the deceased were killed by a bomb from a German Zeppelin. They added the rider that 'The police should have central control of the whole district with regard to lighting.'

The inquests in Ilkeston took place on 3 and 4 February 1916. At one the coroner said the raid was an example of German frightfulness, and at the other an abominable outrage. In both the jury returned a verdict 'That the deceased was killed by the explosion of a bomb discharged from a hostile aircraft.'

The inquests in Scunthorpe all took place on Wednesday, 2 February 1916, under Phillip Gamble, the Lincolnshire coroner. The verdict recorded on all three victims was that death occurred due to 'injuries sustained through the explosion of bombs from a German Zeppelin Airship'. The coroner said that the probable result of the raid was that Britishers would redouble their efforts, so that the raid would rebound on the heads of those responsible for it. He expressed his sympathy for the bereaved but the knowledge that the Zeppelin dropped about fifty bombs, but only three lives were sacrificed, was cause for congratulations. The reaction to this from the families of the victims was not recorded. All the Scunthorpe victims were married with families.

After the inquests came the funerals. The victims in Wednesbury and Tipton were given public funerals, and large processions of local people followed the corteges to the cemeteries at Wood Green and Alexander Road.

Hackwood described the procession in Wednesbury as the saddest and most solemn function the town had ever known. Public subscriptions were raised for the victims in both towns, that in Tipton collecting £1,264.

In Burton a local relief fund was started and 'some deserving individuals were assisted'. We have no record of the actual amounts. We do know, however, that some people were paid reparations under the terms of the Treaty of Versailles. In 1922 a woman whose husband was killed in the raid received an interim award of £75, while in 1924 payments were made for twelve claims for property damage.

In Loughborough a relief fund was started by the mayor and over £500 collected. This paid for the funerals of the victims, and the rest was given as relief or compensation for wages to the families of the dead or to the injured. The mayor let it be known no compensation was paid out of the fund to landlords whose property was damaged. That comment is very interesting and shows that by then politicians were careful about public opinion and matters of fairness. If the Germans were attempting to reduce Britain's capacity to make war by hitting industry and the morale of munitions workers, the British Government knew it had to maintain it. Labour unrest was a major concern. We should remember that when King Street in Wednesbury was bombed a large factory in the street was empty because the workers were on strike. By 1915 David Lloyd George, then Minister of Munitions, was negotiating directly with trade union leaders. The Munitions Act not only agreed to the dilution of skilled labour, indirectly allowing the employment of many more women, but raised wages and introduced measures like rent controls. The war profiteer had become a bogy man. We can see this in the riders to their verdicts by coroner's juries in Derby and Burton.

In Derby the mayor opened a fund for the victims' families. We learn a little about the victims from their obituaries. Harry Hitherway left a young wife and child. He was described as a lifelong member of the London Road Wesleyan Methodist Chapel. James Gibbs Hardy was a well-known preacher with the Brook Street United Methodist Church. We can now only guess what status differences in Edwardian working class society were indicated by the different affiliations. Both Sarah Constantine and James Hardy had been active members of the Derby Temperance Society, probably a good thing for an engine driver and headmistress. William Bancroft on the other hand was a member of the Lilly of the Valley Lodge of Oddfellows who certainly didn't hate the demon drink.

It is not recorded if a fund was established for the Scunthorpe victims. All three were steelworkers, and were married with children. Ernest Wilkinson Benson had seven children. Thomas Danson and Cyril Wright both had one son. Probably the saddest thing to record is that two of the men's wives, Annie Benson and Grace Danson, were pregnant when their husbands were killed. Both had daughters later in the year. So the raid left many widows and orphans, but then so did Henrich Mathy, shot down a few months later, who left a wife and baby daughter.

Ernest Benson and Thomas Danson were buried in the West Street Cemetery in Scunthorpe and Cyril Jack Weight in Bottesford Cemetery.

*Chapter Ten*

# How to Shoot Down a Zeppelin

**How the Zeppelins were defeated, the development of the British air defence system**

There was considerable public anger at the role of the Government. People asked why there had been no advance warning of the Zeppelin attack? Did the authorities know the Zeppelins were approaching? Why were the airships able to fly unhindered over England for many hours, unopposed by British aircraft? Why was there no blackout in many of the target areas?

At the time it was difficult to give effective answers to these questions. For reasons of military secrecy, and to avoid political embarrassment, it was years before some were answered. Certainly the Government knew from about noon on 31 January 1916, that there was to be a raid. Intercepted German radio signals alerted them to it. The problem was that they had no way of knowing where the Zeppelins would attack. In the past the main target had been London, and most defence aerodromes were near the capital. In addition to this most fighter aircraft of early 1916 were ineffective against the Zeppelins. While generally faster, they had great difficulty operating at the sort of altitudes the Zeppelins did and were easily out climbed by the airships. In addition to this, in an era without radar and with very primitive radio communication, simply finding the raiders was a very difficult task. Zeppelins were big enough to carry radio equipment, British fighters were not.

The British Defence Forces were almost totally ineffective. Only one Zeppelin, L.17, was troubled. She dropped her bombs almost immediately after being caught in a searchlight. Most aircraft operated from airfields around London as defence planning assumed that most raids would be on the capital. Fog caused considerable problems to British pilots. No Zeppelins were seen, and many of the returning aircraft were unable to find their landing flares, and crashed. Six aircraft were wrecked and two pilots killed in accidents. Only one aircraft operated in the Midlands, an RE7 based at Castle Bromwich.

The report of the pilot demonstrated some of the problems with the blackout. Birmingham was dark and could not be seen, smaller towns around were well lit and easily seen. While large cities were subject to lighting restrictions, small towns and railways were not. There does not appear to be any logical reason for this, it was probably assumed they were not vulnerable to attack. The raid of 31 January changed all that. The whole country became subject to blackout regulations. Statistically it is probable the blackout cost, rather than saved, lives. The Black Country was never again subject to a Zeppelin raid, and undoubtedly many people died as a result of road accidents and the like. However, civilian morale demanded something be done, and the blackout seemed to provide protection against the raider from the sky. At the very least it showed the government was doing something.

The partial blackout was almost certainly the reason most of the areas bombed were in small towns. The big cities on the Zeppelins route – Birmingham, Leicester and Nottingham – were subject to a full blackout. Smaller towns or railways were not. Zeppelins were drawn like moths by the lights of Burton, Loughborough and the Black Country. This was not a cynical plot to preserve the cities at the expense of the towns; it was just that the British authorities, like the Zeppelin commanders, over-estimated the ability of the airships to hit selected targets. The fact that the Zeppelins were hopelessly lost was suspected after the Germans claimed to have hit Liverpool and Sheffield in press releases in the USA. It was confirmed by interviews with captured crewmen months after the event.

Within days most local councils in the affected areas held emergency meetings. They made local plans and criticised the government for its lack of defence measures. One of the most vocal critics of the government was the Mayor of Walsall, Alderman Samuel Mills Slater. The press gave no hint of the strong personal interest he had in this, his wife Mary dying in a Walsall hospital. At a meeting of Walsall Council Mayor Slater pointed out that though several Midland towns were warned of a Zeppelin attack, Walsall was not. He asked for an independent and official inquiry to find out why. Other politicians were quick to make statements.

The Mayor of Dudley was strident. He said: 'I am disgusted at the gross carelessness shown by the War Office. It is established there was ample time to warn the people of the Midlands. They seem unable to grapple with an emergency of any kind, such dilly-dallying is fatal to public safety.' He went on to call for the arrest of aliens who were a threat to public peace and whose own lives were at danger at the hands of the people.

The Mayor of Nottingham was not much more measured: 'We need more prompt warnings. The first step should be to put the air defence of the country under one man, whose power to introduce new methods should be unhampered. We should also adopt reprisals and bombard Rhine towns, especially those of strategic value, Cologne for instance.'

In Walsall a council member made a very perceptive remark, one that shows the north/south political divide is nothing new. He said: 'Protection does not rest in the defence of London, but by measures to prevent the Zeppelins crossing the coast.' We do not know whether his advice was taken to heart. However, defence of the coast was to become central to British anti-Zeppelin strategy, and was to spell doom for Max Dietrich and Zeppelin L.21, a few months later.

As well as Walsall other local councils held emergency meetings to deal with the Zeppelin crisis. The deliberations of Bilston Urban District Council were well minuted. A special meeting on 2 February resolved that all public lighting be discontinued, except for certain lights at dangerous places, and that these be masked. The same restrictions applied to shops and houses. Wolverhampton Council was asked to reduce the lighting on the town trams. At a later meeting Bilston UDC resolved to insure civic property against air raids. Property to the value of £44,580 was insured by the Royal Insurance Company for an annual premium of £70 13s 3d. Most importantly a system for giving air raid warnings was introduced. On official notification by the police, five long blasts, followed by a further five long blasts on three factory hooters, would be given. On hearing this all persons were to take cover, and all external lights put out. The factory hooters designated to give warning were at: John Thompson Ltd, Ettingshall; J Sankey and Son, Bankfield Works; and Bradley and Company, Albion Works, Mount Pleasant. Other councils passed similar by-laws setting up blackout regulations and air raid warning systems. In the first few weeks after the raid there was little standardisation.

Many years after the tragedy the edict of Smethwick Council seems amusing. A factory hooter at the carriage works was to sound 'cock-a-doodle-doo' at the approach of Zeppelins.

Some of the confusion of the night is reflected in the minutes of the Wolverhampton Watch Committee of 7 February 1916: 'Resolved. That this Committee are astounded to hear that the Mayor of this Borough was not advised by the Chief Constable either on Monday or Wednesday last of the visit or anticipated visit of hostile aircraft and that the Chief Constable be instructed to explain why this was not done and to give the Mayor and Committee information in the future.' It would have surely been a comfort to the worried citizens that it took more than a Zeppelin attack to destroy bureaucracy at its best.

In Burton the day after the raid the council introduced a number of restrictions of its own. All windows of houses and shops had to be screened, all outside lights turned off by 18.00. No lighting was allowed on the tops of trams. Air raid warning sirens were to be installed, and lamplighters given yet another responsibility: at night men with long poles would patrol the streets and tap on bedroom windows when Zeppelins were reported to have crossed the coast.

Fortunately for the war effort these local initiatives were to be superseded by the national air raid warning system. The government was taking the issue of air raids very seriously. In a report on 12 February 1916, the Ministry of Munitions reported there was a complete lack of faith in official warning arrangements, and that 'Workmen are refusing to work at night at all unless guaranteed that warnings will be given in sufficient time for them to disperse.' It was not merely a question of putting out the lights. A circular was put out to police forces asking them to notify all munitions factories in their area if hostile aircraft were approaching. This was to be done either by telephone or by a system of public warning such as hooters or sirens.

A major political initiative came on 8 February 1916 when a conference for all Midland mayors was held at Birmingham Council House. The meeting was chaired by a man much better known for his role in another war, the Lord Mayor of Birmingham, Neville Chamberlain. It is interesting to speculate to what extent his experience of the Zeppelin raids had on his policy of 'appeasement'. One of the ideas behind appeasement was the concept that 'the bomber will always get through', and that civilian morale would quickly collapse following the destruction bought about by the large-scale bombing of cities. As the RAF was less powerful than the Luftwaffe, appeasement of Hitler was necessary. People who attended the Birmingham conference included the Earl of Dartmouth, the mayors of most West Midland boroughs, as well as their town clerks and chief constables. The meeting took place in private, but a press statement was issued. Neville Chamberlain said he had expressed in strong terms his opinion that the arrangements for warnings were inadequate on the night of the raid. However, he felt it more important to improve the system rather than apportion blame. The conference then agreed a uniform system of lighting regulations and discussed ways in which telephone warnings could be given to the local police forces.

The conference also elected a committee to meet with the military authorities to discuss an effective air raid warning system. This group included Neville Chamberlain, the Earl of Dartmouth, and the mayors of Coventry, Dudley and Walsall. They travelled to London to meet Field Marshal Sir John French. The result of his meeting was an improved air defence system.

The meeting with Field Marshal French was opportune. French had just been sacked as commander of the British Forces on the Western Front, mainly because of the debacle at Loos. He was replaced by his bitter rival Douglas Haig. As a sop to his feelings French was made a viscount and given what seemed to be a non-job, Head of Home Defence. Determined and bitter, considering himself to be a scapegoat, the now Lord French was probably the only man with the background, contacts and clout to produce a workable system of air defence out of an existing system, which was undermined by inter-service rivalry and poor communication with the civil powers. This had led to an operation on the night of 31 January 1916 described as: 'A disaster for the defences, producing the highest proportion of aircraft losses, casualties and accidents per sortie of any home defence operation of the entire war.' Moreover none of the casualties were a result of enemy action, just poor equipment, leadership and communication.

We need to look at the air defence system and how it operated on the night. Plans had been made to transfer command responsibility for air defence from the Admiralty to the War Office, but they had not come into effect at the time of the raid. One fact of the raid was kept secret for many years for military and political reasons. British Naval Intelligence knew at about noon there was to be an attack in strength. Zeppelins were fitted with powerful radio transmitters and, in the early days of radio communication, their radio discipline was non-existent. All signals were monitored by British Intelligence. The Royal Navy had a series of radio stations all down the East Coast from Lerwick in the Shetland Isles to Lowestoft. They had been erected to monitor all radio signals from the German High Seas Fleet. Intercepts were instantly transmitted by telephone cable to the Admiralty in London. The Naval cryptography and code breaking section, usually known as 'Room 40', monitored all radio communications. Zeppelins were fitted with powerful radio transmitters and, in the early days of radio communication, commanders were probably not aware of the range their signals could be picked up from. The British radio receivers were very sensitive. They had been developed to intercept signals from ships, even a low power transmission from a Zeppelin at altitude on the other side of the North Sea could be picked up. The Royal Navy had captured some German codebooks early in the war; these were used for military-merchant ship communication and were known as the *Handelsschiffsvekehrsbuch* or HVB. Because of this Room 40 was able to decode most radio signals from Zeppelins. The unsophisticated nature of German radio discipline was shown when the Admiralty intercepted a signal from each of the Zeppelins to their base. It was: 'Scouting mission: Only HVB on board.' They had left behind the top secret German Navy codebook, in case they were shot down over England. It did not take a genius to work out why this was, and experience of other raids had shown the Admiralty that this was confirmation there was to be a raid on Britain.

Though Admiralty Intelligence knew at noon that there was to be a raid on 31 January, they did not know where it was to take place. Police across the country were told an air raid was possible. However, no public air raid warnings were given. Ground observers were also alerted that a raid was likely and good observations and excellent records were kept. The main problem seems to have been that there was no satisfactory system to cope with all the intelligence coming in. It seems to have been communicated on an *ad hoc* basis, and did not provide a clear basis for decision making.

The fact that British defences were on the alert did lead to an advantage for historians. The path of the Zeppelins over England were well tracked. This is very useful as the logs of the Zeppelin commanders were wildly out. The excellent records kept by ground observers on the route of the nine airships enable an account of the individual actions of each of them, and give us a picture of the whole operation.

At first the system worked well, probably because communication went directly from the Admiralty to naval vessels. A number of anti-aircraft trawlers and one light cruiser were sent from Lowestoft to try to intercept the raiders. Unfortunately fog prevented contact. The first Zeppelins crossed the coast as dusk fell. Searchlights were in operation and Zeppelin L.17 was fired on by a 4.7-inch gun. She then dropped her bombs to try to kill the searchlight. These fell on open fields without effect and shortly after she turned for home. After this the defence measures proved to be utterly unsuccessful. By 19.00, seven Zeppelins had crossed the coast and unaware of their location the War Office made the assumption that London was the target, and that their estimated time of arrival was about 20.15.

This decision was to have fatal consequences, because of the foggy weather in the London area. The defence operation was a mixture of chaos and bravery. Based on previous experience the decision that London was the main target was rational, all previous raids had been on the East Coast or the capital. Most of England's defences were based there. British night fighter aircraft were ordered to take off from airfields on the outskirts of London from about 19.15. Again this was a rational decision, in normal conditions, because the slow rate of climb of the BE2c meant the fighters would be at the height of the airships when they arrived. There was no effective way of communication with the pilots once they were in the air. There was a system where searchlights would point in the direction of Zeppelins, but it was largely ineffective. It was only if a Zeppelin was caught in a searchlight beam that pilots could easily find them.

The real problem for the pilots was the weather. There was patchy drifting fog all around London. Aeroplanes took off during breaks in the fog. Their pilots were brave young men, but their senior officers should have known better. In all twenty-two sorties were flown during which pilots flew around London looking for non-existent Zeppelins. Some pilots reported seeing them – the 'Phantom Zeppelin Phenomenon', we have previously discussed. The problems mainly occurred when the fighter was low on fuel and oil and needed to land. In the calm weather the drifting fog had got worse. The landing flares on most airfields were obscured, and most aircraft crashed on landing. Six aircraft were totally wrecked, many more damaged, and sadly two very experienced pilots, Major Leslie Penn-Gaskell and Major Ernest Unwin, flying BE2cs were killed. Both pilots hit trees and caught fire, Major Penn-Gaskell while taking off and Major Unwin while landing. The operation produced the highest number of casualties and accidents per sortie of any home defence mission in the entire war and was subsequently described as 'one of the biggest fiascos in British air defence history'.

It is always easy to criticise operational decisions with the benefit of hindsight, but there were a number of obvious failures. The first summed up by the old RAF saying 'Take-offs are discretionary, landings are compulsory.' If it was foggy at 19.15, it was almost certainly going to be foggy at 22.15, and this made the loss of pilots and aircraft almost inevitable. The fact that it was impossible to communicate with pilots after take-off makes the decision to launch even more irresponsible. It says much about the command structure that no one was able to question an order sending men on a suicide mission. The second problem goes right to the top: the total lack of organisation and system. After the Zeppelins crossed the coast, intelligence about their position was coming in from ground observers, being recorded and presumably sent to the War Office, but there was no system to collate it and use it to make decisions.

Only one aeroplane was available for defence in the Midlands. It was an RE7, a very slow, two-seat night fighter armed with one Lewis gun. The RE7 was produced by the Royal Aircraft Factory and attached to the 5th Reserve Aeroplane Squadron operating out of Castle Bromwich, near Birmingham. It was piloted by Major A B Burdett with Second Lieutenant R A Cresswell as the Observer/Gunner. The pair had no idea at the time that Zeppelins were in the area. They took off at about 20.20, just as L.21 was bombing the Black Country. Burdett and Creswell saw nothing of this. They flew towards Birmingham city centre, noting that the blackout of the city was effective, though the suburbs, not subject to blackout restrictions, were easily visible. Major Burdett wrote later that visibility over Birmingham was generally good. Sadly this did not apply to Castle Bromwich. When he returned at 21.50 the flare path was hidden by mist, and the aircraft was destroyed on landing. Fortunately both crewmembers were unhurt.

Major changes took place in February 1916 with the blackout imposed on smaller towns and cities. A nationwide air raid warning system was introduced, and sirens appeared and were tested on factory buildings all over the Black Country. The War Office reorganised the air defence of Britain. The Army, through the Royal Flying Corps, was given the responsibility for the defence of inland cities, while the Navy, with the Royal Naval Air Service, concentrated on the defence of the coast. As part of this effort there were four aerodromes established around the Black Country: at Perton, Wall Heath, Chasetown and Great Barr. In the East Midlands they included Royston, Lillington, Castle Donnington, and Loughborough. The county with the most new aerodromes was Lincolnshire. During the war thirty-eight aerodromes were built, most in response to the Zeppelin raids. A number became bomber bases in the Second World War. Three remain as RAF bases today: RAF Cranwell, RAF Scampton and RAF Waddington.

Broadly speaking the air raid warning system worked, at a cost. There were several months of false alarms, which declined after the first Zeppelins were shot down. The alarms and the blackout certainly caused a temporary fall in industrial production. The railway companies were for some time scapegoats and seen as symbolising war profiteering. But it is difficult to run a railway system in the dark, and railways were essential for war production. Compromises were made and Zeppelin raids became just another hardship to be endured. The Government after all promised victory and a land fit for heroes. At least it kept one of its promises.

Most importantly a system of centralised control, based in the War Office was established. This air defence system which resulted in part from the Chamberlain/French meeting was probably the finest achievement of two men whose failures define them in history. The system worked and can probably be seen as the embryo of the fighter control system which served this country so well twenty-five years later in the Battle of Britain. The basis of the system was that the gathering and communication of intelligence was made separate from decision-making. It was a simple system. When a Zeppelin crossed the coast it was given a simple code name, usually a girl's name. This was put on a counter and moved around a large map. As intelligence came in from ground observers the position of the Zeppelin was updated and the counter moved accordingly. The officers responsible for decision-making could decide when to order fighters from different airfields to take off. They could also alert searchlights and anti-aircraft batteries, and order the civil powers to sound the air raid warning sirens. We know that when L21 was shot down on 27 November 1916 she was given the name 'Mary' and her position tracked across the country to Stoke-on-Trent, which she bombed. She returned over Peterborough. Fighters were scrambled but failed to find her. However, as she flew on her course continued to be plotted and it was predicted that Mary would cross the coast near Lowestoft. Fighters were ordered to take off to wait for her, and Mary was shot down over the sea a few miles from Lowestoft. It was a very different outcome from the shambles ten months earlier.

Along with an effective system of fighter control and air raid warnings, the other important factor in the defeat of the Zeppelin menace was the contribution of technology. After a long period of development, the summer of 1916 saw the mass production of effective incendiary and explosive ammunition for aircraft machine guns. Buckingham incendiary bullets and Pomeroy and Brock explosive bullets were reliable enough for use in night fighters and spelled doom for the highly inflammable, hydrogen-filled Zeppelins.

Before the introduction of reliable incendiary ammunition, a number of weapons were developed many of which demonstrated a triumph of hope over intellect, and showed the degree of panic in some sections of the High Command about the Zeppelin menace. The cause of this was a mistaken belief that the Germans had invented a system for piping inert exhaust gas around the hydrogen to prevent ignition. Hydrogen is such an inflammable gas it was at first thought a few tracer bullets would set the gas cells alight. When this did not happen it was believed that an inert gas must have been used to isolate the hydrogen. This led to the mistaken belief that bombing was the only way to bring down an airship.

The first Zeppelin to be destroyed by a British airman was brought down by bombing. This was army Zeppelin LZ.37, commanded by *Oberleuntnant* van der Haegen, destroyed on 7 June 1915 by Flight Sub-Lieutenant Reginald

Warneford of the RNAS. It was not a planned attack. Warneford was flying a French Morane Parasol monoplane on a mission to bomb Zeppelin sheds in Belgium. He was flying at about 11,000ft when he saw the Zeppelin about 4000ft below him over Ostend. He gave chase and after about an hour caught her over Ghent. He flew about 150ft above her and dropped six 20lbs bombs. The Zeppelin immediately exploded, the blast throwing the Morane on its back. Warneford managed to regain control and saw the blazing Zeppelin fall like a stone, landing around a Belgian convent. He was awarded the VC for the action. The commander of the Zeppelin and most of the crew were burned to death. However, in one of the strangest escapes of the war the helmsman *Oberleutnant* Alfred Muhler fell over a mile from the front gondola as the blazing Zeppelin crashed to earth. He went straight through the roof of the convent and landed on a bed, surviving with fairly serious injuries. A number of nuns were killed when the burning Zeppelin hit the convent. It has to be recognised that Warneford's victory was the result of a number of favourable coincidences: he was already in the air and higher than the Zeppelin when he saw her,

This led to the development of the 'Ranken Dart', essentially a small bomb with vanes at the tail that would spread out in the airflow on release and stick in the envelope of the Zeppelin giving time for its incendiary charge to set the airship on fire. The pilot had a box of 24 darts and was expected to drop them on the Zeppelin three at a time, a very difficult feat as in 1916 Zeppelins could easily out-climb the cumbersome aircraft we used as night fighters. It proved a technological blind alley.

While the Ranken Dart was ineffective, it was a masterpiece of rational design in comparison to some of the other anti-Zeppelin weapons considered by the High Command. The most memorable of these was the 'Fiery Grapnel'. This was a simply a four pronged grapnel which was towed on a wire about 190ft behind a fighter. The fighter was expected to approach the Zeppelin from the side, and climb over it. The grapnel would then hook on to the envelope of the airship and burst into flames. Hopefully at that point the wire would detach from the fighter, and the Zeppelin too would catch fire. The device seemed to work when tested on a captive balloon and a number of BE2c aircraft were fitted with two grapnels under the fuselage.

To the possible relief of Zeppelin crews and the certain relief of British pilots, the grapnel was never used in action.

While the Fiery Grapnel was as close as Britain ever got to the production of a suicide weapon, we should not fail to recognise the contribution made to the security of the nation by Major Charles Burke, the Commanding Officer of No 2 Squadron RFC. He told his pilots in 1914 that if they failed to shoot down a Zeppelin they should take other measures, that is: ram it. The effect on morale is not recorded. While it is easy to doubt either the sincerity or sanity of Major Burke we should not forget that the solution to the Zeppelin problem suggested by Admiral Fisher, the First Sea Lord was to tell the Germans that if Britain was bombed we would shoot German prisoners of war as a reprisal measure. A slightly more sensible idea was put forward by E R Calthorpe, a year later. Calthorpe was a parachute designer. The fighter was to ram the Zeppelin, but the pilot was to jump just before the impact and float down, presumably on one of Mr Calthorpe's parachutes.

Another weapon considered was the 'Davis Gun', a large calibre recoilless rifle which fired a six-pounder shell while discharging a similar weight of lead shot behind. Also fitted to a number of planes were Le Prieur rockets. These were tested, but not used against Zeppelins.

It is probable that the idea that bombing was a viable way to destroy airships held back the only realistic method: firing incendiary bullets into the belly of the Zeppelin. In the early months of 1916 night fighters were armed with both Lewis guns and a box of Rankin Darts. The weight of gun and darts made the poor climb rate of the BE2c night fighter even worse.

The production of reliable incendiary ammunition showed the strength of research and development in wartime Britain. Incendiary and explosive bullets are not difficult to make, and they had been used in rifles for years, though there was doubt about their legality under the terms of The Hague Convention. The problem is not making them explode, but ensuring they don't go off too soon in over-heated ammunition boxes, or the hot breech or magazine of a machine gun. For all their scientific ingenuity the Germans were behind Britain in this technology. As late as 1918 the German Air Force lost a number of Fokker DVII fighters due to incendiary ammunition igniting in poorly cooled ammunition boxes fitted near the engine.

The answer to the problem of producing ammunition capable of bringing down a Zeppelin was learned by a process of trial and error using a combination of incendiary and explosive ammunition in the magazine of the Lewis gun. Pure hydrogen is not easy to ignite, and tracer bullets passed straight through the gas cells without causing ignition. The gas only became really inflammable when mixed with air. Loading the Lewis gun magazine with a mixture of incendiary and explosive ammunition brought this about. The explosive bullets would cause the gas bags to tear and leak hydrogen, which mixed with air. The incendiary bullets would ignite the mixture. British airmen soon worked out how to defeat the Zeppelin. Most fighters had Lewis guns angled to fire upwards. The pilot would fire incendiary and explosive bullets into one area on the hull of the Zeppelin. It usually took dozens of bullets to cause a fire, but once ignited, the airships burned like a furnace in the sky, machine and crew being completely destroyed in a matter of minutes. We have a number of descriptions of the shooting down of Zeppelins. As it first caught fire the airship would glow like a huge Chinese lantern, then as the fire spread the machine would fall like a stone as the hydrogen lifting gas burned away. The blaze created by over a million cubic feet of hydrogen meant a burning Zeppelin would be visible to other airships or aircraft as much as a hundred miles away.

We have a description of what it was like to be shot down in a Zeppelin from one of the very few survivors. He was Heinrich Ellerkamm, shot down in Zeppelin L.48 at Theberton, Norfolk on 7 June 1917. He was an engine mechanic and was climbing up a ladder from his engine gondola into the hull to check the fuel supply. He heard a machine gun firing. He looked down and saw an English fighter firing its tracer bullets at L.48. As he looked up into the hull he saw bullets like fireflies in the dark shooting through the gas cells. There was an explosion 'not loud but a dull woof as when you light a gas stove', then a burst of flame and more explosions as one gas cell after another caught fire. The Zeppelin fell very quickly as its hydrogen lifting gas burned. Luckily for Ellerkamm the wind created by the fall kept the flames away from him, and he survived badly burned when the Zeppelin hit the ground.

The other problem in 1916 was the aircraft used as night fighters. These were mainly BE2c biplanes, a pre-war design by the Royal Aircraft Factory first used in 1912. The initial BE stands for Bleriot Experimental which explains some of the problem. While they look very old fashioned, completely un-streamlined, wire braced biplanes, they were by the standards of the time sturdy and reliable aircraft. The problem was they were built to a design specification which made them the world's first 'inherently stable' aeroplane. In ordinary language this seems to be a good thing, no one wants to go on their holidays in an inherently unstable aeroplane. However in aeronautical terms 'inherently stable' has a more precise meaning: the plane will naturally fly straight and level unless the pilot moves the controls. The down side of this was that the BE2c was stable but very difficult to manoeuvre. It was so slow and clumsy that it was a death-trap when used during the day in its original role as a reconnaissance aeroplane on the Western Front where it was easy prey for fighters.

The BE2c is usually considered the worst aircraft of the war. An MP, Noel Pemberton Billing described them as 'Fokker fodder' in March 1916, saying in a debate in Parliament that pilots on the Western Front had been murdered rather than killed, being sent to fight in aircraft so outdated and outclassed. A result of this was the setting up of a Parliamentary committee which perhaps inevitably came up with the conclusion that the BE2 was aerodynamically sound, and capable of being built by companies that had never built aeroplanes before. This was indeed an advantage. The aircraft was designed for mass production, there were detailed drawings for every component and it was built by non-specialist companies such as furniture makers and car manufacturers. In 1916 it was fitted with the RAF 1a engine, also designed by the Royal Aircraft Factory. This was a simple reliable eight-cylinder engine of about nine litres, producing 90hp. This engine gave it just enough performance to defeat the Zeppelin.

As a night fighter the BE2 was a major success. Nine airships were shot down over England, two of these, L.15 and L.33, by anti-aircraft fire. One Zeppelin, L.70, was shot down by a DH4 aeroplane. All the rest by BE-types. Zeppelin L.48 was shot down by a BE12. This was in fact just a B.E2 with a larger 140hp RAF 4a engine. All the rest S.L.11, L.21, L.31, L.32, L.34 were shot down by BE2cs. The inherent stability made the BE2c relatively easy to fly at night. Its top speed of about 85mph made it faster than the Zeppelin, though as it took sixteen minutes to reach 6000ft, its rate of climb was much slower. The usual armament of one or two Lewis guns angled to fire upwards over the wings was a necessary result of this. The usual method of attack was to fly under the Zeppelin and fire at a small area in the belly. This was very effective. As higher performance aeroplanes were introduced later in the war most kept the upward firing Lewis guns as their main armament.

The upward firing gun was a British invention, which basically made a virtue out of necessity, allowing fighters with very little performance advantage over the Zeppelins to shoot them down. It was a very successful weapon in the Second World War, used not by the RAF but by the German Luftwaffe in all their twin-engine night fighters from 1943 onwards. The Germans called the system *Schrage Musik*, literally 'oblique music' or colloquially 'jazz music'. A fighter would attack from underneath and slightly behind a bomber, usually remaining undetected until the cannon shells hit their target.

The major advantage of the BE2c at night was its reliability, slow landing speed of about 40mph, and robust construction. If we return to the shambolic air defence operation on 31 January 1916, the strength of the BE2 can be seen. Twenty-one sorties were flown by BE2cs, twelve of these resulted in crashes on take-off or landing, most if not all caused by pilots unable to see because of fog. Two pilots died both a result of hitting trees, causing their aeroplanes to catch fire. The other ten pilots all survived with minor injuries, though many of the aircraft were wrecked, a testament to the strength of the aircraft.

In 1916 stability was seen as vital for a night fighter. It was believed that agile day fighters were simply un-flyable at night. This changed in the next few years as experienced pilots proved they were able to fly high performance aircraft such as the Sopwith Camel, SE5a and Bristol Fighter at night. However in 1916 the BE2c was probably the best we had. It is a tribute to the bravery of our pilots that they were able to shoot down the airships with such a limited performance advantage.

The reorganisation of home defence began to show results within a few weeks. On 1 April Zeppelin L15 was damaged by anti-aircraft fire. Due to the loss of gas she landed in the sea near Margate. Her commander *Kapitanleutnant* Breithaupt and most of her crew were captured.

The real prize came later, the shooting down of a Zeppelin over British soil. In fact, the first airship shot down over England was not a Zeppelin. It was Schutte-Lanz SL.11 of the German Army. The Schutte-Lanz Company was a business rival of the Zeppelin Company. SL.11 was roughly the same size as a 'Q' class Zeppelin like L.21. It looked much the same, too. The major difference was under the skin. The Schutte-Lanz had a wooden rather than duralumin airframe. The airship's commander was *Hauptmann* Wilhelm Schramm. He was 34-years-old and a professional soldier. He had been born in London when his father worked there for the Siemens Company. He was to die at Cuffley, Hertfordshire a few miles from his birthplace. SL.11 left her base at Spich near Cologne in the afternoon of Saturday, 2 September 1916, with a crew of sixteen. She was part of the largest airship raid of the war, so far. Sixteen airships, four from the army, the rest from the navy flew towards London.

The airships were tracked from when they left their bases, and as they approached London a number of fighters took off to intercept. The raiders were also met by searchlights and anti-aircraft fire. Lieutenant William Leefe Robinson of 39 Squadron RFC took off from Suttons Farm at about 23.08. He flew over London for more than three hours sighting at least one airship. He saw SL.11 caught in a searchlight beam flying about 12000ft over north-east London. He flew between 500ft and 800ft below her, and fired three magazines loaded with Brock and Pomeroy ammunition into her belly. He reported her hull started to glow and then in seconds her whole rear was blazing. He landed almost out of petrol at 02.45. The blazing SL.11 was seen by tens of thousands of people from all over London as she fell to earth near Cuffley. All sixteen crew members were killed. The wreckage became a major attraction. Special trains were put on and in two days 10,000 people made use of them.

William Leefe Robinson was a national hero. He was awarded the Victoria Cross. He also received reward money of several thousand pounds mainly raised by national newspapers. In a macabre publicity stunt they had promised a cash prize to the first man to shoot down a Zeppelin. The same newspapers had headlines in the next few days campaigning against the 'Zeppelin baby killers' being given a military funeral. British pilots voiced their disgust at this attitude, and the crew were given a military escort at their funeral. After many years their bodies were moved and buried in 1964, with other airship crews, in a special plot at Cannock German Military Cemetery.

For some time after the destruction of SL.11 the British claimed she had been destroyed by bombs. This was both for military reasons, not to let the Germans know the British had developed workable incendiary ammunition, and probably for political reasons too, for there was still concern about the legality of incendiary bullets under the Hague Convention.

Over the next few months more Zeppelins were shot down. By 1917 the German Navy was attempting to counter British air defences by building even larger Zeppelins, known a 'height climbers', which were able to operate at 20,000ft, well above the ceiling of British fighters. Though they had some limited success, the day of the Zeppelin as a terror bomber was over. By the end of the war they could be out climbed by fighter aircraft, and their vulnerability to incendiary ammunition made them flying death traps. It is notable that even the Zeppelin Company began to produce large aeroplanes, the so called 'Giant' bombers. Along with the Gotha bombers these would kill many more people on bombing raids than the airships ever did, and were a much more difficult problem for the Home Defence Force. During the First World War airships dropped 196 tons of bombs on Britain and killed 557 people. Aeroplanes, mainly large bombers, killed 857 people.

*Chapter Eleven*

# The Burning

## The shooting down of the Zeppelins

The raid of 31 January 1916 was carried out by nine Zeppelins crewed by 154 men. By the end of 1916 half of them were dead. This is what happened to them. In this chapter I look at the fate of the commanders of the nine Zeppelins. It was normal practice for a successful commander to take his crew with him when he was assigned to a new airship, so in practice a commander and crew would live and die together. The policy of the airship service was to give the new more efficient ships to the best commanders. New and less experienced officers went to the older ships. This was indeed the same policy for pilots in the German air force and the RFC and RAF.

I cannot be certain in every case that the crew killed with the same commander at a later date were identical with those on the 31 January. Sickness, injury and leave meant that some men were replaced. However, this was exceptional. One such case is that of Zeppelin L.21. When L.21 was shot down on 27 November 1916 it was commanded by Kurt Frankenberg. He had served as second officer on L.14 under *Kapitanleutnant* Alois Bocker. He had been promoted from *Oberleutnant* to *Kapitanleutnant* and given command of his own airship. He must have been proud of his promotion, but it killed him. Bocker survived the war, Frankenberg was shot down in flames. I will now describe the fate of the commanders of the airships in the raid.

## L.11 *Kapitanleutnant* Horst Julius Freiheer Treusch von Buttlar-Brandenfels

Von Buttlar was the only Zeppelin commander to serve in Zeppelins from the beginning to the end of the war. It seems likely that his aristocratic background allowed him to advance his career more quickly than other commanders. He was not popular in the Airship Service and was accused of falsifying his combat records to advance his career. In May 1916 he was assigned to the first of the new 'R' class Zeppelins L.30. Buttlar collected it from the Zeppelin Works at Friedrichshafen and took the old Count von Zeppelin as a passenger with him to Nordholz. At about this time he was promoted from *Oberleutnant zur See* to *Kapitanleutnant*.

The 'R' class Zeppelin was called by the British the 'Super' Zeppelin and this can cause confusion with the later height climbers. The 'R' class ships were bigger and better than the 'Q' class, but not significantly different in tactical operation. They were longer at 649ft, of greater diameter at 78ft and had a more streamlined hull. With six engines and a gas capacity of almost two million cubic feet of hydrogen, they had better range and about twice the bomb load. However, they did not fly significantly higher or faster, and were no more difficult to shoot down. Flying no higher than the BE2c and relying on machine guns for defence was to prove a fatal weakness.

Buttlar was involved in some of the testing and development work on the 'R' series. He was involved in scouting missions from 5 July 1916. He is recorded as having bombed a British armed trawler on 19 August 1916. His first raid was on 8 August 1916. As more 'R' type Zeppelins went into service Strasser began to increase the raids on England. On that day nine Zeppelins bombed the coast of England: Harwich, Redcar and Hull were hit. Ten people were killed, sixteen injured and £13,196 worth of damage done.

Zeppelin L.30 next raided England on 2 September 1916. Twelve airships of the army and navy set out on the night SL.11 was shot down. The target was southern England with London as the main target. Buttlar left Ahlhorn at about noon. We then get a distinct difference between Buttlar's combat report and British observations. Buttlar claimed to have bombed London. British observers spotted L.30 crossing the coast, near Lowestoft. She then bombed villages and hamlets on the Norfolk–Suffolk border. Eight high explosive bombs and twelve incendiary bombs fell on Bungay, nine high explosive bombs and one incendiary bomb fell on Earsham, eight high explosive bombs fell on Ditchingham, and four high explosive bombs fell on Broome. It seems Buttlar's bombs injured one man, and badly damaged two farmhouses. The bombs killed two cows and injured three more. Buttlar then turned for home near Lowestoft.

Zeppelin L.30 next raided England on 23 September 1916. On that night twelve Zeppelins set out. The main target was London. This was the night Peterson and Bocker were shot down. Buttlar again claimed to have bombed London, though the British have no record of it. It is impossible to tell where L.30 dropped her bombs, almost certainly not near London. In fact the GHQ Intelligence report says only that Zeppelin L.30 made Happisburgh, in Norfolk and skirted the coast in her usual ineffective manner.

Buttlar raided again on 25 September, alongside eight other Zeppelins. Buttlar claimed to have bombed Ramsgate and Margate, but the British have no record of any bombs falling in the area. They say L.30 was probably off Cromer at 20.15 and approached Yarmouth at about 20.50. She wandered up and down the coast for some time dropping a large number of heavy bombs in the sea at about 22.25. The GHQ report further comments: 'Two airships L.23 and L.30 were becoming notorious for their pusillanimous conduct when near our shores.'

The Zeppelins attacked in two waves. The larger 'R' class ships raided London and the south while the smaller 'P' and 'Q' class ships bombed the north. A number of cities were bombed in the north of England including York, Bolton and Sheffield. There were heavy casualties: forty-three killed and thirty-one injured. £39,698 worth of damage was caused.

Buttlar raided next on 2 October 1916, the night Mathy was shot down. Eleven Zeppelins set out and it appears Buttlar returned early. The British in their GHQ reports were growing quite caustic about the commander of L.30. It appears they did not know who he was when the report was written, commenting only that 'these ships habitually seem to avoid coming far inland'.

On 27 November 1916, ten Zeppelins set out. This was the night Max Dietrich in L.34 and Kurt Frankenberg in L.21 were shot down. It seems Buttlar had a genuine reason for turning back this time – two engines on L.30 failed on the voyage out. The British obviously did not know this and the GHQ report mentioned the timidity of the commanders of Zeppelins L.23 and L.30. (The commander of L.23 at the time was *Kapitanleutnant* Ganzel.)

It may be that Peter Strasser had some concerns about the determination of Buttlar because he didn't raid again for another year. On 11 January 1917, the command of L.30 was transferred to *Oberleutnant zur See* Kurt Friemel, and Buttlar wasn't assigned to another ship until 16 September 1917 when he was assigned to the much more advanced 'height climber', Zeppelin L.54.

His first raid in L.54 was on 19 October 1917, when eleven Zeppelins raided the Midlands and London. This was the so called 'silent raid'. The Zeppelins flew at about 20,000ft and because of strong winds were not heard from the ground. Buttlar reported after the raid that because of the strength of the wind he had abandoned attacking Sheffield or Manchester but had instead dropped his bombs on Derby and Nottingham, from 21,000 feet. The British report tells a different tale. L.54 was observed crossing the Norfolk coast near Happisburgh at 20.55, she turned south towards Harwich and dropped her bombs between Ipswich and Colchester causing no damage, and then went out to sea near Clacton. Because of the high winds Buttlar descended to about 5000ft and was pursued by a BE2c from Great Yarmouth. It was unable to catch him. L.54 returned to Tonder at about 08.45 the next morning.

Buttlar raided England for the last time on 12 March 1918, one of five airships to do so that night. He claimed to have bombed Grimsby, and said he had come under heavy anti-aircraft fire. One of the gas cells of L.54 was damaged and empty. Though it is possible that the damage was caused by anti-aircraft fire, it could also have been caused by ice particles thrown by the propellers. The British believed Buttlar dropped his bomb load out at sea; some bombs were reported as having fallen near a group of British armed trawlers which fired at the airship. They didn't hit her and she returned safely to her base a Tondern.

Zeppelin L.54 was destroyed a few months later on the ground. On 19 July 1918 seven British Sopwith Camel fighters took off from a new kind of ship, the aircraft carrier, HMS *Furious*. The carrier was sailing off the Schleswig coast of Germany and the target was Tonder Airship Base. Three airship sheds were bombed, Toska, Tobias and Toni. Zeppelins L.54 and L.60 in the Toska shed were completely destroyed.

Buttlar is probably the most difficult Zeppelin commander to assess. On 9 April 1918 he was awarded Germany's highest bravery award the *Pour le Merite*, the so called Blue Max. He was only the second Zeppelin officer to get it. Buttlar has been described as unpopular among Zeppelin commanders. It was thought his aristocratic background allowed him more privileges than other men and he was a shameless self-promoter making extravagant claims about the targets he attacked. This was certainly the view the British had of him. He was undoubtedly more cautious than most of his colleagues, which was exactly what was required to stay alive. On paper he had a distinguished career commanding a number of Zeppelins and flying combat missions from 1915 to 1918. In all he was involved in 221 sorties.

Probably the strangest thing about Buttlar is that, if the British casualty reports are accurate, he may not have killed anyone from his various Zeppelins. He is recorded as injuring one man and killing two cows on the raid of 2 September 1916, but that seems the worst he did. He wasn't the best or bravest Zeppelin Commander but if that was his memorial, looking back it is as good as you can get.

Buttlar remained in the navy after the war, commanding a torpedo boat. In July 1920 he commanded a new Zeppelin L.72 on a test flight. He left the navy in September 1920. He worked as an insurance broker and as a business executive, employed by Lufthansa for some years. He wrote a number of books, including one translated as *Zeppelins over England* published in 1932.

When Germany re-armed under Hitler, Buttlar re-joined the military, becoming a major in the Luftwaffe in 1935. By 1939 he was a colonel and by 1945 a general. He commanded the Frankfurt-am-Main airfield at the end of the war. He died on 3 September 1962.

Some of Zeppelin L.30, Buttlar's airship still survives. L.30 was handed over to Belgium as part of war reparations under the Treaty of Versailles. Her front engine gondola is on display in the Brussels Army and Military Museum.

The Executive Officer on L.11, *Leutnant zur See* Hans von Schiller also survived the war. He continued to serve with Buttlar, completing 221 sorties with him. He was employed by the Zeppelin Company after the war, finishing his career as captain of the civilian airship the *Graf Zeppelin*.

### L.13 *Kapitanleutnant* Heinrich Mathy. Shot down in flames on the 1st October 1916 in Zeppelin L.31

Heinrich Mathy was back in action in his lucky ship Zeppelin L.13 on 5 March 1916, when three Zeppelins set out to bomb 'England North'. The main target was to be the Firth of Forth in Scotland. There was a severe decline in the weather as the Zeppelins approached the coast and the target was changed to 'England Middle'. Mathy had engine trouble over the North Sea and crossed the coast further south than he estimated. He had to jettison some of his bombs. British records show L.13 dropped bombs from Newark to Sheerness, but it seemed the commander was unable to properly aim them. The raid was deemed a success as the other two Zeppelins reached Hull. Eighteen people were killed, fifty-two injured and £25,005 worth of damage done.

Mathy next raided on 31 March 1916, part of an intensive operation by Strasser that saw Zeppelins bomb England almost every day for a week. Seven navy airships took off. Mathy reached Stowmarket, having correctly navigated there. He intended to bomb the Explosive Works, but had problems finding the factory because of mist. He circled and dropped a flare when he was over the town searching for his target. He came under anti-aircraft fire, but continued to look for the works. His bombs landed near the factory but failed to do much damage, only breaking windows. Demonstrating the bravery which made him admired by both sides, Mathy then flew towards the gun battery and aimed twelve bombs. The British reported they did little damage. The anti-aircraft gun then hit the Zeppelin and damaged some gas cells. The British had an interesting piece of intelligence, about exactly what happened. A German Navy message blank was found in Stowmarket the next day. Mathy had scribbled a note to the Executive Officer and wireless operator, ordering a radio message to be sent to the Commander in Chief High Seas Fleet: 10.00pm (21.00 GMT). 'Have attacked and hit a battery at Stowmarket with 12 bombs. Am hit, have turned back, hope to land in Hage towards 4.00 am. L.13.' The message must have found its way out of the command gondola in the chaos following the damage. Flying home with the ship losing height Mathy dropped the rest of his bombs near Lowestoft as he crossed the coast. L.13 got back to Hage safely, but needed repairs.

The raid of 31 March was damaging for the British and the Germans. The bombs killed forty-eight people and injured sixty-four more, damage was done worth £19,431. Most of the casualties occurred in Cleethorpes. Soldiers of the Manchester Regiment were billeted in a chapel, which was hit by a single bomb. Thirty-two men were killed and forty-eight injured.

The Germans lost Zeppelin L.15, hit by anti-aircraft fire. It came down in the sea, Joachim Breithaupt and most of the crew were rescued and became prisoners of war.

Zeppelin L.13 was repaired by 2 April 1916. A force of six airships from the army and navy set out to bomb 'England North': that is, Scotland. Bocker in L.14 bombed Edinburgh. Mathy was less lucky in L.13 and had to return home because of engine trouble.

On 14 July 1916 Mathy was assigned to a new 'R' type ship, Zeppelin L.31. His first raid on England was on 31 July 1916. Strasser had again planned an intensive campaign with a lot of raids over a few days. It was to be largely ineffective. Ten airships set out against London and 'England South', but low cloud and fog restricted their bombing. No injuries were caused and only £139 worth of damage done.

Eight Zeppelins were involved a few days later, on 2 August 1916, a raid which was almost as ineffective: one person was injured and £796 worth of damage done. Mathy set out to bomb London and the other ships to hit East Anglia. L.31 reached Kent, but was forced back by strong anti-aircraft fire.

Mathy's third raid in just over a week was on 8 August 1916. This time the target was 'England Middle', raided by nine airships. Hull was hit by several. The raid was more effective. Ten people were killed, sixteen injured and £13,196 worth of damage done.

In the first two raids Mathy claimed in his combat report to have bombed London, but realised his mistake. He wrote of the three raids that they show: 'It is dangerous to fly for long periods at night, and over solid cloud ceilings, because winds that cannot be estimated and which are often very strong can produce significant and even serious drift errors unless wireless bearings are used freely.' The comment shows how Mathy was analysing and passing on his experience. He knew how difficult it was to navigate over clouds, yet he still overestimated the usefulness and underestimated the danger of wireless bearings.

The next series of raids began on moonless nights in late August. Mathy took off in L.31 on 24 August 1916. Thirteen airships took off to bomb England South, only Mathy reached London. Using mist to avoid searchlights he reported bombing houses in South East London. It seems L.31 dropped thirty-six high explosive and eight incendiary bombs, killing nine people and injuring forty, damage was done to the tune of £13,000. On the way home the weather worsened and Mathy made a heavy landing at Nordholz because of the weight of rain water on the envelope of his ship. L.31 needed to have extensive repairs and was not airworthy until 21 September 1916.

As a result of this Mathy next raided on 23 September 1916, as part of a raid by twelve Zeppelins. The smaller 'P' and 'Q' type ships were to raid England Middle, and the new 'R' class ships were to raid London. Mathy in L.31 and Peterson in L.32 flew towards London over occupied Belgium and the English Channel, rather than the normal North Sea route. Mathy reached London, there are detailed British GHQ reports on the raid and the damage he did. The British thought Mathy was using a new technique. He was caught by searchlights over Croydon, but escaped them by dropping a parachute flare to dazzle the opposition. He bombed Brixton and Streatham dropping a total of thirty-three high explosive and forty-one incendiary bombs, destroying a number of houses, shops and a tram. In Streatham six men and one woman were killed. In Brixton three men, three women and one child. In Leyton four men and one child and in Lea Bridge two men and one woman. In all twenty-one people were killed and seventy-two injured.

The raid was very damaging for both sides. The Zeppelins killed forty people, injured 130 and caused £135,068 worth of damage. For the Germans it was worse. They lost two Zeppelins. Peterson in L.32 was shot down in flames by a fighter. Bocker in L.33 was lucky – he was hit by anti-aircraft fire and captured. Mathy saw the end of Peterson and L.32. He seems to think his compatriot was shot down by anti-aircraft fire. His report, as quoted by Robinson, was unemotional. 'The ship was also heavily fired on, and after dropping her bombs appeared to have reached safety when additional searchlights opened up ahead of her and, after a brief very intense bombardment, the destruction followed, the ship fell in flames.'

Mathy was in action again two days later. On 25 September 1916 nine Zeppelins raided England. Again the smaller ships were to raid England Middle, the larger ships England South. Mathy again approached the coast via Belgium and the English Channel. Because of the very clear night sky he decided not to attack London, but targeted Portsmouth. He dropped most of his bombs on Portsmouth Harbour and dockyards, under heavy anti-aircraft fire, from about 11,000 feet. None of the bombs were traced by the British probably because they were aimed at ships and missed, falling into the sea. It seems the main reason for this was a combination of the altitude and being confused by searchlights and gun fire. The British, however, put it down to a failure of the bomb release gear on L.31. The GHQ report says of L.31: 'Her bold flight over Portsmouth Harbour on 25 September fortunately had no results owing to the possible failure of her bomb releasing gear, but her success in flying over the Portsmouth defences remains. The decision of *Kap Leut* Mathy and the boldness of his navigation were alike remarkable.' Mathy flew back along the south coast, dropped three bombs which were recorded by the British, probably aimed at shipping near Dover. He returned home safely.

The raid by the smaller ships on England Middle was very successful. York, Bolton and Sheffield were bombed. Forty-three people were killed, thirty-one injured and £39,698 worth of damage done.

Heinrich Mathy set out on his last raid from Nordholz in the afternoon of Sunday, 1 October 1916, along with ten other airships. Again the smaller Zeppelins were to raid the Midlands, the bigger 'R' class ships to raid London. Despite, or possibly because, he was regarded by Strasser (and by the British) as the boldest and best Zeppelin Commander, Mathy was under terrible psychological pressure, the destruction and burning of his comrades was severely affecting him. He said: 'It is only a matter of time before we join the rest. Our nerves are ruined by this mistreatment. If anyone should say he was not haunted by visions of burning airships, then he would be a braggart.'

Mathy was asked by a newspaper reporter what he would do if his ship was on fire, would he jump or burn? He said 'I won't know until it happens.' He made his choice over Potters Bar just before midnight on Sunday, 1 October 1916.

The route of L.31 was tracked by the British. She was seen by the Cross Sand Light Vessel at 19.45. She crossed the coast at Corton and flew over Lowestoft, was again spotted at Wrentham at 20.05, Blythborough at 20.15, Framlingham at 20.30 and Needham Market at 20.50. She flew in the same general direction passing Hadleigh (21.00) south of Sudbury (21.10) and Halstead at 21.15. She then seemed to stop her engines, as if Mathy was checking his position. She then changed course, flying more to the south. Between Braintree and Terling at 21.25 and north of Chelsford (21.30), Writtle (21.35) and Blackmore (21.40 pm). As she got nearer to London Mathy could see the searchlights. She was caught in one near Klivedon Heath (21.45.) and changed to a north-easterly course. Mathy was near Ongar at 22.00, and Harlow at 22.10. She stopped again to verify her position near Much Hadham (22.20) and then, when near Buntingford, turned north with a view to attacking London from that direction. Mathy flew north of Stevenage (22.55), and at 23.00 was west of Welwyn. She flew over Hatfield (23.05) and Hertford (23.10). She again stopped and drifted in the direction of Ware. It may be that Mathy was drifting un-powered to confuse the defenders, if so it didn't work as he came under heavy fire from the guns at Newmans and Temple House. He then dropped most of his bombs at Cheshunt at about 23.40. The thirty high explosive and twenty-six incendiary bombs destroyed four houses and slightly damaged about 300 buildings including a large number of green houses. There was fortunately only one casualty, a woman who was injured. Mathy then seemed to give up the attack on central London and started weaving to avoid the searchlights. He was by this time being followed by an aircraft, a BE2c flown by Second Lieutenant Wulstan Tempest. Like William Leefe Robinson and Frederick Sowrey, Wulstan Tempest was a member of 37 Squadron RFC. It seems Mathy saw the fighter as he dropped the last of his bombs at Potters Bar. Moments later Wulstan Tempest attacked. Tempest wrote in his combat report that the Zeppelin was at 15,000ft and climbing like a rocket. He dived to catch her and flew under her, then sat under her tail 'and pumped lead into her for all I was worth'. He could see tracer bullets from her machine guns flying in all directions. As he fired he noticed her begin to go red inside like a giant Chinese lantern, and a flame shot out of the front of her. She shot up 200ft, and then began to fall straight at him. He put the BE2c into a spin and just managed to corkscrew out of the way as she shot past 'roaring like a furnace'.

The red hot wreckage of L.31 came to earth in a field just outside Potters Bar. People quickly reached the site. They found in a field a man half embedded in the soil. He was still alive but soon died. It was Mathy. He knew what to do, and he jumped rather than burned. The nineteen crew members of L.31 are all now buried at Cannock Chase.

**L.14 *Kapitanleutnant* Alois Bocker shot down and captured on 24 September 1916 in Zeppelin L.33**

Alois Bocker took part in five raids after January. On 5 March he bombed Beverley and Hull in Zeppelin L.14. His was the second airship to bomb Hull that night so it is not possible to determine the damage he did. However, eighteen people were killed and fifty-two injured in the bombing. The day after a Royal Flying Corps vehicle was stoned by the enraged population.

On 31 March, with Strasser on board L.14, Bocker set out to bomb London. In his combat report Bocker claimed he hit the city, but the British report shows he bombed Sudbury, Braintree, Brentwood and Thameshaven. As this was a major raid with seven Zeppelins killing forty-eight and injuring sixty-four, doing £19,431 of damage it is not possible to determine exactly what Bocker did, however, he certainly was responsible for many of the deaths.

The first week in April 1916 was the busiest time for Zeppelin raids in the entire war. Strasser planned five raids in the week. On 2 April 1916 Bocker could claim a first. He bombed Scotland, hitting Leith and Edinburgh, causing £44,000 worth of damage. He destroyed a whisky warehouse and killed a baby in Leith and damaged many houses in Princes Street Station in Edinburgh, killing eleven people. There is an inscribed paving stone commemorating the raid at the place a bomb fell in the Grassmarket.

He bombed Scotland again on 2 May 1916. It seems he did no damage this time. His bombs fell in a field near Arbroath. He thought he had bombed Edinburgh again, but because of strong winds and poor visibility was further north than he believed.

Bocker took over a new Zeppelin L.33 on 3 September 1916. His first and last raid in her was on 23 September 1916. As was normal, Bocker took most of the crew of L.14 with him. The executive officer of L.14 *Oberleutnant zur See* Kurt Frankenberg, did not move with Bocker, however. He had been promoted to *Kapitanleutnant* to command Zeppelin L.21. He was replaced by *Leutnant zur See* Ernst Wilhelm Schirlitz, who had been Franz Stabbert's executive officer before the crash in Norway. Frankenberg would not live long to enjoy his promotion

We have good records of the last flight of Zeppelin L.33. She had twenty-two members of crew. She left Nordholz at about 13.30. She was spotted as she flew into the Thames Estuary at 22.00. She was fired on by a destroyer at 22.12, but avoided damage. She went inland between Southminster and Burnham at 22.45. She dropped an incendiary bomb at South Fombridge at 23.00 – it did no damage. She was spotted flying directly towards London, over Rayleigh at 23.05, south of Wickford at 23.20, west of Ingrave at 23.25, over Billericay at 23.27. Now looking for targets, she dropped a flare south of Brentford at 23.35. She dropped four incendiary bombs on Upminster Common at about 23.40. At about 23.50 she dropped six high explosive bombs at South Hornchurch. She dropped another flare at Chadwell Heath and was picked up by a searchlight. She got away from this and arrived over Wanstead at midnight. Going towards East London she then came under steady anti-aircraft fire. She was fired at by guns at West Ham, Victoria Park, Becton and Wanstead. A number of these batteries claimed to have hit her. It is difficult to say for certain which did, but shrapnel appears to have damaged her and she began to lose gas.

She flew over East London dropping bombs both high explosive and incendiary. Six people were killed in Bromley. The Black Swan public house in Bow was hit by a 100kg high explosive bomb which killed three women and two children. She then turned towards Stratford dropping more bombs as she flew. All this time she was still under anti-aircraft fire. At about 00.15 on 24 September witnesses on the ground said she appeared to be running badly and was making a 'knocking noise'. It appeared a shell had damaged one of her propellers. She was also losing gas. She was again picked up by a searchlight at Kelvedon Common at 00.30, and attacked by a BE2c piloted by Second Lieutenant Alfred de Bathe Brandon from Hainault Farm RFC field in Essex. The chase continued over Ongar and south of Chelmsford at 00.30. Bocker was either very skilful or very lucky as L.33 was hit by several incendiary bullets without catching fire. Bocker managed to shake off the aeroplane, but was in serious trouble because of loss of gas.

Her path became even easier to track as she began to jettison cargo. At Broomfield spare parts, a machine gun at Boreham, another machine gun at Wickham Bishops, a third and fourth machine gun at near Tiptree. She reached the coast near West Mersea but Bocker, realising she had only minutes left in the air, turned around and crash landed at 01.20 in a field near Great Wigborough and Peldon. All the twenty-two members of the crew survived. Bocker set the wreckage alight with a flare pistol. The crew were then arrested by Special Constable Edgar Nicholas. After a night guarded in Wigborough Church Hall, the crew were taken to London for days of interrogation by the redoubtable Major Trench and his team. Many captured Zeppelin crews seem to have held a lifelong resentment about their treatment during these interrogations, and a particular grudge about Major Trench, the head of the German Section of Naval Intelligence.

Bernard Trench was a Royal Marine officer. He was fluent in French and German and had worked mainly as an interpreter before the war. In 1908 and 1910 he and a fellow Marine officer, Lieutenant Vivian Brandon were recruited by Naval Intelligence for *ad hoc* spying missions. In 1908 he received an official commendation for his useful report on coastal defences around Kiel. In 1910 he was recruited to prepare a report on defences on the Friesian Islands. In what appears to be a very amateurish operation, Trench and Brandon were given the cover story that they were officers on leave going on a walking tour of Borkum Island. A day or so after the start of the mission in August 1910, Brandon was arrested taking photographs of a restricted area. The fact that it was during the night and he was using a flash does indicate a certain lack of professionalism. When his colleague was captured, Trench hid his intelligence material under the bolster in his hotel room and tried to get to Holland, but was arrested.

The men were held in custody and interrogated. The story Brandon told, that he had photographed defences to write a newspaper article, was seen as less than the whole truth by the cynical Germans. It was not until December that the rest of the material under Trench's bolster was discovered by the hotel proprietor. The time period casts some doubt on the efficiency of the German Intelligence Service, as well as standards of hygiene at the hotel. The material was found to have details of military sites at Kiel, Wilhelmshaven, Borkum and the Kaiser Wilhelm Canal. Trench and Brandon were put on trial in Leipzig, just before Christmas, and unsurprisingly found guilty. They were both sentenced to four years imprisonment in a fortress. Trench was sent to Glatz in Silesia. Along with some other British spies the men were released in 1913, after the Kaiser granted an amnesty following the marriage of his daughter Victoria Louise to the Duke of Cumberland.

It is said the two-and-a-half years in Germany left Trench with 'a fluent command of the language and a thorough dislike of anyone who spoke it'. Though it is always claimed, probably correctly, that captured Zeppelin crews were never physically tortured, they were subject to enormous psychological pressure. The threat that they would not be treated as prisoners of war, but put on trial for murder was very much part of this. Trench was a clever and devious interrogator. Agents impersonating German prisoners were put in the cells of Zeppelin crews. There was a lot of use of hidden microphones and shorthand writers. The real strength of Trench and his team was an almost encyclopaedic knowledge of the Airship Force; crew members having been drilled with the need for secrecy were confronted by interrogators who talked openly not only about technical matters but service gossip, who was in favour and who was not and such like. Trench was in fact a very good intelligence officer with one big advantage: the Zeppelin Works was based in Friedrichshafen on Lake Constance. Spies based across the border in Switzerland were able to pass on up-to-date information about the factory and Airship Service. Indirect discussion about issues the Zeppelin men believed the British knew all about, and oblique questioning could gather enough intelligence to build a full picture. Trench spent most of the war as an Intelligence Officer. He retired as a Lieutenant Colonel in 1927. Such was his reputation as an interrogator that he was recalled during the Second World War. He died in 1967.

We still don't know if threats to put Zeppelin commanders on trial for murder were complete bluff, it was certainly discussed at higher political levels. Certainly Major Trench would have had little say in the matter. In all cases when as much intelligence as possible was gathered, the crew all went to POW camps. The officers went to Donington Hall, now the site of the Donington Park Motor Racing Circuit, near East Midlands Airport. After two years in Donington Hall, Bocker was repatriated to Germany with the usual stipulation he would not serve in combat. He returned to Nordholz as Director of Airship Training often flying his old ship L.14, which had been retained as a training machine. He saw out the war training airship crews. They probably appreciated the knowledge a very skilful and lucky commander could pass on to them.

Zeppelin L.14 survived until just after the war. The terms of the Armistice were that all airships were to be handed over to the Allies. This led to the scuttling of the High Seas Fleet at Scapa Flow on 21 June 1919. On the 23 July 1919, a conspiracy of former Zeppelin crews at Nordholz let the Zeppelins, empty of gas, fall on to the floor of their sheds. The weight of the unsupported ships damaged the fragile duralumin structures severely. When in their sheds, Zeppelins were suspended from the roof. They were too weakly constructed to sit on the ground and if they did the structure would partially collapse under its own weight. All the Nordholz ships, L.14, L.41, L.42, L.63 and L.65 were damaged beyond repair.

To understand why this happened we need briefly to look at the political situation at the time. By October 1918 Germany was falling apart under Allied military pressure. The *de facto* political leaders Hindenburg and Ludendorff were desperately seeking to end the war. The leaders of the navy then behaved with extraordinary stupidity, making plans for a last ditch attack on the British Royal Navy. It was a mission they claimed would improve armistice conditions, though everyone knew it had so little chance of success as to be essentially a suicide mission designed to save the honour of the German Navy. The rank and file sailors were having none of it. Mutiny broke out at Kiel then spread to all the ports, reaching Cuxhaven within days. By 11 November 1918, most ships were flying the red flag and were controlled by workers and sailors' councils. Sailors began hunting down their officers, stripping them of rank insignia and decorations.

During the next few months Germany was in a state of civil war as the Social Democratic Government used the right wing *Freikorps* to put down the revolution. It was in this situation that the Treaty of Versailles was imposed on Germany. One of the provisions was that most of the High Seas Fleet be handed to the various Allies. This led to the scuttling of the surrendered High Seas Fleet in Scapa Flow on 21 June 1919. The same was to happen to the airship fleet. During the winter and spring of 1919, Allied officers had inspected the airship bases and Zeppelins and plans were made for them to be handed to the various Allies. To prevent this happening, groups of officers and flying crews, supporters of the old regime, planned to 'scuttle' their ships. Though all the Nordholz ships were destroyed, the plot was discovered in other bases and some Zeppelins were handed over. Douglas

Robinson interviewed a member of a Zeppelin flight crew almost forty years later, who told him 'We weren't thinking about the Allies getting the ships, we didn't want them falling into the hands of those dammed Communists in Berlin.' Comments which neatly sum up much of the tragedy of German history in the twentieth century.

**L.15 *Kapitanleutnant* Joachim Breithaupt, shot down and captured on 31 March 1916. Survived the war, as a POW**

Like many of the Zeppelins fitted with the 240hp engines, Zeppelin L.15 was out of action for some time while they were returned for modification to the Maybach factory at Friedrichshafen. She had modified engines fitted and was readied for action in March 1916. On 31 March 1916 seven Zeppelins, including Breithaupt in L.15, set out to bomb London. He crossed the coast at Dunwich, Suffolk at 19.45 and flew towards the Thames, via Ipswich and Chelmsford. While London was a difficult target because of effective defence, the city was easy to find with the Thames an excellent signpost. He was over north-east London at 22.30. He dropped fourteen HE bombs near Dartford. At about the same time he was picked up by searchlights. He manoeuvred to avoid them but was caught again. At about 22.45 he was hit by two shells from the Woolwich anti-aircraft battery. The shells destroyed a number of gas cells and punctured others. Breithaupt dropped the rest of his bombs to lighten the ship. Lucky not to catch fire, L.15 rapidly lost height as she leaked hydrogen. To add to his problems Breithaupt was seen and attacked by an aeroplane. The pilot, Second Lieutenant Alfred de Bathe Brandon, from Hainault Farm RFC station climbed above L.15 in his BE2c and attacked with Ranken Darts. For once the Zeppelin was not a sitting duck, and machine gunners stationed on the top of the hull fired to some affect. On landing Brandon found a number of bullet holes in his plane – one of the few cases of damage to a fighter by a Zeppelin. All the darts missed and L.15 was able to shake off Brandon.

Breithaupt knew he was in deep trouble. He radioed his base to say he intended to try to reach the Belgian coast near Ostend. He jettisoned most of his fuel, keeping just enough to reach German occupied territory. After the fuel, the machine guns were thrown overboard. All this was in vain. At around 23.15 the Zeppelin went into the sea about fifteen miles from

Margate, near the Kentish Knock lightship. After several hours seventeen members of the crew, standing on top of the floating hull, were rescued by British armed trawlers. One crew member drowned. Breithaupt had a number of complaints about his treatment. The first was that the crew of the trawler, obviously thinking about the *King Stephen* affair, forced the Zeppelin crew to strip naked before taking them aboard. They were then taken to Chatham and were subject to intense interrogation by the formidable Major Trench. It is said that Breithaupt never lost his deep sense of grievance of his treatment during his interrogation. There is no doubt much useful material was collected, including the fact that most of the crew were convinced they had bombed Liverpool, on 31 January. When they had given as much information as Major Trench calculated he was going to get, the crew were treated as prisoners of war. Breithaupt and the executive officer went to Donington Hall. *Leutnant* Kuhne was repatriated on the condition he would not participate in combat operations. He spent the rest of the war on Strasser's staff. Breithaupt spent the rest of the war as a POW.

The decision to repatriate Alois Bocker and Otto Kuhne has always seemed to me to be strange. Both were senior officers and even in a formal non-combat role had a lot to contribute to the German war effort in terms of planning and training. Along with this they had personal experience of British interrogation methods and how much the British knew about the Airship Service. Undoubtedly on their return repatriated prisoners would give a very full account of their interrogation.

There is an interesting story by Ernst Lehmann – a Zeppelin commander who later worked for the Zeppelin Company and died in the Hindenburg disaster at Lakenhurst New Jersey in 1937 – about the methods used by Major Trench. He wrote that when Bocker was a POW he was visited by a friendly RAF Captain. (It must have been RFC.) The officer said he had been at Friedrichshafen during the commissioning of L.33, when Bocker visited the Zeppelin Works. He was able to describe in detail where Bocker had been on different days. He even said he had been in a pub, the Bayerischer Hof in Lindau, Bavaria, one afternoon and had been listening at the next table while Bocker discussed the development of a type of automatic cannon for Zeppelins with his watch officer. While it seems unlikely that the officer who visited Bocker had been present, it seems to be certain that there was an effective spy network in place. Robinson wrote that, after an investigation following a report on Trench's interrogation methods, given by a repatriated prisoner, three men from Tondern and two from Nordholz were shot, though no further details were given.

Breithaupt returned home after the war. He was a Luftwaffe General in the Second World War. He retired in 1943 but spent some years in Soviet captivity as a POW. He was released in 1949. He died on 18 July 1960.

### L.16 *Oberleutnant zur See* Werner Peterson. Shot down in flames on 2 September 1916 in Zeppelin L.32

After the January raid, Peterson and his crew took part in six more raids on England. In late March, early April 1916 Strasser ordered a week of intensive raiding, Zeppelins would raid every day if possible. Peterson took part in the first on 31 March 1916. He bombed Bury St Edmunds and Lowestoft. A total of ten army and navy Zeppelins took off. Peter Strasser ordered that the usual radio signals were not transmitted after take-off, so the British had less warning. The raid was a success in terms of damage: it killed forty-eight people, injured sixty-four and did £19,431 worth of damage. However, Zeppelin L.15 was shot down by anti-aircraft fire, and most of the crew captured.

Peterson flew again on 2 April 1916, in a mission of six army and navy Zeppelins. They did £73,113 worth of damage and killed thirteen people, injuring twenty-four. L.16 is recorded as having bombed Cramlington airfield. Peterson flew again the next day, 3 April 1916. He bombed Bishop Auckland, killing one person, injuring nine and doing £7,883 worth of damage. He was in action again on 24 April 1916, one of six navy Zeppelins. It seems he dropped his bombs without effect, as only one person was killed and that was when Hull was bombed by L.11. Peterson was in action again on 2 May 1916. The raid took place in very poor weather, which led to a number of problems. Nine Zeppelins were involved, eight from the navy. The target was England North – Rosyth, the Forth Bridge and the north of England. The first Zeppelin to cross the coast, probably L.23 commanded by *Kapitanleutnant* Otto von Schubert, dropped incendiary bombs on Danby High Moor, near Middlesbrough and set fire to the heather on the heath. Three more Zeppelins were attracted by the fire and bombed the open moor,

*Kapitanleutnant* Prolss in L.13, Peterson in L.16 and Herbert Ehrlich in L.17. The raid did £12,030 worth of damage and killed nine and injured thirty, none probably resulting from Peterson's bombs. It is interesting to note that in his combat report Peterson claimed to have bombed Stockton-on-Tees. He said he set buildings on fire as well as clearly recognisable railway tracks and embankments. This seems to have been an honest mistake, all the East Coast towns had blackouts and visibility was poor due to heavy snow clouds.

On 7 August 1916 Peterson was assigned to a new ship, Zeppelin L.32. His Executive Officer *Leutnant zur See* Karl Brodruck, and most of his crew went with him. Zeppelin L.16 after fifty-six combat missions was reassigned as a training ship. She was wrecked in a landing accident at Nordholz on 19 October 1917.

Peterson's first raid on England in L.32 was on 24 August 1916, His target was London. He got as far as Dover, came under anti-aircraft fire and dropped all his bombs in the sea. He claimed in his combat report to have bombed numerous ships, a hit on one causing a devastating explosion. The British Intelligence report does not bear this out. It says all his bombs fell in the sea off Dover making a grand spectacle for watchers on the coast and throwing up fountains of water and spray. Peterson was followed out to sea by a fighter but it lost him. He was later fired on by Dutch guns as he crossed the territory of neutral Holland, but he got back to Nordholz safely.

Zeppelin L.32 next raided England on 2 September 1916. In the biggest raid of the war sixteen airships of the army and navy set out to bomb London. Peterson left Nordholz in the early afternoon. He crossed the coast at Cromer, and dropped a few bombs in Norfolk. He was over Tring in Hertfordshire at about 02.25 when he saw SL.11 shot down in flames. He described the event: 'A great fire which shone out with a reddish-yellow light and lit the surroundings within a large radius and then fell to the ground slowly.' He was about twenty miles away from SL.11 when she was shot down. After this his combat report and the British GHQ report differ substantially. Peterson claimed he went on to bomb London. The GHQ report is very uncomplimentary. It seems a copy of Peterson's combat report was found intact in the wreckage of L.32 after she was shot down. In it Peterson claimed to have bombed Kensington, which the British knew was untrue. They say that after seeing the catastrophe of SL.11, Zeppelin L.32 turned away from the Metropolis. They imply that Peterson quite deliberately put misleading information in his report. He went on to bomb Hertford Heath where he dropped five high explosive and eleven incendiary bombs killing two horses, and Great Amwell where he dropped sixteen high explosive and eight incendiary bombs, killing a pony. Peterson went on to Ware where he dropped his last two high explosive bombs. He then went home crossing the coast at Corton. He arrived safely at Nordholz at about 09.40, the next morning.

On 23 September 1916, L.32 set out from her base at Ahlhorn, near Bremen. She was part of a large raid. Eight 'P' and 'Q' class ships were to attack the Midlands, four new 'R' class ships – L.30 commanded by Buttlar, L.31 commanded by Mathy, L.32 commanded by Peterson and L.33 commanded by Bocker – were to attack London. Zeppelin L.32 was spotted by the British when she crossed the coast at Dungeness at 22.50 where she dropped six HE bombs. She was spotted at Tunbridge Wells at 00.10 on 24 September. She reached Ide Hill near Sevenoaks at 00.30 and dropped an incendiary bomb. She was caught by the searchlight at Crokenhall at 00.50. She dropped seven HE bombs, but just broke some windows. She crossed the Thames near Purfleet at about 01.00. As she reached London she was fired on by a number of anti-aircraft guns. The battery at Tunnell Hill claimed definite hits. She dropped the rest of her bombs, twenty-three HE and twenty-one incendiary over South Oakenden at about 01.05. As she crossed London she was much bothered by searchlights, which enabled Second Lieutenant Frederick Sowrey of 39 Squadron RFC to attack her in his BE2c at 01.10. He used the tried and tested method of flying under her and firing upwards with his Lewis gun. It seems he sprayed bullets all along her hull, as it took three drums of ammunition loaded with a mixture of Brock, Pomeroy and tracer to set her on fire. He reported the first two drums seemed to have no effect, but the third caused her envelope to glow and catch fire. He watched her fall to the ground in flames. L.32 crashed at Great Burstead, near Billericay. All twenty-two crew members were killed. They are now buried at Cannock Chase

Peterson was one of the youngest commanders, but with more than sixty combat missions was regarded as one of the best ship handlers. The

British in their GHQ Intelligence report described him as hesitant, but his loss along with that of Bocker in a single night was a severe setback for the Airship Service.

### L.17 *Kapitanleutnant* Herbert Ehrlich. Survived the war

Zeppelin L.17 took part in her next raid on 1 April 1916. Two Zeppelins raided the north of England. L.11 and L.17. Sunderland and Middlesbrough were bombed. Twenty-two people were killed, thirteen injured and there was £25,568 worth of damage. Most of the casualties were in Sunderland and caused by L.11. Ehrlich had engine problems as he crossed the English coast and dropped his bombs in the sea. L.17 raided again a few days later on 3 April 1916, Ehrlich was again forced to abandon the mission off the coast of Norfolk because of engine problems.

Ehrlich next raided England on 24 April 1916, in Zeppelin L.17. Eight airships set out. The main target was London. Due to bad weather, mist and heavy rain clouds, the ships just flew over East Anglia. Only one person was killed – a woman in the village of Dilham in Norfolk when an unknown Zeppelin unloaded forty-five bombs. Ehrlich was more successful on his next raid on 2 May 1916. L.17 had bombed the Skinningrove Chemical Works in North Yorkshire, when Ehrlich was attracted by fire on Danby Moor and dropped his bombs on the burning heath land. In his combat report he claimed to have bombed a coastal town in the east, probably Saltburn.

In June 1916 Zeppelin L.17 still commanded by Herbert Ehrlich took part in the Battle of Jutland. The next raid on England was not until 28 July 1916. L.17 was one of five Zeppelins that set out for England. All the Zeppelins dropped their bombs on open ground. There were no injuries and only £257 worth of damage. A few days later Ehrlich was raiding again. On 31 July 1916, L.17 was one of seven Zeppelins to attack England. She bombed Mattishall, near Norwich. Once again the raid was largely ineffective, and there were no injuries and only £139 worth of damage. L.17 flew again on 2 August 1916. This time six airships set out on what was again an ineffective mission, one person was injured and damage worth £796 was done.

On 18 October 1916 Ehrlich was assigned a new Zeppelin, L.35. He took *Leutnant zur See* Dietsch and his crew with him. His first raid in the new ship was on 27 November 1916, when ten Zeppelins set out to bomb England North. Ehrlich had problems with some of the automatic gas pressure valves on some of his gas cells, and had to fly low at about 8000ft. L.35 had just crossed the coast near Seaham in County Durham when he saw Zeppelin L.34 commanded by Max Dietrich caught in a searchlight near Hartlepool. More searchlights caught her, holding her fast and brightly illuminated. He saw an anti-aircraft gun fire at the Zeppelin. After about five minutes a rocket or flare was fired and the gun stopped firing. A few minutes later L.34 became a brightly glowing ball of fire. She tipped up vertically burning over her entire length. As she fell there was a bright ball of burning gas streaming behind the ship. Another rocket was fired and the search lights went out. Lookouts in the gondola saw two aircraft in the vicinity. At that Ehrlich turned for home.

That was Ehrlich's last raid of 1916. During the winter L.35 served in the Baltic, operating in very cold conditions. Her next raid on England was on 16 March 1917. Five Zeppelins set out but because of poor weather conditions most dropped their bombs in open country. According to the GHQ report there were no injuries and only £163 worth of damage.

It was 21 August 1917 when Ehrlich set out on his next raid. Eight airships set out to bomb England North. L.35 had engine trouble and returned early. He raided England again on 24 September 1917, when eleven Zeppelins set out to bomb the North. Zeppelin L.35 bombed the Parkgate Steel Works and Silverwood Colliery north of Rotherham. Ehrlich was attracted by lights, but they were put out before he reached his target, some damage was done but there were no casualties.

In December 1917 Ehrlich was assigned to another Zeppelin, L.61. This was a much more advanced high altitude machine. Her first raid was on 12 March 1918, one of five Zeppelins that took part. Again the North was the target, but because visibility was poor and there was solid cloud below the Zeppelins, which were flying at 16,000 to 18,000ft, accuracy was poor. Zeppelin commanders claimed to have bombed Leeds, Bradford and Grimsby, but British records show these cities were untouched. The raid was largely ineffective, one man was killed and £3,474 worth of damage done. Ehrlich reported he attacked a heavily fortified place on the Humber, but the British have no record of his bombs. It is probably fair to Ehrlich to say he genuinely believed he had attacked a city, the fact he didn't try to name it makes it more believable, but he was bombing through cloud and had no real idea where his bombs landed.

Ehrlich's last raid was on 12 April 1918, five Zeppelins set out to bomb the English Midlands. Zeppelin L.61 left her base at Wittmund at about 11.00. She crossed the English coast at about 20.45 at Withernsea. Ehrlich's target was Sheffield. He recorded in his combat log that he was over Sheffield at an altitude of 18,400ft at 22.07. He dropped all his bombs between 22.17 and 22.35. He was in fact over Wigan. The British reported that the blast furnaces of the Wigan Coal and Iron Company were in operation. Eight high explosive bombs fell on the suburb of Lace, injuring a man and causing some damage. Ehrlich dropped fifteen high explosive bombs on Wigan killing seven people and injuring twelve. The last four bombs of 300kgs fell in open fields near Aspull, but damaged cottages and injured four people. In the whole raid seven people were killed, twenty injured and £11,673 worth of damage done, most of it by L.61. With the bombs gone Ehrlich climbed to 22,000ft and the log shows he crossed the coast near Spurn Point, after midnight, at 00.30. British observers noted he crossed the coast later than that near Hull.

It demonstrates the strength of British air defences that Ehrlich's problems were not over when he crossed the coast. An F2a twin-engine flying boat had left Great Yarmouth at 03.30 to find a Zeppelin sighted some 60 miles from Yarmouth. The flying boat crew and crew of L.61 saw each other at about 04.45, in the early morning. Luckily for Ehrlich it was still dark enough for him to get away. Zeppelin L.61 landed at Wittmund at about 11.00 on 13 April 1918.

Herbert Ehrlich is probably the least well-known Zeppelin commander. He seems to have been a careful and competent pilot and he and his Executive Officer *Oberleutnant zur See* Dietsch had flown together since July 1915. He had commanded a number of airships, and flown many missions in his career, including high altitude raids against England and operations in the Baltic. When he bombed Wigan he came closer to Liverpool, the elusive target of so many raids, than any other commander. In May 1918 he retired from active service and took over his old airship L.35. His Executive Officer said at the time that, 'The physical, technical, navigational and metrological difficulties had risen immeasurably, visibility conditions were becoming ever more circumscribed: the zenith of the airships' reign had been passed.'

It is interesting to note the experimental work Ehrlich was involved in – the development of glider bombs or aerial torpedoes. Probably the first guided missiles, controlled by signals sent down a long wire attached to a Zeppelin, these worked – after a fashion – but never saw active service. Ehrlich was also involved in an experimental programme to launch an Albatross fighter from a Zeppelin. He ended the war on the Navy Staff at Wilhelmshaven. He later studied economics and German at the University of Leipzig, but he died following surgery on 12 December 1921.

### L.19. *Kapitanleutnant* Odo Loewe. Drowned in the North Sea on or around 3 February 1916

Probably the only thing to add to the story of L.19 is what happened to the *King Stephen*: she never worked as a trawler again. Captain William Martin died not long after the incident. The trawler was taken into the Royal Navy as an armed 'Q' ship, a ship that looked like an unarmed merchantman but was able to shed her disguise, if approached by unsuspecting enemy ships. She was sunk by a German torpedo boat, and her crew taken to Germany as prisoners of war. The captors knew all about the ship's history, her crew were subject to intense interrogation and threats, but in the end finished the war as POWs like the luckier Zeppelin crews.

### L.20 *Kapitanleutnant* Franz Stabbert, shot down in flames on 20 October 1917, in Zeppelin L.44

The subsequent history of Franz Stabbert seems to confirm the RAF saying that 'you can have bold pilots, or old pilots: you never have an old, bold pilot'. Stabbert's story at times reads like a Biggles novel, albeit without the happy ending. He was undoubtedly a brave man, though his skill as a Zeppelin commander is less obvious. Most Zeppelins were out of action for some weeks following their safe return on 1 February 1916. Their HSLu engines were removed in early March and returned to the Maybach works at Friedrichshafen for modification. L.20 returned to active service in May when Newcastle and Scotland, described by the Germans as England North, were attacked by eight airships. Rosyth was the main target. Stabbert with a crew of eighteen left

Tondern in the early afternoon of 2 May 1916. His target was Dundee. It seems he reached the coast at about 19.00, but the weather changed as it tends to do in Scotland, and a strong north-westerly wind sprang up. By about 20.00 L.20 was flying over dense cloud and in heavy rain and snow squalls. The hull began to ice up and Stabbert had to drop ballast and jettison fuel. The weather cleared by about 01.00 the next morning, and Stabbert found he was over Loch Ness, far north in the Highlands. He dropped his bombs on Craig Castle, near Rhynie, a ruin he took to be a pit head. He attempted to fly south but was drifting in the strong wind. He crossed the coast near Newburgh, north of Aberdeen at about 04.00. By 06.00 he had requested a radio position, and was told he was near the Orkney Islands. He saw a neutral ship the *Holland* and descended to 60ft to get an exact position. It was 58 degrees north, 3 degrees east. Basically he was in the middle of the North Sea between the Orkneys and the south of Norway. He realised he had no chance of getting back to Germany, so decided to land in Northern Denmark. However, he failed due to the strong south-easterly wind. To add to the challenge his mechanic told him two engines were about to break down. By 11.00 he reached the coast of Norway near Stavanger. In the fierce wind he made a successful crash landing near the beach, destroying L.20, but saving the crew. Some scrambled ashore, others were rescued by fishing boats. This led to a strange legal situation in neutral Norway. The crew rescued by boat, including *Leutnant* Schirlitz the Executive Officer, were classed as shipwrecked mariners and returned home. Those including Stabbert who scrambled ashore were classed as combatants and interned.

The story then gets even more like Biggles. After seven months in captivity Stabbert escaped and returned to Germany. He was soon returned to active service. He got the latest Zeppelin, the 'height climber' L.44 in April 1917. He raided England again on 23 May 1917 in Zeppelin L.44. The raid, in which Strasser was on board, was not a success. L.44 only briefly crossed the coast coming over at Lowestoft and going out a few minutes later at Great Yarmouth. In his combat report Stabbert said he dropped all his bombs on Harwich. As the British have no record of this they must have fallen in the sea. Stabbert and Strasser had major problems. They had suffered from engine problems over the North Sea and when they reached the coast all the six engines failed. The mechanics managed to get one going again, and after a long slow flight, L.44 got back to Nordholz. The cause of the problem seems mainly to have been lack of experience in operating the new high altitude Zeppelins, as they flew at 20,000ft – twice the height of the older ships. The crew suffered severely from altitude sickness, and it seems the cause of the engine problems was the loss of radiator water due to evaporation at high altitude. If the raid was a failure it did at least demonstrate some of the problems with the new ships that needed to be solved.

The engine issue seems to have been solved, though considerable problems with altitude sickness still remained when Stabbert set out in L.44 on 21 August 1917. There were no casualties caused on this raid and little damage was done. L.44 raided again on 24 September 1916 along with ten other airships. Little damage was done and no one killed.

On 19 October 1917 Stabbert in L.44 left his base at Ahlhorn near Bremen at about noon. His target was London. Eleven Zeppelins took part in the raid. L.44 was one of the four Zeppelins lost in this, the so called 'silent raid'. Stabbert quickly got into trouble as the weather changed to a north-easterly gale. We don't know exactly what happened after that as all his logs were lost. It seems L.44 crossed the coast east of the Wash at 19.45. She then flew down the south-east coast, and was spotted at Herne Bay at 21.40, where Stabbert dropped a few bombs. After this she was seen again at 21.52 between Dover and the North Foreland. It seems that by this time Stabbert had major engine trouble and was drifting with only partial control of the airship. From Dover he crossed the Channel and spent much of the night over northern France. He reached the Western Front, in daylight, at about 07.40, crossing French lines at St Clement near Luneville in Lorraine. He was fired on by French 75mm anti-aircraft artillery, from the 63rd Colonial Artillery Regiment. The first salvo missed, and Stabbert increased height to 5800m. L.44 was hit by an incendiary shell in the second salvo and immediately burst into flames. The airship came down near the town of Chenevieres. All eighteen crew members were killed. The bodies of most crew members were badly burned, but five were found some distance from the wreck which indicates they jumped to escape the flames. The French published photographs of the bodies of the crew, some still recognisable. They included *Oberleutnant zur See* Armin Rothe the Executive Officer. Most of the crew are buried at the Military Cemetery at Gerbeviller, France.

*Leutnant zur See* Ernst Schirlitz had a less interesting time after he returned from Norway. He was a young man, the son of a pastor, born 7 September 1893. He got back home, a few days after the wreck of L.20. He was soon assigned to another ship. This was Zeppelin L.33 commanded by Bocker. She was shot down on her first raid on England, at Great Wigsborough on 23 September 1916. All the crew were captured. Schirlitz was interrogated by the menacing Major Trench. He was threatened with trial for murder, but when his interrogators, who described Schirlitz as discourteous and rude, decided they had got as much information as they were going to get from him, he was transferred to Donington Hall as a POW. He went back to the German Navy after the war. In the Second World War he reached the rank of *Vizeadmiral*. He was commander of the Atlantic Coast defences and the fortress of La Rochelle in France. He was tried as a war criminal after the war, but acquitted. He died on 29 November 1978.

## L.21. *Kapitanleutnant* Max Dietrich shot down in flames on 27 November 1916 in Zeppelin L.34

Max Dietrich was next in action in Zeppelin L.21 on 24 April 1916, with Peter Strasser as a passenger. Eight Zeppelins set out. The main target was London. However, due to weather conditions mist and rain clouds restricting visibility, little damage was done. None of the airships seems to have got further than East Anglia, and some brought their bombs home. A number of commanders claimed to have bombed Cambridge and Norwich, but the British had no record of this there was only one casualty: a woman died in Dilham in Norfolk.

Dietrich set out again on a raid on 2 May 1916, when eight airships set out for England North. Zeppelin L.21 bombed York. She arrived over the city at about 22.30 and dropped eighteen bombs, killing nine people and injuring forty more. The streets bombed included Nunthorpe Avenue and Upper Price Street. Dietrich did not take part in any more raids in L.21, though he took part in a number of scouting missions and the Battle of Jutland.

He took over a new 'R' class Zeppelin L.34 on 27 September 1916. He was soon in action again on 1 October 1916. Dietrich left Nordholz, one of a fleet of eleven Zeppelins. She was spotted crossing the coast at Overstrand at 21.42, and she reached the Corby area at about midnight. A searchlight and anti-aircraft gun based at Corby fired on L.34. The GHQ report states that

Dietrich turned towards the gun and then dropped seventeen high explosive bombs on the railway near Corby tunnel, and thirteen incendiary bombs near the road from Rockingham to Gretton. She then turned for home and crossed the coast between Palling and Horsay at about 01.40 on 20 October. She then dropped her remaining high explosive bombs in the sea. The British GHQ report was unsure whether Dietrich saw the fall of Mathy in L.31, which was probably 100 miles away, and dropped his bombs as a result of this, or because he was fired on from Corby. It may be a coincidence that both events took place at about the same time.

Max Dietrich's next and last raid was on 27 November 1916. It was Dietrich's forty-sixth birthday. It is said that the officers' mess at Nordholz was decorated for his birthday celebration. When the officers sat down for lunch at about noon Peter Strasser's adjutant came in and said, 'Gentlemen, we have attack orders, the industrial areas of Middle England, we have to be in the air by 1.00pm. (noon GMT) we have excellent prospects.' It is said that the commander of L.21, Kurt Frankenberg who had taken over the ship from Max Dietrich, said, 'leave the birthday decorations we can celebrate tomorrow.' But his Executive Officer Hans-Werner Salzbrunn, said to a friend 'I know we won't come back from this flight.' Neither Max Dietrich nor Kurt Frankenberg returned for the party, but we can be sure those of their comrades that did needed a drink.

L.34 left Nordholz, with a crew of twenty, at 13.00 on 27 November 1916. Her target was Newcastle. She arrived over England at 22.45 that night near Black Hall Rocks, north of Hartlepool. She was picked up by a searchlight near the Hutton Henry Lighthouse and fired on by anti-aircraft guns. Max Dietrich dropped thirteen high explosive bombs on the searchlight battery, failing to hit it, but striking farm buildings and injuring two cows.

We have good records of what happened next. Dietrich turned for home, heading over West Hartlepool where he was again caught by searchlights. He dropped sixteen high explosive bombs on West Hartlepool. Two fell in the Ward Jackson Park, where there is now a memorial stone plaque. He then bombed working class housing in the Harley Street, Lowthian Road and Poplar Grove area, killing four people and injuring eleven. A number of houses were damaged. He then bombed allotments and hit the grandstand of Hartlepool United Football Club, causing major damage.

The bombing of Hartlepool was to be the last act of Max Dietrich. Zeppelin L.34 had been spotted in the searchlight beams by a British night fighter. The pilot was Second Lieutenant Ian Vernon Pyatt, a member of 36 Home Defence Squadron of the Royal Flying Corps. He was flying a BE2c aircraft. He had taken off from Seaton Carew, and chased L.34 over Hartlepool. In his combat report he said he caught up with L.34 at about 23.42 over the mouth of the River Tees and fired seventy-one rounds from his Lewis gun. He noticed a small patch on her envelope become incandescent where he had seen his tracer bullets entering. 'This patch rapidly spread and the next thing was that the whole Zeppelin was in flames.' He watched L.34 fall into the sea, still burning, half a mile off shore. The next day only a patch of oil marked the spot where Max Dietrich and nineteen other crew members had died. A few parts of L.34 were later washed up on shore.

## Zeppelin L.21 shot down in flames on 27 November 1916. Commanded by *Kapitanleutnant* Kurt Frankenberg

Zeppelin L.21 was to meet the same fate as her old commander that same night. Since the raid on the Black Country, L.21 had seen a lot of action. She had been involved in twelve more bombing raids, and seventeen reconnaissance operations, including taking part in the Battle of Jutland. She had a new commander *Kapitanleutnant* Kurt Frankenberg. It was normal for less experienced commanders to be given older Zeppelins. He had previously been executive officer on L.14. On this flight his Executive Officer was *Leutnant zur See* Hans-Werner von Salzbrunn. Zeppelin L.21 took off from Nordholz at about the same time as L.34. She crossed the English coast, near Atwick at 22.20, on 27 November 1916. She spent several hours over England. She flew over Leeds and bombed Wakefield and Barnsley before reaching the Stoke-on-Trent area. Over the Potteries she dropped bombs on Kitsgrove, Goldenhill, Tunstall, Chesterton, Fenton and Trentham. We know that a bomb dropped in the garden of a house at 8 Sun Street, Tunstall. The blast demolished the outhouses and sculleries of four houses, and damaged a church. One man, a Mr Cantliff of 8 Sun Street, was injured, but recovered in hospital.

After leaving the Stoke area, Frankenberg headed back to the coast. On her way over the East Midlands L.21 made slow progress. She probably had engine trouble. She passed south of Nottingham and was caught in an airfield searchlight at Buckminster. She was passing over dangerous territory as by this stage of the war there was a concentration of home defence aerodromes in the Lincolnshire area. Sure enough, she was attacked by two BE2c aircraft near Peterborough at about 03.00, but escaped. An hour later near East Derham she was attacked again, but the aeroplane, a FE2b, had an engine failure and crash landed.

L.21's luck ran out when she reached the English coast near Lowestoft in the early dawn light at 06.05. The system of air defence introduced after the 31 January raids was in operation, and working well. Given the code name 'Mary', L.21 had been tracked on her nine-hour flight over the country. When she reached the Lowestoft area three aeroplanes from the Royal Naval Air Service were in the air waiting for her. The pilots were Flight Lieutenant Egbert Cadbury (of the Birmingham chocolate family), Flight Sub-Lieutenant Gerard Fane and Flight Sub-Lieutenant Edward Laston Pulling. All three pilots attacked L.21, but Sub-Lieutenant Pulling received the credit for her destruction as he fired the last shots, and was scorched by the flames as the Zeppelin caught fire. Pulling also had the grizzly experience of seeing the machine gunner stationed on top of the airship's envelope leave his platform and run straight off the nose of the Zeppelin to escape the flames. He reported that the Zeppelin caught fire after a few shots and 'was in a few seconds a fiery furnace'.

L.21 fell into the sea about eight miles east of Lowestoft at 06.42 on 28 November 1916. All seventeen crewmembers were killed. Vessels searching the spot found only a broken propeller blade floating in a great pool of petrol and oil. The rest of L.21 sank to the bottom of the North Sea. As far as we know it is still there.

It is fitting to end with the destruction of L.21. The Zeppelin had roamed over the Midlands on 31 January 1916 without opposition. Though she again roamed over the Midlands ten months later, on 27 and 28 November she was the hunted not the hunter. The British had learned the lessons of the January raid, but the Germans had not. At the time the British had seen the raid as a defeat. Zeppelins had roamed at will over the Midlands. The air defence operations were a total failure. It is much to their credit that the people responsible for home defence were willing and able to accept this and build an effective air defence system in response. In a war where the biggest criticism of those in command is usually that they lacked the moral courage to acknowledge and learn from their mistakes, the development of the Air Defence System deserves special credit. In some ways the defeat of the Zeppelins was more to do with the efforts of failed generals, politicians and bureaucrats, than the bravery of pilots and the genius of scientists. It was developed by a system of trial and error, but above all it was based on a judgement of what worked.

That is, basically, the end of the story of the 31 January 1916 raid. There were few Zeppelin raids on the Midlands in the rest of the war, though Hull was bombed several times. The Black Country was never bombed again, though other Midlands towns were.

In Lincolnshire the worst raid was on 31 March 1916 at Cleethorpes. Zeppelin L.22 commanded by Martin Dietrich (no relation to Max) thought he was bombing Grimsby, and dropped all his bombs on the town. Most fell in the sea, but one hit a Baptist Chapel in Alexander Road. The building was completely destroyed. Soldiers from the 3rd Battalion, the Manchester Regiment were billeted in it. Thirty-one soldiers were killed, and another forty-eight were injured. Most are buried in the town cemetery.

Nottingham was bombed on 23 September 1916, the night Peterson and Bocker were shot down, by Zeppelin L. 17 commanded by *Kapitanleutnant* Hermann Kraushaar. He had taken over L.17 from Herbert Ehrlich, and this was his second raid over England. His first had been on 2 September 1916, when SL.11 was shot down by William Leefe Robinson. Kraushaar set out at about noon from Tondern intending to bomb Sheffield. He thought he was near Sheffield when he saw fire belching from factory chimneys. In fact he was over Nottingham. At about midnight he dropped eight high explosive and eleven incendiary bombs damaging two railway stations and killing three people. There was considerable public anger at the failure of rail companies to extinguish lights. On the way back home he was near Lincoln, at about 01.00 on 24 September, when he reported seeing what he and his crew described as an evil omen, a burning airship. This must have been Zeppelin L.32 with Werner Peterson and his crew. Kraushaar had seen the fall of L.32 from near Lincoln, when he was some 150miles from Billericay where she crashed.

Kraushaar was shot down on 14 June 1917 off the Dutch coast near Vlieland, in a new Zeppelin L.43. He was on a scouting flight. The attack by a RNAS Curtis H12 flying boat showed the advances the British were making in the anti-Zeppelin campaign. The Curtis 'Large America' flying boat was a four-seat aeroplane with twin 275hp engines. It was fitted with radio. There were seaplane bases at Felixstowe and Yarmouth. When it was known by radio interception that Zeppelins were out, the seaplanes would be made ready to take off at a moment's notice. When British shore bases picked out transmissions to the Zeppelin giving her approximate position, the seaplanes were scrambled. As new information was gathered this was sent by radio to the flying boat. As a result of this the Curtiss H12, piloted by Flight Sub-Lieutenant Hobbs, was able to find and intercept L.43. The large flying boat was able to out-climb and out-perform the Zeppelin. The airship was shot down in flames. All twenty-four crew members were killed. This was the second successful attack by Curtis flying boat. On 14 May 1917 Zeppelin L.22, the Zeppelin that had bombed Cleethorpes, now commanded by *Kapitanleutnant* Ulrich Lehmann, was shot down in flames by a seaplane piloted by Flight Lieutenant Gilpin. Her crew of twenty-one were all killed.

The last two raids on the Midlands were both carried out by *Hauptman* Kuno Manger. Manger was an army officer commanding a navy Zeppelin. His Executive Officer *Oberleutnant zur See* Bruno Gruner and crew were all navy men. Manger had started his airship career in an unfashionable ship, the Perseval PL.25, a small non-rigid machine, similar to the later Goodyear Blimps. He took over Zeppelin L.14 from Bocker in June 1916 and was assigned to the 'height climber' L.41 in January 1917. He was an experienced commander with a number of raids on England to his credit.

He took off from Ahlhorn at about noon on 19 October 1917 in Zeppelin L.41. He was taking part in the last major Zeppelin raid of the war. Eleven Zeppelins were setting out to bomb Middle England, and the principal targets were to be Sheffield, Manchester and Liverpool. The raid became known as the 'silent raid', because the airships flew above 16,000ft and because of the wind direction they were not heard from the ground. Though the raid caused a great deal of destruction (250 bombs were dropped, causing £54,346 worth of damage, thirty-six people were killed and fifty-five injured), it was a disaster for the Naval Airship Service. The weather forecast before the raid had been inaccurate, and the Zeppelins were caught in a gale on the way home leading to the loss of four ships.

Manger set out to bomb Manchester, and reported hitting the city. In his combat report he said he bombed a brightly lit, big new factory and an iron foundry with blast furnaces. He was in fact over the outskirts of Birmingham. He had bombed the Austin Motor Works at Longbridge. Two men were injured and some buildings damaged. L.41 was affected by the gale, but returned to Ahlhorn, sustaining some damage in a heavy landing.

On 21 January 1918 Manger was assigned to Zeppelin L.62. He took part in a raid on England on 12 March 1918, with Peter Strasser aboard. Because of the heavy cloud below their height of 16,000 to 18,000ft they were unable to see the ground. Manger's bombs fell in open country some three miles east of Leeds causing no casualties. His last attack on England was on 12 April 1918. Zeppelin L.62 left Nordholz at about 13.00. The intended target was the industrial Midlands. At 22.05 Manger bombed a lit night flying field, he believed was near Lincoln. In fact it was at Tydd St Mary which is about forty miles south-east of Lincoln. He then claimed to have bombed Nottingham, but no traces of his bombs were found by the British. He then claimed to have bombed Birmingham with the rest of his 300kg (660lbs) bombs. He claimed to have seen the damage done by the 300kg bombs as black craters on the lit up streets. It seems he was flying further south than he calculated. We now know where the bombs landed. It seems he dropped two 300kg bombs close together. One fell south of Coventry on the Baginton sewerage works, near the present day Coventry Airport. The next bomb fell on Whitley Common, killing two cows and making a crater twenty-five-foot wide and eight-feet deep. In a recent newspaper report a man who lived in the area as a boy in the 1930s, said the Zeppelin crater was widely known and used by boys on their bikes like a modern BMX track. Manger continued west. He dropped his last two bombs in the Birmingham area. The first landed on the Manor Farm in Shirley, and the second the Robin Hood Golf Course in Solihull. A lot of windows were broken in the Hall Green area, but there was no other damage. H A Jones remarked in his *War in the Air* how lucky it was that no more damage was done. If Manger had been two or three miles further north he would have bombed the centre of Coventry and Birmingham, undoubtedly causing considerable casualties.

Manger was under attack from anti-aircraft fire and fighters during this part of the raid. He was fired at by guns in Coventry and in Birmingham. According to official reports he was attacked by Lieutenant Cecil Henry Noble-Campbell, from B Flight, 38th Squadron R.A.F, who took off from Buckminster, near Melton Mowbray in a FE2b. Nobel-Campbell was a New Zealander who had previously served as a sergeant with the Wellington Mounted Rifles in the Gallipoli campaign.

Another pilot Lieutenant William Alfred Brown took off from Stamford to intercept, he reported seeing the Zeppelin but could not catch it. Nobel-Campbell reported that he had been patrolling at 16,000ft when he attacked the airship. Unfortunately he enters the history books as the only pilot ever to have been shot down by a Zeppelin. He said he chased L.62 for about half-an-hour, failing to hit her. He was fired at by crew in the gondolas, and was wounded in the head, and his propeller broken. He made a forced landing at Radford near Coventry. William Alfred Brown also landed there, the pilots only then finding out they had been chasing the same Zeppelin. There is some mystery about the circumstances of the injury to Nobel-Campbell. Manger did not mention a fighter attack in his combat report. The FE2b was an old design with a performance only slightly better than the BE2c. It had a top speed of about 80mph and a ceiling of about 16,000ft. It is unlikely that Manger was as low as this. His log shows he reached 21,650ft during the flight and it is unlikely he would have gone down to 16,000ft when under anti-aircraft fire. So it is difficult to understand how the FE2b and the Zeppelin got close enough to exchange fire. It has been suggested that Nobel-Campbell and William Brown were attempting to reach the Zeppelin and shooting at it. In the dark Brown shot Nobel-Campbell, luckily only wounding him. We will never know for sure. Manger's problems were not over, however. As she journeyed home L.62 came under anti-aircraft fire near Norwich. She was hit and a gas cell damaged. She lost a lot of height but returned safely to Nordholz.

There is a mystery about the final flight of Zeppelin L.62. On the morning of 10 May 1918 she took off from Nordholz on a scouting flight. She was seen by a German ship about ten miles north-west of Heligoland, flying low. She was seen to fly into a large cloud. Seconds later there was a loud explosion. L.62 had broken into two pieces and fell into the sea a blazing wreck. Five bodies were recovered but the entire crew were killed. It has never been established what happened. Peter Strasser thought the cause was lightning in the cloud. Rumours among Zeppelin crew veterans interviewed by Douglas Robinson many years after the event was that it was an act of sabotage.

While this has to be seen in the context of when it was said, we cannot totally rule out the idea. Many of the Zeppelin flight crews served in the Second World War as senior officers in the Luftwaffe or Navy. Discussing their experiences with an admiring and sympathetic American at the height of the Cold War probably developed conspiracy theories about communist plots. However, the German Navy in May 1918 had severe morale problems, in particular on the capital ships of the High Seas fleet. The men had been inactive since the battle of Jutland and there were massive divisions between officers and crew. The conflict occurred over what seems a trivial issue, but certainly wasn't trivial in blockaded Germany: food. Officers were well fed, ordinary seamen got little more than the rations of civilians, and they could see, day after day, how much time and money went on the preparation of officers' food. Mutiny broke out on a number of battleships. The Navy High Command established food committees to discuss these issues. In the next few years these committees were to develop into sailors' councils, the main form of organisation in the mutinies of 1918, and in the German revolution. The High Command dealt ruthlessly with the ringleaders. Most were sentenced to long terms in prison, and two sailors, Max Reichpietsch and Albin Kobis, were shot. They were quickly regarded as heroes and martyrs by the rank and file sailors. We will never know the cause of the explosion on Zeppelin L.62, but can understand why some people suspected sabotage.

The last act in the Zeppelin campaign against England came on 5 August 1918. Peter Strasser never gave up the belief that precision night bombing would win the war. The L.40 class of Zeppelins, the 'height climber' machines able to operate at 20,000ft, had limited success, but even if the crews were able to cope with the lack of oxygen and intense cold at that height, a basic problem remained: if you couldn't navigate and bomb accurately from 9000ft you certainly couldn't from 20,000ft. By 1918 fighter aircraft could out climb the Zeppelin. It is fitting that Strasser accompanied the last bombing raid of the war in his latest most developed Zeppelin, L.70. It was shot down in flames by a DH4 two-seater aeroplane that out-performed the Zeppelin in every way.

On the afternoon of 5 of August 1918 Strasser took off from Nordholz. Zeppelin L.70 was the latest ship in the airship force, a huge machine 693ft long, and 78ft in diameter, with six engines. She could operate at 23,000ft and reach speeds of almost 80mph. L.70 was one of five airships raiding England. The formal commander was the inexperienced *Kapitanleutnant* Johann von Lossnitzer, with *Leutnant zur See* Kurt Kruger as his executive officer. In practice the ship was commanded by Peter Strasser. In 1916 L.70 would have been invincible; by 1918 fixed wing aircraft had developed much more. The BE2c was replaced by a number of different aircraft that could out climb any Zeppelin.

The British air defence system worked perfectly. The airships were tracked as they approached the Norfolk coast. As dusk fell thirteen aircraft took off from Great Yarmouth Air Station. Ten flew inland to wait for any Zeppelins that crossed the coast; three flew out to sea to intercept. They saw three Zeppelins at about 17,000ft. The first aircraft to attack was a DH4 two-seater flown by Major Egbert Cadbury, with Captain Robert Leckie as his observer. Cadbury had participated in the destruction of L.21 almost two years before. Robert Leckie had been part of the crew of a Curtis flying boat that shot down Zeppelin L.22 a year before. Cadbury attacked head on, flying just below L.70 as Leckie fired a magazine of Pomeroy explosive ammunition from his Lewis gun at the rear of her hull. A fire started quickly, which spread along the length of the Zeppelin. She fell, a blazing mass, hitting the sea north of Wells-next-the-Sea, Norfolk. The crew of twenty-two were all killed. Parts of the Zeppelin were recovered and examined by the British, as were the bodies of a number of crew members. However, following protests from local people they were not buried in the locality, but were given military burial at sea. Most of the other airships saw the conflagration of L.70. They jettisoned their bombs and turned back. All escaped.

There is one man who learned the lessons of the Zeppelin war very well during the chaos of January 1916. He was Arthur Harris, who in January 1916 was a pilot in 11th Reserve Squadron Royal Flying Corps. By March 1916 he had been promoted to flight commander in 39th Squadron, RFC, based at Hornchurch. In his flight were three pilots who would shoot down Zeppelins, William Leefe Robinson, Frederick Sowrey and Wulstan Tempest. Captain Arthur Harris did a lot of the development work on incendiary and explosive ammunition; he had used the still experimental Brock explosive bullets in an attack on a Zeppelin on 25 April 1916. Harris survived the war, became a career RAF officer, and became head of Bomber Command in the Second World War. Air Marshall 'Bomber' Harris knew from bitter experience just how hard it was for a night bomber to find and hit its target. He also believed that there was no such thing as a non-combatant in modern war. The solution was area bombing, in a sense German cities would reap the whirlwind sown a generation earlier by the Zeppelin raids.

A statistic from the Stanton Iron Works at Ilkeston illustrates this. On 31 January 1916 Zeppelin L.20 dropped fifteen high explosive bombs on the works killing two men. In the Second World War the Stanton Iron Works produced steel castings for 500lbs bombs, most destined for the RAF and US Army Air Force, and hence Germany. Between 1942 and 1945 it produced 873,500.

The RAF learned one even more important lesson from the Zeppelin raids. In the ten months between January and November 1916 Britain had developed an efficient air defence system. L.21 was shot down by brave men in barely adequate aeroplanes helped by a new technology, incendiary ammunition. They were able to do this because of a working fighter control system. People in a command centre moving a counter named 'Mary' around a map enabled the route of L.21 to be predicted. Observers on the ground phoned in sightings to a central control centre, the position of the Zeppelin was constantly updated. Decisions were made, in modern parlance, virtually in real time. Fighters were scrambled to intercept. Zeppelin L.21 managed to evade them twice, the third time Cadbury, Fane and Pulling were waiting for her as she neared the coast.

A quarter of a century later, an evolved version of this system won the Battle of Britain. New radar and radio communication technology in fighters made the whole thing more efficient. Brave men in more than adequate fighters were scrambled and directed onto German raiders. When we look at the Battle of Britain we first think of the Spitfire and the Few, but without effective fighter control they would have been useless. The RAF operations room with WAAFs moving counters around a large map as intelligence was updated. The senior officers sitting on a balcony looking down at the map, making life and death decisions when and where to deploy fighters based on constantly updated information was crucial in the defeat of the Luftwaffe. It is, of course, likely we would have developed an effective air defence system without the debacle of 31 January 1916, but I have no doubt that nine Zeppelins bombing at will a completely undefended and unprepared Middle England, concentrated minds wonderfully.

The people of the many Midland towns never forgot the night the Zeppelins came. In 1919 following the signing of the Treaty of Versailles, the people of Tipton marched through the town demanding revenge for Union Street. They hanged an effigy of the Kaiser. These days hardly anyone has personal memories of that frosty foggy night in January 1916. However, in another way the Zeppelin raids are part of the folk memory of many. Parents told their children and grandparents told their grandchildren of their memories of the night the Zeppelins came. I hope this book helps to put some of these experiences into context.

### What now remains?

While researching this book I visited every town where people were killed in January/February 1916, and walked around the bomb sites. I think I was expecting there to be massive change. There is change, it is true, but it is more complex than that. The areas bombed were very largely industrial – factories surrounded by working class terraced housing. The first thing you notice is that most people lived very close to where they worked. Many of the casualties were at work or going to and from work. They lived at most a few hundred yards from where they worked, the vast majority in terraced houses. A few of these houses were destroyed by bombing. Some were damaged and repaired, and a lot remain all across Britain. The massive change has not been the houses, but the industry. Much of it has gone. Since 1979 successive governments have allowed the systematic deindustrialisation of this country. The destruction of our manufacturing capacity was the aim of the bombers. What the Zeppelins and Luftwaffe failed to do, unthinking ideology and short term economics have achieved. Most of the targeted factories have been replaced by modern housing, on brownfield sites.

## The Black Country

The Black Country in the twenty-first century is very different from the one of 1916. The bombed towns of Tipton, Bradley and Wednesbury are struggling to keep their identity in the unitary authorities of Sandwell and Wolverhampton. Union Street, Tipton and King Street, Wednesbury still remain, though they are much changed. In Union Street all the old courts and terraced houses have been replaced by new council housing, though one building – the Conservative Club – seems little changed from 1916. I didn't go inside to check if it had many estate agents, or people who didn't much like Germans. Nothing remains in King Street. All the old terraced houses have been replaced by modern housing. The original terraced houses were demolished in the 1950s and high density council maisonettes built, but in the last few years these too were demolished and new larger properties built. At the end of the First World War both streets had memorial plaques to the victims. It is sad that neither has survived the rebuilding programme. In the last few years local historians have erected a memorial in Wood Green Cemetery to most of the Wednesbury victims. They are buried together in three common graves.

It is surprising how much remains in the centre of Walsall. Some of the outer walls of the Wednesbury Road Congregational Church remain, though the Church itself was demolished in the 1970s, even though it had been rebuilt in 1917 at a cost of £6,200. In Birchills, Saint Andrew's Church, damaged by Zeppelin L.19, seems little changed. The Art and Science Building in Bradford Place remains largely unchanged, as does the Town Arcade. There is a memorial plaque in Bradford Place, and a small section of wall displaying shrapnel damage. It is still possible to catch a bus to Pleck from outside the Institute. Even so it is difficult to imagine, as we stand near the busy town centre, what it was like when a bomb landed on the site of the Cenotaph, and shrapnel ripped through Bradford Place and the number 16 tram killing three people. Walsall Museum has the rusty remains of an incendiary bomb dropped in the Hospital grounds.

The best memorial in the Black Country is in Bradley. The pumping station on the canal bank, where Maud and William Fellows died, seems almost completely unchanged. As does the nearby Old Bush pub in Bradley Lane where Maud was given first aid on a bar table. There is a memorial on the old pump house. It was erected by British Waterways who own the site, following requests by local historians, including Maud's son Wilfred, and unveiled in 1994, by the local MP. It reads:

> To The Memory Of
> Maud Fellows and Frederick Fellows
> Of Daisy Bank
> Who Were Killed By Enemy Action
> When a Zeppelin Bomb Was Dropped On This Spot
> 31st January 1916.

While the plaque gets the name wrong, I am assured it was not a mistake, for some strange unremembered reason William Fellows was known as Fred to his friends and neighbours.

## Burton-on-Trent

I was not able to find any memorials to the Zeppelin victims in Burton. The tourist office didn't even have a leaflet. When I asked about the site of the church mission in Moor Street I was told Burton had probably changed beyond all recognition. In fact it hasn't, as the main industries were brewing and railways the town has changed much less than most others in the Midlands. There is a modern ring road system which has cut a wide swath through the outskirts of the town, but inside this there are a lot of grand Victorian buildings, pubs and breweries that haven't changed much since the nineteenth century. Sadly the ring road development has massively altered the Lichfield Street area, where the local hero Bertie Geary was killed climbing a lamppost to put out the light. The street remains, but most of the buildings have been replaced by modern industrial units and shops. The corner of Lichfield Street and Bond Street where Bertie died is the site of a car park. Outside the ring road Shobnal Street is much as it was: working class terraced housing with the ubiquitous double-glazing. Number 109 must have been repaired – it is like all the others. A few streets away Wellington Road is a long line of terraced houses. It seems that 34 Wellington Street must have been too badly damaged to repair, because there are now a few 1930-type council houses with the same numbers in the line of Victorian terraces. Though the wooden Christ Church Mission Hall was too badly damaged to be repaired, it is nice to know that another single storey community building has been built on the same site. The site at 346 Uxbridge Street is now occupied by the Burton Caribbean Association.

## Loughborough

Loughborough probably remembers its victims better than any other. The town has a very unusual and impressive war memorial, the Carillon Tower, a bell tower in the style of many in Belgium. There is a small impressive war museum, in the tower, which includes Zeppelin raid photographs and relics. A brass plaque which commemorates the victims is displayed and they are all named. The plaques was originally erected in The Rushes but moved when the shopping centre was built. The Rushes, where the first two bombs fell, is the site of a major shopping centre. It is difficult to get any impression of what happened in 1916, because of the extensive redevelopment. There is a small memorial: a granite paving stone with an inscribed iron cross marking where the second bomb fell. It is difficult to find because it is in the middle of the road. To find it visitors should look in the road between the Tesco steps and the kebab shop on the opposite side. It is unfortunate that the cross is on one of the few non-pedestrian parts of 'The Rushes'. The Loughborough traffic isn't quite as dangerous as a Zeppelin, but be careful!

There is a similar iron cross marking on Empress Road, and opposite it a memorial to the victims. These mark the spot where the last bomb fell. The Empress Road site is well worth a visit. It demonstrates very well what successive British Governments have done to destroy the manufacturing industry, something the Zeppelins never came close to doing. In 1916 the area was a mixture of factories and working class terraced houses. Most of the factories have been demolished and modern housing built on the brownfield sites. The terraced houses remain and, except for almost ubiquitous double glazing, from the outside look exactly as they were in 1916. Even the house numbers are the same. The memorials are near the junction of Empress Road and Judges Street.

## Derby

The industrial area bombed in Derby has probably changed less than any other. The bombs all fell within 100yards or so of the Osmaston Road:

the first a mile or so from the city centre and last near the railway station. Though Derby city centre has the same soulless modern shopping centre as most other cities, the Osmaston Road area is a major industrial centre. There are a lot of railway workshops stretching for about a mile to the south. Many are owned and operated by Rail Track and Bombardier. The industrial area is smaller than it was at the time of the raid, but is in almost exactly the same place as it was in 1916. Many of the industrial buildings have obviously, been renewed, but it is organic functional renewal. The area even has the faint smell of engineering: oil, slurry and burnt metal. Looking towards the city centre the factories are to the right. The T W Fletcher Lace Works remains, the building almost unchanged, though it must have been decades since lace was produced there. In its prime it employed 500 people. Eighteen of them are commemorated on a war memorial dating from 1918. On the left Osmaston Road is lined with the same working class terraced houses as it was in 1914. There are a few fairly new houses built on brownfield sites, but the area is largely unchanged. The streets of working class terraced houses from where the four victims walked to work, Fleet Street, Devonshire Street and Strutt Street, that Monday night are unchanged. Rose Hill Street, where Sarah Constantine died of shock, still has the grand Victorian terraced villas, showing the class distinctions in Edwardian Derby society. Much of the site of the Railway Engine Works has been taken over by Derby College and has been redeveloped. The Roundhouse, part of the Railway Engine Works, though not damaged in the raid, has been renovated. It is well worth visiting. Built by George Stephenson in 1839 for the North Midland Railway Engineering Company, it was the world's first railway engine turntable. After years of campaigning by local people it has been preserved and is used as a function and conference centre. Sadly the same cannot be said for the Rolls-Royce Works off Nightingale Road. Most of the site has been cleared, and housing development is starting. The building that housed the Metalite Works still stands, surrounded by the terraced houses in Gresham Road where many of its workers lived.

### Ilkeston

Though I doubt if the town's thriving Local History Society would agree, Ilkeston is probably a dormitory suburb of Derby and Nottingham. It is a pleasant, largely Victorian market town, which makes much of its industrial history: mining and steelmaking. It has a very good museum with some Zeppelin raid relics, stained glass and stone window frames blown out by the bombs. Unfortunately that is about it. St Bartholomew's the church where Walter Wilson was killed still exists, though it is no longer a consecrated building. A few terraced houses built as part of the factory estate still exist, though most of the factory estate has been demolished. The Stanton Steel Works was finally closed in 2007, much to the disgust of the local population. There are some small factories and recycling units around the old Stanton Steel Works site, but most of Hallam Fields consists of modern housing. Anyone who doubts the damage three decades of de-industrialisation has done should go to Hallam Fields.

The terraced house at Stapleford which James Hall left for the last time to go to work at the Stanton Works on 31 January still remains, from the outside largely unchanged. It still has the same number.

### Scunthorpe
Scunthorpe still has a very large steelworks – now owned by TATA – on the site of the Frodingham and Redbourn Works. It is not possible to determine exactly where the bombs landed, but the site must look and smell much like it did in 1916. As this book goes to the printers there is mounting concern in the town over plans to sell the steelworks and a local campaign is being organised to save it and the jobs of the thousands still employed there.

The area of working class housing in the bombed Ravendale Street area, where two of the victims Thomas Danson and Ernest Benson lived has completely gone, replaced by a shopping centre and town library. Cyril Wright's house in Ashby is now a betting shop – we can but hope its customers are luckier than Cyril. Scunthorpe has a very good museum in the old Victorian Vicarage. There is an interesting Great War exhibition, which has a few relics of the raid including shrapnel from one of Mathy's bombs. Ernest Wilkinson Benson and Thomas Danson are buried in West Street Cemetery, Scunthorpe, while Cyril Jack Wright is buried in Bottesford.

As for the Zeppelins themselves, as far as I know only a few macabre relics remain. Wilfred Fellows the son of Maud, had for most of his life the brass fuse cap of the bomb that killed Maud and William Fellows. It was found in the bomb crater by the canal bank, the morning after the raid, and has been kept by the family ever since. This and other pieces of shrapnel have been exhibited in a number of interesting exhibitions on the Great War over the years. People in Burton, Loughborough and Derbyshire have similar relics.

In 2000 an underwater archaeology team recovered some remains of Zeppelin L.19, off the coast of Holland, and from April 2001 they have been exhibited at the National Maritime Museum in Greenwich, London. While other remains of Zeppelin L.19 and L.21 lie deep below the North Sea, the Imperial War Museum in London has an excellent exhibition on the Zeppelin raids on Britain. Most of the exhibits come from Zeppelin L.33 forced down virtually intact later in 1916. The display room contains crew uniforms, machine guns, bombs, flying instruments and sections of the duralamin frame, along with a very impressive model Zeppelin hanging from the ceiling – well worth a visit. The IWM also has a BE2c in perfect condition hanging from the roof.

In Europe two Zeppelin bases remain, and were until recently still in use as modern NATO military bases: Nordholz and Tondern. Nordholz still has some buildings from the Zeppelin period. It is still a German Navy base. It contains an impressive museum, *Aeronauticum* Nordholz recording the history of the German Naval aviation. Its address harks back to the days of the Zeppelin: '*Aeronauticum*, Peter-Strasser-Platz 3, Nordholz, Niedersachsen, Germany'. Many exhibits relating to the Zeppelin raids are on show. They include the letters put in bottles by crew members of L.19, before they drowned in February 1916. It has dozens of relics of actual Zeppelins, framework, engines, instruments and fabric. It has a life size model of a control gondolier, and many smaller models including a large diorama of L.19 floating while the *King Stephen* looks on. It is interesting to note the different approach to history taken by a German military museum. It has to record events from the operation of German float planes in the Nazi era, to the events of the Cuxhaven Soviet. It takes a very factual neutral approach. Not much about glory there.

Tondern Zeppelin base still exists, until a few years ago it was a Danish Army base. Germany annexed the Danish area of Sonderjylland in 1864; it became part of Schleswig Holstein. It was returned to Denmark in 1920, as a result Tondern became Tonder. A Zeppelin hanger, Toska and remains of the hydrogen gasworks still exist. There is a small museum, telling the story of the Zeppelin base. The address also harks back to its use as an airship base, though less militaristically than that of Nordholz: 'The Zeppelin Museum of Tonder, Gasvaerksvej 1, Tonder, Denmark.'

There is a final sombre memorial to the Zeppelin raids in the Midlands, a few miles from the Black Country, at Cannock Chase. In the German War Cemetery there is a memorial garden containing the bodies of 73 men, shot down over England in four airships. Many of them took part in the raid of 31 January 1916. They include William Schramm army commander of SL.11 shot down on 3 September 1916; Werner Patterson commander of L.16 shot down in Zeppelin L.32, on 24 September 1916; Heinrich Mathy commander of L.13, shot down on 2 October 1916 in Zeppelin L.31 and Franz Eichler shot down in L.48 on 17 June 1917.

I sometimes go to Cannock. It is a beautiful, quiet, peaceful place. Looking at the list of airship crew, I think of brave patriotic men, the sound of a Zeppelin starting to burn, a whoosh, not a bang, like a giant gas cooker. Whether to jump or burn?

I think of the British pilots, brave patriotic men who took off in a break in the fog, and had to crash when they couldn't find their landing flares. Men who not only defeated the Zeppelins, but worked out by trial and error and teamwork how to shoot them down. Men who insisted their enemies had a proper military funeral. Men who had a monument erected: 'Who art thou that judges another man's servant' at the grave of a Zeppelin crew.

But most of all I think about my granny, covered in blood and broken glass, sheltering in a doorway with two babies. She was one of the lucky ones. War can bring out many human qualities, courage and ingenuity, but there is no glory in it.

### The Unknown Zeppelin Victim

I will finish this book with a mystery that I have so far been unable to solve. I found it in a number of Lincolnshire newspapers in late February 1916. It concerns an inquest held on Monday, 21 February 1916, on a man, described as a young Lincolnshire farmer. The previous Friday, 18 February 1916, his sister found a mechanism described as a ring with a ball and a propeller on the ground, almost certainly the fuse mechanism of a Carbonit bomb. She took it home and the victim and several of his friends, probably teenage boys, passed it around and generally played with it. Several people twisted the propeller and it is said when it seemed to get stiff they hammered it around. The deceased finding it would not turn gave it an extra twist, and it exploded. He was killed almost instantly. A doctor told the inquest his body had about 200 wounds. The verdict of the coroner was that death resulted from the explosion of a fuse from an enemy aircraft. It seems very likely this was the seventy-first victim of the 31 January raid. Because of wartime censorship the newspapers were unable to name the victim or the area where the death occurred in Lincolnshire. We know several Zeppelins flew over Lincolnshire on 31 January; did the fuse become detached from a jettisoned bomb. Was it thrown out to save weight, or was it a deliberate booby trap?

The answer will be difficult but not impossible to find. We do not know the name of the victim, or where he died. If a coroner's inquest report survives it will be difficult to find without this information. We can be certain a young man was buried in the last week of February 1916, somewhere in Lincolnshire. He must have had parents, we know he had a sister and friends; the manner of his death must have been talked about and passed down the generations. It may have found its way into newspapers or family histories. If we can identify him it will be a memorial not only to him, but the seventy other victims of the day the Zeppelins attacked Middle England.

*Appendix A*

# A List of Casualties of the Zeppelin Raid

This is an attempt to identify everyone killed in the raid of 31 January 1916. It is not an exhaustive list. It is based on census records, post-First World War local histories, coroners' inquest reports and burial records.

**One: The Black Country** Thirty-five people were killed, thirteen men, thirteen women and nine children.

All the Black Country victims were killed by Zeppelin L.21 and Max Dietrich, between 20.00 and 20.30. It is unlikely L.19 commanded by Odo Loewe killed anyone directly. One man, William Henry Haycock, died of shock. A bomb dropped by L.19 may have been a cause of this.

**Tipton** Total number of casualties from Home Office Records: fourteen killed (five men, five women and four children).

| Name | Age | Address |
| --- | --- | --- |
| Thomas Henry Church | 57 | 111 Dudley Road, Tipton |
| Elizabeth Cartwright | 35 | 1 Coppice Street, Tipton |
| Arthur Edwards | 27 | 69 Union Street, Tipton |
| Mary Greensill | 67 | 1 Court, 8 Union Street, Tipton |
| William Greensill | 64 | 1 Court, 8 Union Street, Tipton |
| Benjamin Goldie | 43 | 58 Queens Road, Tipton |
| Martin Morris | 11 | 10 Union Street, Tipton |
| Nellie Morris | 8 | 10 Union Street, Tipton |
| Sarah Jane Morris | 44 | 10 Union Street, Tipton |
| George Henry Onions | 12 | 66 New Road, Great Bridge, Tipton |
| Daniel Whitehouse | 34 | 31 Union Street, Tipton |
| Anne Wilkinson | 44 | 18 Union Street, Tipton |
| Frederick N Yates | 9 | 5 Queens Street, Tipton |
| Louisa Yorke | 30 | 15 Waterloo Street Tipton |

**Bradley** Total number of casualties from Home Office records: two killed (one man and one woman).

| Name | Age | Address |
| --- | --- | --- |
| Maud Fellows | 24 | 45 Daisy Street, Bradley |
| William Fellows | 23 | 33 Castle Street, Coseley |

**Wednesbury** Total number of casualties from Home Office records: fifteen killed (four men, six women and five children).

| Name | Age | Address |
| --- | --- | --- |
| Matilda May Birt | 10 | Dale Street, Wednesbury |
| Mary Emma Evans | 57 | 32 High Bullen, Wednesbury |
| Rachel Higgs | 36 | 13 King Street, Wednesbury |
| Susan Howells | 50 | 12 King Street, Wednesbury |
| Mary Ann Lee | 59 | 13 King Street Wednesbury |
| Albert Gordon Madeley | 21 | 48 Great Western Street, Wednesbury |
| Ina Smith | 7 | 14 King Street, Wednesbury |
| Joseph Horton Smith | 37 | 14 King Street, Wednesbury |
| Nellie Smith | 13 | 14 King Street, Wednesbury |
| Thomas Horton Smith | 11 | 14 King Street, Wednesbury |
| Betsy Shilton | 39 | 13 King Street, Wednesbury |
| Edward Shilton | 33 | 13 King Street, Wednesbury |
| Rebecca Sutton | 51 | 28 King Street, Wednesbury |

**Walsall** Total number of casualties from Home Office records: four killed (three men and one woman). An additional two men died of shock. They are not included in the official casualty figures.

| Name | Age | Address |
| --- | --- | --- |
| Charles Cope | 34 | 84 Crankhall Lane, Wednesbury |
| Frank Thomas Linney | 36 | Perry Street, Wednesbury |
| Thomas Merrylees | 28 | 58 Hillary Street, Walsall |
| Mary Julia Slater | 55 | The Elms, Bescot Road, Walsall |
| *John Thomas Powell (Died of shock)* | 59 | *Walsall Workhouse* |
| *William Henry Haycock (Died of shock)* | 50 | *53 Bescot Street Walsall* |

**Two: Burton-on-Trent** Total number of casualties from Home Office records: fifteen killed (three men, six woman and six children). Three

Zeppelins bombed Burton probably L.15, L.19 and L.20. We cannot be sure which airship was responsible for individual casualties.

| Name | Age | Address |
|------|-----|---------|
| Margaret Anderson | 60 | 195 Scalpcliffe Road, Burton |
| Ada Brittain | 15 | Waterside Road, Burton |
| John Lees Finney | 53 | 5 Slaters Yard, Burton |
| Berty Geary | 13 | 89 Blackpool Road, Burton |
| Charles Gilson | 52 | 34 Wellington. Street, Burton |
| Edith Meashan | 10 | 32 Wellington Road, Burton |
| Mary Rose Morris | 55 | 32 Eaton Place, Brighton |
| Lucy Simnett | 15 | 150 Branstone Rd, Burton |
| Elizabeth Smith | 45 | 73 Park Street, Burton |
| George Stephens | 16 | 332 Blackpool Rd, Burton |
| Rachel Wait | 78 | 72 New Street, Burton |
| Flora L Warden | 16 | 206 Uxbridge Street, Burton |
| George Warrington | 6 | 108 Shobnal, Street Burton |
| Mary Warrington | 11 | 108 Shobnall, Street Burton |
| Florence Jane Wilson | 23 | 8 Casey Lane, Burton |

**Three: Loughborough and Ilkeston** Twelve killed (six men and six women). All the victims in Loughborough and Ilkeston were killed by L.20 commanded by Franz Stabbert.

**Loughborough** Total number of casualties from Home Office records: ten killed (four men and six women).

| Name | Age | Address |
|------|-----|---------|
| Annie Adcock | 42 | 13 The Rushes, Loughborough |
| Alice Elizabeth Adkin | 29 | Kingthorp Street, Loughborough |
| Joseph Williamson Adkin | 27 | Kingthorp Street, Loughborough |
| Ethel Higgs | 25 | 104 Station Street, Loughborough |
| Joseph Gilbert | 49 | Empress Road, Loughborough |
| Elsie Page | 16 | 87 Empress Road, Loughborough |
| Joseph Page | 18 | 87 Empress Road, Loughborough |
| Mary Anne Page | 44 | 87 Empress Road, Loughborough |
| Martha Shipman | 49 | 5 Orchard Street, Loughborough |
| Arthur Christian Turnill | 50 | 83 Station Street, Loughborough |

**Ilkeston** Total number of casualties from Home Office records: Two killed (both men).

| Name | Age | Address |
| --- | --- | --- |
| James Hall | 56 | Homer Cottage, 12 Frederick Street, Stapleford |
| Walter Wilson | 41 | 2 Albert Villas, Station Road, Ilkeston |

**Four: Derby** Total number of casualties from Home Office records: four killed (all men). One woman died of shock and is not included in official records. All the victims were killed by Zeppelin L.14 commanded by Alois Bocker.

| Name | Age | Address |
| --- | --- | --- |
| William Bancroft | 32 | 34 Strutt Street Derby. |
| Charles Henry Champion | 41 | 33 Fleet Street Derby. |
| James Gibbs Hardy | 55 | 11 Strutt Street Derby. |
| Harry Hitherway | 23 | 73 Devonshire Street, Derby |
| *Sarah Constantine* | 71 | *Malvern House, Rose Hill Street, Derby.* |

**Five: Scunthorpe** Total number of casualties from Home Office records: three killed (all men). All the Scunthorpe victims were killed by Zeppelin L.13 commanded by Heinrich Mathy.

| Name | Age | Address |
| --- | --- | --- |
| Ernest Wilkinson Benson | 31 | 3 Ethel Terrace, Scunthorpe |
| Thomas William Danson | 29 | 2 Park Street, Scunthorpe |
| Cyril J Wright | 24 | 43 Ashby High Street, Ashby |

# Zeppelin Graves at Cannock Chase War Cemetery

I n 1966 Zeppelin crews buried at various cemeteries around England were moved to a special memorial at the German Military Cemetery at Cannock Chase. It only contains the remains of men killed over land. The bodies of crews shot down over the coast that landed in the sea were either not recovered, or were recovered and reburied at sea. This includes the body of Peter Strasser.

**Schutte-Lanz SL.11: shot down in flames 3 September 1916**
*Hauptmann* Wilhelm Schram
*Obermaschinist* Jakob Baumann
*Leutnant* Hans Geitel
*Vizefeldwebel* Rudoft Goltz
*Feldwebel-Leutnant* Karl Hassenmuller
*Gerfreiter* Bernhard Jeziorski
*Untermaschinist* Fritz Jourdan
*Untermaschinist* Karl Kachele
*Obermaschinist* Friedrich Modinger
*Obersteuermann* Rudolf Sendzick
*Obermaschinist* Reinhold Porath
*Unteroffizier* Heinrich Schlichting
*Unteroffizier* Anton Tristran
*Oberleutnant* Wilhelm Vohdin
*Untermaschinist* Hans Winkler

**Zeppelin L.32: shot down in flames 24 September 1916**
*Oberleutnant zur See* Werner Patterson
*Obersignalmaat* Adolf Bley

*Obermaschinistenmaat* Albin Bocksch
*Funkentelegraftobermaat* Karl Bortscheller
*Oberheizer* Wilhelm Brockhaus
*Leutnant zur See* Karl Brodruck
*Maschinistenmaatm* Paul Dorfmuller
*Obermaschinistenmaat* Richard Fankhanel
*Obermaschinistenmaat* Georg Hagedorn
*Oberbootsmannsmaat* Friedrich Heider
*Funkentelegraftobermaat* Robert Klisch
*Obermaschinist* Hermann Maegdlfrau
*Obersegelmachersgast* Bernhard Mohr
*Matrose* August Muller
*Bootsmannsmaat* Friedrich Pasche
*Oberbootsmannsmaat* Karl Paust
*Obersignalmaat* Ewald Picard
*Maschinistenmaatm* Walter Pruss
*Obermatrose* Paul Schiering
*Steuermann* Bernhard Scheibmuller
*Oberbootsmannsmaa*t Karl Volker
*Oberbootsmannsmaat* Alfred Zopel

**Zeppelin L.31: shot down in flames on 2 October 1916**
*Kapitanleutnant* Heinrich Mathy.
*Maschinistenmaat* Euen Boudange
*Bootsmannamaat* Arthur Budwitz
*Obermatrose* Karl Dornbusch
*Maschinistenmaat* Nikolaus Hemmerling
*Obermaschinistenmaat* Karl Hiort
*Segelmashermaat* Ernst Kaiser
*Funkentelegrafieobergast* Ernst Klee
*Steurmann* Siegried Korber
*Signalmaat* Gustav Kunish
*Maschinistenmaat* Karl Mensing
*Obersteuermannsmaat* Friedrich Peters
*Obermatrose* Heinrich Phillips

*Maschinistenmaat* Friedrich Rohr
*Maschinistenmaat* Hubert Stender
*Leutnant zur See* Jochen Werner
*Bootsmannsmaat* Heinrich Witthoff
*Obersteuermannsmaat* Viktor Woellert

**Zeppelin L.48 shot down 17 June 1917**
*Kapitanleutnant* Franz Eichler
*Obermaschinistenmaat* Heinrich Ahrens
*Maat* Wilhelm Betz
*Obersignalmaat* Walter Dippmann
*Obermaschinistenmaat* Wilhelm Gluckel
*Bootsmannsmaat* Paul Hannemann
*Signalmaat* Heinrich Herbst
*Bootsmannsmaat* Franz Konig
*Funkentelegrafiemaat* Wilhelm Meyer
*Obermaschinistenmaat* Karl Milich
*Obermaschinistenmaat* Michael Neunzig
*Obermatrose* Karl Ploger
*Obermaschinistenmaat* Paul Suchlich
*Korvettenkapitan* Victor Schutze
*Obermaschinistenmaat* Hermann van Stockum
*Steuermann* Paul Westphal

Three members of the crew of L.48 survived the crash they were:

*Maschinistenmaat* Heinrich Ellerkamm. This is the man who survived to tell what it was like to be shot down in flames in a Zeppelin.
*Leutnant zur See* Otto Mieth
*Maschinistenmaat* Wilhelm Uecker. He was one of the unluckiest men in the war. He survived the crash and spent the rest of the war in hospital in considerable pain from his burns. He died on 11 November 1918. He is buried at Cannock Chase though not in the 'Zeppelin' plot.

# Bibliography

**Documents and Articles**

Tom Cope. *Zeppelins over the Black Country*. Article in the *Blackcountryman*.

Harold Dudley *The History and Antiquities of Scunthorpe and Frodingham*. Written 1931. Republished by Scunthorpe Corporation 1975.

Frederick Wm Hackwood. *The History of Wednesbury* The Borough News Press. 1920.

John Hook. *Airs from Heaven*. Self-published 1984.

Intelligence Section GHQ Home Forces. Secret document. Probably written by Lieutenant Colonel H G de Watterville. *Air raids 31 January – 1 February 1916. Air Raids, 1916. 2 – 3 September 1916. Air Raids, 1916 23 September to 2 October 1916*. HBM Government. GHQ. H.F (1) November and December 1916.

David Mechan. *The Silent Raid – The Untold Story*. Cross and Cockade International. Volume 45/4 2014

The Reverend W L T Merson. *Zeppelin Raid on Walsall*. Article in *Borough of Walsall, Programme of the Peace Celebrations*. Borough of Walsall. 1919.

Chris Percy and Noel Ryan. *Lincolnshire Aviation in World War 1*. Airfield Research Group. 2012.

Mick Powis. *Zeppelins over the Black Country*. Article in the *Blackcountryman*. Numbers 3 and 4, Vol. 29. 1996.

E W Sockett. Article in *Fortress*. Number 13. May 1992.

Walsall Local History Centre. *Walsall Chronicle* No 8: *Walsall at War*. Walsall Library and Museum Service. 1986.

*Wolverhampton and the Great War*. Wolverhampton Archives and Local Studies 2014.

**Newspapers**

The *Black Country Bugle*. August, September, October 1983. July, November 1994.

The *Daily Sketch*. Editions from February 1916

The *Derby Telegraph*. Editions from 1916 and article 2014.

The *Dudley Herald*. Editions from 1916.

The *Express and Star*. Editions from February and March 1916. Also see articles by Mick Powis in the editions of 25 January 1996 and 6 January 2000.

The *Guardian*. 4 April 2001.

*Hartlepool History Now and Then* 2014
The *Ilkeston Advertiser*. Editions from 1916
The *Ilkeston Pioneer*. Editions from 1916
The *Lincolnshire Star*. Editions from 1916
The *Loughborough Echo*. Editions from 1916
The *Stoke-on-Trent Sentinel*. 2014
The *Tipton Herald*. Editions from 1916.
The *Walsall Herald*. Editions from 1916.
The *Walsall Pioneer*. Editions from 1916.
The *Wednesbury Herald*. Editions from 1916.

**Books**
Alec Brew. *The History of Black Country Aviation*. Alan Sutton 1993.
Ian Castle. *London 1914 – 1917 The Zeppelin Menace*. Osprey 2008
Christopher Cole and F G Cheeseman. *The Air Defence of Great Britain. 1914– 1918*. Putnam 1984.
Gwynne Dyer. *War*. The Bodley Head. 1986
Stephen Flinders and Danny Corns. Stanton. *Gone But Not Forgotten*. Ilkeston and District History Society 2013.
Bill Gunston. *Night Fighters. A development and combat history*. Patrick Stephens 1976
H A Jones. *The War in the Air*. Claredon Press 1931.
Alan Judd. *The Quest for C. Mansfield Cummings and the Founding of the Secret Service*. Harper Collins 1999.
Peter Kirk, Peter Felix and Gunter Bartnik. *The Bombing of Rolls-Royce at Derby in Two World Wars- with Diversions*. Rolls-Royce Heritage Trust. 2002
Ernest A Lehmann and Howard Mingos. *The Zeppelins. The Development of the Airship, with the Story of the Zeppelin Raids in the World War*. J. H. Sears 1927. Reprint by P S Chapman 2014.
Raymond Rimell. *Zeppelin* Vol 1. Albatros Publications 2006.
Raymond Rimell *Zeppelin* Vol 2. Albatros Publications 2008.
Raymond Rimell. *The Last Flight of the L.48*. Windsock 2006.
Raymond Rimell. *Zeppelins at War! 1914 – 1915* Albatross Publications 2014
Raymond Rimell. *The Airship VC*. Aston Publications 1989.
Douglas H Robinson. *The Zeppelin in Combat*. Schiffer Publishing 1994.
Dennis Stuart. *History of Burton-on-Trent*. Wood Mitchel and Co. 1977.
David Wainwright. *Cranes and Craftsman. The Story of Herbert Morris Limited*. Hutchinson Benham 1974.
Richard M Watt. *The Kings Depart. The German Revolution and the Treaty of Versailles 1918-19*. Pelican 1973.

## Maps

H A Jones has a fairly detailed GHQ map of the route of each Zeppelin over a ten-miles-to-the-inch Ordnance Survey Map of the time. While this appears to be very detailed putting the routes of all the Zeppelins on one page makes it look rather like spaghetti. I am not sure how accurate it is. Certainly Jones has been able to plot the position of each Zeppelin recorded by ground observers, however, the nicely curved paths shown for each Zeppelin probably owe a lot to artistic licence. Though the Zeppelins certainly circled looking for targets any attempt to portray this on a small scale map is questionable.

I have found two types of map particularly useful. The first is the modern edition of the humble A-to-Z or Phillips Street Atlas of the bombed areas. Drawn to a scale of about four-inches-to-the-mile they are very useful in plotting the course of the Zeppelin and locating where the bombs landed. The second are the Godfrey Edition 'Old Ordnance Survey Maps' reproduced at a scale of about fifteen-inches-to-the-mile. Most date from between 1900 and 1910; they not only show the changes in the name of roads over 100 years but often allow houses to be identified. The following maps cover most of the areas where people were killed:

Bradley, Coseley and Wednesbury Oak, 1901. Staffordshire sheet 67.04
Burton-on-Trent, 1900. Staffordshire sheet 40.16
Burton-on-Trent (North), 1900. Staffordshire sheet 40.12
Derby (South), 1899. Derbyshire sheet 50.13
Dudley Castle and Tipton Green, 1901. Staffordshire sheet 67.12
Loughborough, 1901. Leicestershire sheet, 17.08.
Scunthorpe, 1906. Lincolnshire sheet, 18.04
Tipton, 1904. Staffordshire sheet 67.08
Walsall (SW) and Pleck, 1901. Staffordshire Sheet 63.10
Wednesbury, 1902. Staffordshire sheet 68.01

## Websites

There are numerous websites on World War One and Zeppelins. I have found those below particularly useful. With the centenary of the start of the First World War in 2014, many local newspapers and local history societies produced articles on different aspects of the conflict, quite a few on the Zeppelin raids. There are too many to separately list here but it is well worth using Google to look at a location and Zeppelin, as the 100th anniversary draws near, many more articles will appear.

www.aeronauticum.de
This is the site of the Aeronauticum Museum at Nordholz, some sections in English.

www.crossandcockade.com
The website of the British magazine about all things concerning First World War aviation.

www.zeppelin-museum.dk
The site of the Zeppelin and Garrison Museum Tonder, the museum is on the site of Tondern airship base, now part of Denmark. A very good website, many pictures of the base, ships and crews. Almost everything in English.

www.frontflieger.de
A site commemorating German airmen who died in WW1, good section on Zeppelin men. Some sections in English.

www.loughborough-rollofhonour.com
Certainly the best British site on the Zeppelin raids from a local point of view. Has a list of the entire Loughborough victims and many of the damaged buildings in the town.

# Index